Theory of Crisis

Historical Materialism Book Series

The Historical Materialism Book Series is a major publishing initiative of the radical left. The capitalist crisis of the twenty-first century has been met by a resurgence of interest in critical Marxist theory. At the same time, the publishing institutions committed to Marxism have contracted markedly since the high point of the 1970s. The Historical Materialism Book Series is dedicated to addressing this situation by making available important works of Marxist theory. The aim of the series is to publish important theoretical contributions as the basis for vigorous intellectual debate and exchange on the left.

The peer-reviewed series publishes original monographs, translated texts, and reprints of classics across the bounds of academic disciplinary agendas and across the divisions of the left. The series is particularly concerned to encourage the internationalization of Marxist debate and aims to translate significant studies from beyond the English-speaking world.

For a full list of titles in the Historical Materialism Book Series available in paperback from Haymarket Books, visit: www.haymarketbooks.org/series_collections/1-historical-materialism.

Theory of Crisis

Kōzō Uno

Edited and translated by
Ken C. Kawashima

Haymarket Books
Chicago, IL

First published in 2021 by Brill Academic Publishers, The Netherlands

Published in paperback in 2026 by
Haymarket Books
P.O. Box 180165
Chicago, IL 60618
773-583-7884
www.haymarketbooks.org

ISBN: 978-1-64259-790-5

Distributed to the trade in the US through Consortium Book Sales and Distribution (www.cbsd.com) and internationally through Ingram Publisher Services International (www.ingramcontent.com).

This book was published with the generous support of Lannan Foundation, Wallace Action Fund, and the Marguerite Casey Foundation.

Cover art and design by David Mabb. Cover art is a detail of *Construct 63, Morris, Golden Lily / Malevich, Suprematist Composition*, paint and wallpaper on canvas (2006).

Printed in the United States.

Library of Congress Cataloging-in-Publication data is available.

Dedicated to Mouna and to Comrades in Japan, Korea and China

Photo taken from "Introduction to *Capital*", Kuramoto Bunko, 1952

Contents

Translator's Preface XI
Ken C. Kawashima
Author's Preface XVIII

Uno Kōzō, Kyōkō Ron (*Theory of Crisis*)

Introduction 3
1 Classical Phenomena of Crises 18
2 The Theory of Crisis and Foreign Trade 27
3 The Role of Commercial Capital in Relation to the Phenomena of Crisis 36
4 The Possibility and Inevitability of Crisis in Capitalist Society 42

1 **Prosperity** 52
1 The Accumulation of Capital in the Phase of Prosperity 53
2 The Role Performed by Credit 58
3 Speculative Development and the Rise in Prices 65

2 **Crisis** 70
1 The Collision between the Profit Rate and the Interest Rate 71
1.1 *The Falling Rate of Profit That Accompanies the Advance of the Accumulation of Capital* 71
1.2 *The Sharp Rise in the Interest Rate at the Highest Point of Prosperity* 74
1.3 *The So-called Shortage of Capital* 77
2 The Excess of Capital and the Excess (Surplus) of Populations 81
2.1 *The Rise in Wages and Its Limits* 81
2.2 *The Excess of Capital as an Excess of Commodities* 84
2.3 *'Poverty in the Midst of Affluence'* 89
3 The Destruction of the Value of Capital 91

3 **Depression** 95
1 The Stagnation of the Reproduction Process 95
2 Inaugurating New Accumulation through Improvements to the Production Process 99
3 The Turn towards Prosperity 103

4 The Turnover Period of the Business Cycle 106

5 The Inevitability of Crisis in Capitalist Society 116
1 Mechanical Inevitability and Historical Inevitability 116
2 The Inevitability of Crisis and the Inevitability of Collapse 123
3 The Theory of Crisis and the Analyses of Crises 129

Appendix 1: Problematic Points in the Theory of Crisis in *Capital* 131
Appendix 2: *Capital* and the Demonstration of the Inevitable Ground of Crisis 144
Guiding Comments 158
Makoto Itoh
Supplementary Essay: Uno Kōzō's *Theory of Crisis* Today 177
Ken C. Kawashima and Gavin Walker
Works Cited in *Theory of Crisis* 203
Index 205

Translator's Preface

Published in Japan and in Japanese in 1953, Uno Kōzō (1897–1977) originally wrote his *Theory of Crisis* as a series of special lectures that he delivered at the University of Tokyo, Faculty of Economics. In 1974, *Theory of Crisis* was re-published in Volume 5 of the *Collected Works of Uno Kōzō* (Iwanami Publishers). Then, in 2009, one year after the so-called sub-prime mortgage crisis of 2008, *Theory of Crisis* was re-published as a paperback book, also by Iwanami Publishers. This English translation of Uno's *Theory of Crisis* is the complete translation of his 1953 book that was republished in Volume 5 of the *Collected Works of Uno Kōzō*.

As for the composition of Uno's *Theory of Crisis*, the book begins with a short Preface by the author, which articulates his basic argument on the need to demonstrate the inevitability of crisis based on Marx's *Capital*, and which situates the book in relation to his earlier research. Then there is Uno's Introduction. By Uno's own admission, the Introduction is disproportionately longer than the other chapters. This is because in it, Uno clarifies the three levels of his entire methodology for political economy from the specific perspective of the theory of crisis. Uno also clarifies why, among other things, his theory of crisis 'abstracts' and 'omits' the analysis of foreign trade, and why merchant capital is also 'abstracted' in the pure theory. These are problems that Uno clarifies before he explains his main demonstration of the inevitability of crisis in the process of capital accumulation.

The Introduction is followed by three chapters that demonstrate the inevitability of crisis through a theoretical exposition of the three phases of the cycle of accumulation (Chapter 1, "Prosperity", Chapter 2, "Crisis" and Chapter 3, "Depression"). This is followed by a chapter on the turn-over time of the business cycle (Chapter 4), and by the final chapter, "Mechanical Inevitability and Historical Inevitability", in which Uno discusses capitalist crisis in contrast with the notion of the collapse of capitalism (Chapter 5). Finally, as per Uno's original *Theory of Crisis*, I have translated and included two Appendix chapters by Uno, which deal with specific theoretical problems in Marx's *Capital* that are related to the theory of crisis.

Throughout this translation, all references to Marx's *Capital*, Volumes 1, 2 and 3, come from the Penguin edition unless otherwise noted.

I first read and studied *Theory of Crisis* in 1998–2000 in Japan, at a time when I was conducting historical and archival research on Japan's colonization of Korea, and on the everyday struggles of Korean workers in inter-war Japan. I did this research through an affiliation with the Ohara Institute for Social Problems at Hōsei University, where I met Professor Yutaka Nagahara (Department of Economics). I thank Nagahara for his teachings over the years.[1] Nagahara urged me to read Uno's *Theory of Crisis*, as well as Tsutomu Ouchi's *Nōgyō Kyōkōron*, or *Theory of Agrarian Crisis*, and I slowly began learning how to use Marx's *Capital*, Lenin's *Imperialism, the highest stage of capitalism*, Uno's fundamental principles for political economy, his theory of crisis and his theory of the stages of capitalist development, for the historical and concrete analysis of capitalism and imperialism in Japan, as well as for the analysis of the colonization of Korea (1910–1945).

Of course, Uno's *Theory of Crisis* is not a book about the history of capitalism in Japan in particular, and it generally refrains from speaking about the concrete history of Japanese workers' struggles directly. Moreover, *Theory of Crisis* says nothing directly about the history of Korean workers, or about the colonization of Korea. Yet, this is precisely what I found most useful about Uno's *Theory of Crisis* when I first read it, for, from the outset, it theoretically subverted a certain national(ist) discourse and its eternalizing histories of the nation that commonly blind social scientific analyses of colonialism and capitalism, not to mention those of 'modern Japanese history' or 'modern Korean history'. Instead, Uno's *Theory of Crisis* provided me with two, more theoretically objective and scientific problems to research: "the commodification of labour power" (労働力の商品化) and "imperialism," as a historical stage of capitalism. Through Uno's *Theory of Crisis*, as well as through Uno's tri-level method for research in political economy (Uno's *sandankairon*), I learned how and why I should read Marx's *Capital* for its logical exposition of capital, as well as Lenin's *Imperialism, the highest stage of capitalism*, for its historical analysis of capitalism's stages of development. Uno's method for political economy 'completes' both the theory of capital (based on Marx's *Capital*), as well as the theory of the stages of capitalist development, precisely in order to ground the production of concrete and historical knowledge of contemporary capitalist society (specifically after 1917) for the advancement of socialist and communist struggles. In my research, the concrete analysis shed light upon the everyday struggles of colonized Korean workers that surrounded the process of transforming "Korean" labour power into a commodity after World War One and before the outbreak of World War Two. This research was published as *The Proletarian Gamble: Korean Workers in Interwar Japan* (Duke UP, 2009).

1 Cf., Yutaka Nagahara, *Tennōsei Kokka to Nōmin* (The Emperor System and Peasants), Nihon Keizai Hyōronsha, 1989; and *Warera kashi no arumonotachi: Han 'shihon' ron no tame ni* [We, the Defective Commodities: For an Analytics of Anti-'Capital'-ism], Tokyo: Seidosha (2008).

As I mentioned above, Uno's *Theory of Crisis* was re-published in Japan in 2009, one year after the so-called 'sub-prime mortgage crisis' of 2008. In early 2010, I myself began translating *Theory of Crisis* from Japanese (which is not my native language) into English (which is my native English), but quickly realized that this was not going to be an easy task. Not only was Uno's writing (and lecturing style) extremely difficult, at times, for me to comprehend on the purely linguistic and semiotic level of the Japanese language; it was additionally difficult because of the sheer intensity of Uno's commanding and demanding discourse on Marx's *Capital*. Of course, I had been reading and studying *Capital* for years already and considered myself someone with relatively good knowledge of the text, at least compared to many in my eclectic, postmodern and postcolonial generation. But over the first several years of translating Uno's *Theory of Crisis*, I experienced the sinking feeling of being (and becoming) what can only be described as a 'late-developing Marxist'. In other words, I had a lot of studying and 'catching-up' to do, especially regarding Marx's *Capital*. Similar to so-called 'late-developing countries', all that I could do – just as Marx had said – was to "shorten and lessen the birth pangs" (Marx, *Preface to the First Edition of Capital*).

Ten years later, I was finally able to deliver a complete English translation of *Theory of Crisis*, but its birth still had many linguistic and theoretical 'defects'. Fortunately, in early 2020, I had the great opportunity of working with Professor (Emeritus) Makoto Itoh of The University of Tokyo, who studied with Professor Kōzō Uno himself, and who organized a team of three other professors, all economists and specialists of Uno's theories and research, to meticulously read, revise, and to correct my draft translation. In addition to Professor Itoh, these were professors Kiyoshi Nagatani (Shinshū University, Department of Economics), Kosuke Oki (Kagawa University, Department of Economics); and Professor Thomas Sekine (York University).[2]

2 My debt to these professors goes well beyond their corrections of my translation, and extends to their research and published books. It was around 2010 that I began reading the works (in English) of Professor Makoto Itoh, especially his *Value and Crisis* and *The Basic Theory of Capitalism: The Forms and Substance of the Capitalist Economy* (1988). I also studied Professor Sekine's English translations of two of the most important works in Uno's method for political economy: *Keizai Genron* (*II*), or *Principles of Political Economy: Theory of a Purely Capitalist Society* (Harvester Press, 1980), and *The Types of Economic Policies under Capitalism* (Haymarket Books, 2016). My grasp of Marx's *Capital* and Uno's methodology was also deepened by Professor Kōsuke Oki's *Tomi naki jidai no shihonshugi* (Capitalism in the Age of no Wealth) (Gendai Shōkan, 2019), and *Jōyōkachi no seiji keizaigaku* (The political economy of surplus value), Nihon Keizai Hyōronsha (2012), as well as by Professor Kiyoshi Nagatani's *Shijō keizai toiu yōkai: shihonron no chōsen to gendai* (The Spectre of the Market Economy:

The team divided up the chapters for revision and corrections. Chapters 1 and 2 were corrected by Professor Nagatani; Chapters 3, 4, and 5 by Professor Itoh; the two Appendix chapters by Professor Oki; and the Introduction was read by Professor Sekine. Professor Oki also generously reviewed and corrected my revised translation of the Introduction in July of 2020. Professors Itoh and Nagatani then went over my revisions yet again in the winter of 2020. As a result of this collective effort, my original English translation has been greatly improved, and I simply could not have completed the translation without their help. I thank the professors from the bottom of my heart for their generosity and Promethean effort, and for correcting and forgiving me of my many errors and mistakes. Whatever defects and errors that remain are mine.

Translating Uno's *Theory of Crisis* from Japanese into English has been one of the most difficult yet transformative experiences of my life. It is my hope that it lives up to what Walter Benjamin once wrote of the 'task of the translator': "It is the task of the translator to release in his own language that pure language which is under the spell of another, to liberate the language imprisoned in a work in his re-creation of that work."[3]

As you will read in this volume, the notion of 'the commodification of labour power' is central to Uno's overall method for political economy. The process known as the commodification of labour power represents the essential core of Uno's theory of the fundamental principles of political economy. It is therefore also the core of his *Theory of Crisis*, which Uno considered the conclusion or culmination of the fundamental principles. Moreover, on a lighter note, it is well known by many Japanese readers, researchers and scholars of Uno's theories that Uno himself only half-jokingly considered the phrase, 'the commodification of labour power', as a kind of personal *mantra*, perhaps suggesting that, if repeated (or chanted) enough times, it could bring about sudden (revolutionary) enlightenment. I can only speak for myself, but after nearly twenty years of repeating 'the commodification of labour power' – in discourse, in research, and in concrete, everyday life – I can confirm that it has definitely led to a revolutionary awakening.

Therefore, I have kept "the commodification of labour power" throughout the text, but I should mention that other terms could also be used for 'labour power', such as the 'human ability to work', or 'labour-capacity'. In other words,

Challenging the market economy and the present with Marx's *Capital*), Shakai Hyōronsha, 2013.

3 Benjamin, Walter, "The Task of the Translator," *Illuminations: Essays and Reflections*, New York: Schoken Books, 1968.

the ultimate relevance of the phrase is that it draws our attention to Marx's *concept* of labour power itself. As Marx wrote: "We mean by labour-power, or labour-capacity, the aggregate of those mental and physical capabilities existing in the physical form, the living personality, of a human being, capabilities which he [sic] sets in motion whenever he produces a use-value of any kind."[4]

One could say that Uno's entire method for political economy is built upon Marx's concept of labour-power as a commodity, which represents capitalism's basic contradiction, i.e., where capitalist society is the weakest and most vulnerable. The 'Achilles Heel' of capitalism, so to speak, is found in the fact that, on the one hand, *if* capital is to produce surplus-value and make profit for the capitalist class, which it is designed to do, then capital must necessarily *consume* labour power *as a commodity* in the production and labour process; on the other hand, however, labour power is a peculiar 'thing' that capital actually cannot produce as a commodity directly. As Uno writes in *Theory of Crisis*, "*The establishment of a capitalist commodity economy can only come about with the commodification of that which capital itself cannot produce, namely labour power.*" (p. 44) This reveals how the existence of capital is fundamentally restricted historically and socially, precisely around our labour power, which represents capital's weakness, and therefore – dialectically – our fundamental advantage and point of resistance *to* capital, our potential social and political leverage *over* capital. For this reason, Uno constantly refers to this basic contradiction of capitalist society. In the words of Itoh and Lapavitsas, it points to, "the contradiction of the unavoidable commodification of labour power, on the one hand, and the inevitably incomplete character of this process, on the other."[5] Which is to say that, whenever we consider a capitalist commodity economy and its basic method of dominating a society, we should recognize that, from the outset, its basic method is fundamentally contradictory and incomplete, and therefore fundamentally transient and immanently possible to change, precisely beginning with a radical rethinking of 'the commodification of labour power' and subjectivity.[6]

At the same time, Uno's *Theory of Crisis* also reveals just how much the problem of the commodification of labour power has been consistently repressed theoretically in the political-economic unconscious of Marxist discourse in

4 Marx, *Capital*, Volume 1, 1990, p. 270.

5 Itoh and Lapavitsas, *Political Economy of Money and Finance*, Palgrave-McMillan, 1999, p. 135.

6 On the relation between the commodification of labour power and the politics of subject-formation, see Kawashima and Walker's article, "Uno's *Theory of Crisis* Today", in this volume. See also Gavin Walker's *Sublime Perversion of Capital* (2016), chapter 4, "Labor Power: Capital's Threshold".

general, and in prevailing Marxist theories of crisis, in particular. Uno's method for political economy, which is also, as Professor Itoh would say, "a political economy for socialism", is based on liberating "the commodification of labour power" from its theoretical repression, precisely to shed concrete and historical light upon its sublation and overcoming in actuality, in practice, and in class struggle.

Finally, in addition to the complete English translation of Uno's *Theory of Crisis*, we have also included two additional texts. The first is authored by Professor Makoto Itoh and titled, "Guiding Comments". In this text, Professor Itoh extends Uno's analysis of contemporary capitalism to the era of neoliberalism and to the so-called sub-prime mortgage crisis of 2008–2009. Importantly, Itoh identifies the 'financialization of labour power' in our present conjuncture of contemporary capitalism, which extends Uno's original identification of the commodification of labour power as capitalism's fundamental contradiction and weakness. This is an essay that the professor originally wrote for the 2009 Japanese paperback version of *Theory of Crisis*. For this volume, it has been translated by Guy Yasko and edited by the professor and myself. For those interested in reading more about Uno's work in political economy, I strongly recommend Professor Itoh's recently re-published book, *Value and Crisis: Essays on Marxian Economics in Japan* (2021), which contains a wealth of chapters on different aspects of Uno's research and methodology for political economy, as well as his *Basic Theory of Capitalism: The Forms and Substance of the Capitalist Economy* (1980); *Political Economy for Socialism* (1999); and *Political Economy of Money and Finance* (1999), co-authored with Costas Lapavitsas.

The second text is an article co-authored by myself, Ken C. Kawashima (University of Toronto, Department of East Asian Studies), and Professor Gavin Walker (McGill University, Department of History/East Asian Studies), titled, "Uno Kōzō's *Theory of Crisis* Today". This essay is the result of many years of conversations about Uno's work and its center of possibility for radical theory and politics today. In this text, we discuss Uno's *Theory of Crisis* after the 2008 crisis and in our present conjuncture, as well as Uno's approach to crisis, imperialism, and the question of labour power as a commodity. We also make theoretical inter-connections between Uno's methodology for political economy, on the one hand, and problems of state power and subject-formation in the works of Deleuze-Guattari, Foucault, Althusser and Poulantzas, on the other. Gavin Walker's book, *The Sublime Perversion of Capital: Marxist Theory and the Politics of History in Modern Japan* (2016), is also an inspired and brilliant book that delves into the heart of Uno's method for political economy, not only in relation to the famous debate on capitalism in Japan in the early 1930s, but also in relation to contemporary theories of the subject, and I recommend his book to anyone interested in Uno's thought.

Many people have made this translation possible and, indeed, inevitable. I would like to thank: Mouna Mannai, for her loving support and constant encouragement throughout this whole process; Mama JJ and Sistah Kimi, Brothers Jason, Derek and Luc; Gavin Walker (aka 'Mad Science'), for his friendship and comradeship, and for what we call the "Alongside" project, the first iteration of which is found in our essay in this volume; Harry Harootunian, whose historical and theoretical research in Marxism and Japanese intellectual history originally inspired 'all of this' for me; my students at the University of Toronto, Department of East Asian Studies, for their hard work and for enduring my lectures on *Capital* and Uno; professors and comrades Eric Cazdyn, Bruce Cumings, Mark Driscoll, Katsuhiko Endo, Kanishka Goonewardena, Asad Haider, Andy Higginbottom, Katsu Hirano, Sabu Kohso, Kojin Karatani, Rebecca Karl, Wendy Matsumura, Yutaka Nagahara, Kōsuke Oki, Hyun Ok Park, Kristin Plys, Janet Poole, Kristin Ross, Naoki Sakai, Andre Schmid, Gavin Smith, Jesook Song, Robert Stolz, and Alberto Toscano for their solidarity and encouragement; and Sebastien Budgen and Danny Hayward of the *Historical Materialism* book series, and Jennifer Obdam of Brill Publishers, for their organization, patience and support for this publication.

I wish to especially thank Professor Makoto Itoh for generously overseeing the many revisions and corrections of the translation, and for coaching me not only on the finer and deeper points of Uno's *Theory of Crisis*, but also, inevitably, on the work of Marx himself, who wrote these words about the future of 'the universal crisis', which reverberate so loudly today:

> The contradictions inherent in the movement of capitalist society impress themselves upon the practical bourgeois most strikingly in the changes of the periodic cycle, through which modern industry runs, and *whose crowning point is the universal crisis*. That crisis is once again approaching, although as yet but in its preliminary stage; and by the universality of its theatre and the intensity of its action it will drum dialectics even into the heads of the mushroom-upstarts of the new, holy … empire.[7]

Ken C. Kawashima
Toronto, Canada
March 26, 2021

7 Marx, *Capital*, Vol. 1, "Postface to the Second Edition", p. 103.

Author's Preface

Most people today, it is probably safe to say, will readily recognise how the phenomenon of crisis is an inevitable peculiarity of capitalist society. Indeed, it has already become clear that those who, more recently, deny crisis as an inevitable manifestation of the contradictions of capitalism are not able to demonstrate this denial theoretically. This denial of the inevitability of crisis is inspired by the fact that crisis has taken various forms along with the various stages of capitalist development. Instead of speaking of crisis, however, they speak, for example, of war, thereby adding a further level of difficulty. This raises the problem of why a theory of the fundamental principles of political economy, one that strives to explain the general economic laws of capitalism, has never irrefutably demonstrated the inevitability of the phenomenon of crisis. Even in *Capital*, which, I believe, comes the closest to completing the theory of the fundamental principles of political economy, does not give us such a demonstration. Moreover, among those who study the work of Marx, while there have been many different debates about crisis – not just in our country but all over the world – they often overlap theoretically, yet at the same time, they cannot provide a systematic and consistent explanation of this problem theoretically. It would not be wrong to say that the new condition that we face now, as a result, is that of a decline in concrete analysis, matched by rampant treatments of the so-called business cycles by vulgar economics. However, to substitute a theory of crisis for a theory of business cycles does nothing except to substitute a theory of fundamental principles for a theory of phenomena, or to commit to the mistaken approach of becoming overwhelmed by a theory of phenomena. As a result, foundational theories such as the theory of value unavoidably become buried in a theory of prices, or even become annulled by the latter altogether. No matter how precisely and correctly we develop a systematic theory of fundamental principles out of the theory of value, it would not have any credibility without the demonstration of the inevitability of crisis. For those who accept the Marxist approach to the theory of value, the theory of surplus value, as well as to theories of accumulation, profit, and rent, the clarification of the theory of crisis is still an important, yet unfinished, topic. It still remains unfinished because it is a topic of research that was not completed in *Capital*. In my opinion, this is not a topic that can afford to remain unexamined.

In my *Fundamental Principles of Political Economy*,[1] I tried in my own way to solve this problem, but since I was, as they say, wandering in the dark and

1 [Transl. note: This refers to Uno's *Keizaigenron I, II*, in UKC, Vols. 1 and 2. The English trans-

unaware of many things, I was not able to theorise where, within the theory of the fundamental principles of political economy, a theory of crisis had to be demonstrated. Concretely, I did not theoretically postulate how and why the theory of crisis had to be theoretically developed before the logical exposition of commercial capital and after that of loan capital. There have been many debates on this point in the past and I think it has left many readers unsatisfied. Of course, in a book such as this one, which specifically theorises the phenomena of crisis, I should probably re-examine these old debates and describe my position point by point. At present, however, I have neither the time nor the ability to do this. Instead, I would like to state anew my opinions on matters dealing with my *Principles of Political Economy: Theory of a Purely Capitalist Society*, a text which I mentioned earlier very briefly, and to address those methodological points that I did not consider necessary to enunciate at the time. This should make certain parts of the *Fundamental Principles* easier to understand, but it has also led to a disproportionately long introductory chapter of this book.

Originally, this book was written on the basis of a series of special lectures that I gave at the Faculty of Economics at the University of Tokyo, and that was published as a correspondence lecture at Hōsei University, titled "Principles of Political Economy." While this book cannot avoid repeating many basic problems, these repetitions should at least make my thinking on these matters more accessible. For the publication of this book, therefore, I have only touched up on my words and phrases here and there, and have not revised the texts. As for the two essays in the Appendix – one from *Social Science Research* from Tokyo University's Institute of Social Sciences, the other from *Research in Political Economy* from Hitotsubashi University – both deal with the development of the theory of crisis in the text of *Capital*, and with what I consider to be its most difficult points.[2] While most of these problems are positively represented in the main parts of this book, I have published these essays here, as I believe it is appropriate for me to clarify how my own thinking of these problems has essentially been based on the theoretical exposition of *Capital* itself. The first essay begins with a comment on the work of Professor Kuruma Samezō. His newly published book, *Research in the Theory of Crisis*, contained criticisms of sev-

lation of *Keizaigenron II*, which is a condensed version of *Keizaigenron I*, exists in Thomas Sekine's *Principles of Political Economy: Theory of a Purely Capitalist Society*, Sussex: Harvester Press, 1980.]

2 [Transl. note: The English translations of these articles are found at the end of this book, as Appendix 1 and 2. They were originally published in June (Appendix 1) and October (Appendix 2) of 1952.]

eral points of my understanding of his theory of crisis, but I did not feel it was especially necessary to respond to his criticisms explicitly. And even if my own understanding of his text was insufficient or mistaken, it does not change the point of my argument itself in this essay. I have therefore reprinted the text in its original version. The one and only point that I felt was meaningful in Professor Kuruma's criticisms is whether wages can be theorised, within the fundamental principles, in cases when wages exceed, or else fall beneath, the value of labour power. I address this problem to a certain extent in this book, but depending on the nature of the matter, we must also refer to fluctuations of other commodities, not to mention wage fluctuations. This point is also made in *Capital*, as well. Crucially, on this point, the commodity of labour power, which is unlike any other commodity insofar as it cannot be capitalistically produced directly, discloses extremely profound problems which explain the striking difference between the price fluctuations of labour power and those of other commodities. I would like to take up these matters theoretically, provided that I can clarify these difficult problems, but this will have to wait until another occasion.

On this point, which has been considered the most difficult to solve, and which has been discussed repeatedly, I would like to leave it up to my readers and students to judge, for themselves, the extent to which this book, as well as my *Fundamental Principles*, can clarify these problems and withstand scientific criticism.

Kōzō Uno
28 July, 1954

Uno Kōzō, Kyōkō Ron (*Theory of Crisis*)

Introduction

The crisis that broke out in the wake of the New York stock market crash of October 1929 was the most acute and extensive world crisis of recent times. It was followed by a prolonged depression in the first half of the 1930s. None of the world's leading capitalist nations could stand by idly and do nothing, and every means were carefully considered and put to use to 'save' the economy. In every country throughout the 1930s, it became clear that the fundamental causes of the powerful tendency towards statism, as well as of the outbreak of World War Two, were found in this economic process. Nonetheless, in the preceding year, not a single person in the United States was able to foresee this massive crisis.[1] A year before the crisis, a period of prosperity – known as the so-called Hoover bubble – continued, even to the point of glossing over the chronic world agricultural crisis that followed World War One.[2] In the midst of the 1928 presidential elections, '[Hoover] had informed the American people

1 For example, in the recently translated *Aspirin Age, 1919–1941*, and in the section titled 'The Crash – and What it Meant', we find the following quotation taken from an editorial article from 1 January 1929 in the *New York Times*: 'But it will be hard to get people to think of 1928 as merely a "dead past" which we must make haste to bury. It has been a twelvemonth of unprecedented advance, of wonderful prosperity – in this country at least … If there is any way of judging the future by the past, this new year may well be one of felicitation and hopefulness' (Thurman Wesley Arnold, 1949, p. 215).

2 In order to explain crises stemming from agricultural crises, it is necessary to distinguish agricultural crises from general industrial crisis. Although this point cannot be clarified unless it can be shown how the development of capitalism uniquely influences agriculture, agricultural crisis does not break out periodically. As a result, agricultural crises do not proceed from phases of crisis to depression to prosperity, as with industrial crises. The agricultural crisis in western Europe that accompanied the development of world transportation relations of the late nineteenth century, and especially the world agricultural crisis that accompanied the development of colonial agriculture following the end of World War One, both appeared at definite stages of the development of capitalism. Based on specific relations of the world market, agricultural crisis is fundamentally different from the crises which appear under the general determinations of capitalism. General industrial crisis – which includes within it agriculture, which itself must be assumed theoretically to be managed capitalistically – started later, and appears in concretely different forms depending on the stage of development of capitalism. The world agricultural crisis following World War One, which intensified the depression following the great crisis of 1929, simply cannot be thought apart from industrial crisis in the latest stage of capitalism. However, the crisis which we wish to clarify here must be distinguished from agricultural crisis theoretically. As I will discuss later in terms of general determinations, the changes themselves to the forms of crisis phenomena, which accompany the development of capitalism, must also be abstracted.

that they could expect two chickens in every pot and two cars in every garage as part of the normal standard of living for every family'.[3] Indeed, the phase of prosperity that lasted from 1928 to early 1929 was an unprecedented one, even though, depending on the industrial sector, production did not necessarily rise uniformly and full employment was not enjoyed.[4]

A vivid passage from *The Aspirin Age* describes the autumn of 1929, when the crisis suddenly broke out. It is a bit long but I wish to quote it in its entirety:

> Wall Street was fully in accord with such sentiments [which President Hoover articulated, as mentioned in the passage above]. During May and June, 1928, stocks wavered, but as Election Day approached, the market advanced. And when Hoover rolled in by twenty-one million votes to Al Smith's fifteen million, the Dow Jones industrials soared to 300. The 'New Era' had arrived. A new school of economics argued that when you buy common stocks, you buy the future, not the present. Imaginative projections of earnings, five and ten years ahead, flourished … U.S. Steel, American Telephone, and Eastman Kodak, reached all-time highs.
>
> Inauguration Day – March 4, 1929 – found Wall Street even more ebullient. The Dow Jones industrials were up another 20 points. When stocks faltered in April, Wall Street seers regarded it as a 'buying opportunity'. And so it proved for a few months. By August the Dow Jones industrials

3 Arnold, Thurman Wesley, 1949, p. 216.

4 The monthly average of industrial production in the United States of America was the following, with prices of February 1927 calculated to 100.

	Total industrial factories	Steel and iron ore	Automobiles	Misc. textiles	Leather goods, shoes	Foodstuffs
Feb. 1927	100	100	100	100	100	100
June 1928	111	121	153	103	104	97
Dec. 1928	117	131	197	106	97	109
June 1929	129	165	219	116	108	100

SOURCE: LEAGUE OF NATIONS 1931, P. 124

As for unemployed workers, the unemployment rate was 12% and 13% for card-carrying workers in America in 1928 and 1929 (September), respectively (League of Nations 1931, p. 69).

> hit 380. But somehow, somewhere, the old zip was lacking. Pools worked valiantly, but stocks trashed about getting nowhere. The first in September stocks climbed to 381. That high stands to this day.
>
> The break came early in September. There was a mid-month recovery, but it was the last gasp. Liquidation increased. Brokers' clerks worked long hours sending out margin calls. Came Thursday, October 24. Panic. U.S. Steel, which had been as high as 261 ¾, opened at 205 ½, crashed through 200, and soon was down to 193 ½. General Electric, which only a few weeks before sold above 400, opened at 315, dropped to 283 ...
>
> The climax came November 13, 1929. The Dow Jones average dropped to 198.7. And how the high and mighty fell! American Can was down from 181 7/8 to 86; American Tel. and Tel. from 304 to 197 ¼; General Motors from 72 ¾ to 36; New York Central from 256 3/8 to 160; United States Steel from 261 ¾ to 150. 'The Big Bull Market was dead.' And Coolidge-Hoover Prosperity was dead with it.[5]

In this manner, America after 1930 had fallen into a depression that was unimaginable in 1928. Production fell off, unemployment rose, and it became difficult to reduce goods in stock. General prices fell sharply and suddenly. Particularly big was the fall in prices for agricultural products, and in general a fall in prices for raw materials outdid a fall in prices for finished goods.[6] With the presid-

5 Arnold, Thurman Wesley, 1949, pp. 216–17.

6 The fall in industrial production in America can be gleaned in the following trends (Eugen Varga, *World Economic Crises, 1848–1935*, translated by Michio Nagasumi, Vol. 1, Part 2, Tokyo: Keiō Shobo, 1938, pp. 428–9).

Figures for years 1923 to 1925 have been calculated to 100.

Year	1925	1926	1927	1928	1929	1930	1931	1932	1933	1934
Index	104	108	106	111	119	96	81	64	76	79

Regarding the rise in unemployment, a general trend can be gleaned from the following unemployment rates (Varga, 1938, p. 430).

Year	1925	1926	1927	1928	1929	1930	1931	1932	1933	1934
%	8.9	7.2	14	13	12	21	26	32	31	26

ential election of 1932 going to Roosevelt, the famous New Deal policy was pressed into service, but it only turned out to be an inflationary-type of policy for depression. Nonetheless, what was clearly revealed by this crisis were the results and effects brought on by an increase in the productive forces of capitalist society, which could no longer be taken as a simple matter of putting 'two chickens in every pot and two cars in every garage', as President Hoover waxed. Thus, even if it is true that, on the basis of an advance in productivity, the general standard of everyday life rose, it was never actualised in such simplistic depictions. In the depression of the 1930s, for example, many countries adopted public works projects as relief measures, precisely over capitalism's inability to manage the increase in its own productive forces, and yet these projects could never save capitalism itself. Rather, by 1938, England and the United States had already fallen into a crisis, one which Germany and Japan managed to

---

Varga, moreover, writes: 'In the darkest hour of the crisis, the number of unemployed workers reached between fifteen and seventeen million. After the crisis had been overcome, a rise in production could not increase employment to match this figure' (1938, p. 436).

As for the amount of goods in stock, the following figures give us a glimpse into the matter. Figures for 1923 to 1925 are calculated at 100.

	Raw materials	Manufactured goods
June 1929	120	121
Dec. 1929	186	119
June 1930	125	125
Dec. 1930	195	121
June 1931	144	120

Source: League of Nations 1931, p. 145

Year	1925	1926	1927	1928	1929	1930	1931	1932	1933	1934
General prices	151	146	139	141	139	126	107	95	96	109
Agricultural prices	154	141	139	149	147	124	91	68	72	92

Source: Varga 1938, p. 432

While we cannot generalise this directly for the reason that monopoly capital influences the comparison between raw materials and manufactured (or finished) goods, the prices for the former fell 30% between June of 1929 and June of 1931, while prices for the latter fell 20% (League of Nations 1931, p. 168).

avoid by turning to an expansion of armaments. This is an extremely important phenomenon to consider. The fact that the great crisis of 1929 has not been repeated since then needs to be considered in conjunction with how, during the interim period, the extraordinary and extremely exhausting Second World War broke out.

In the theory of crisis that follows in this book, however, my intention is neither to analyse the processes of individual crises, nor to elucidate their causes. Of course, it is extremely important for political economic research to analyse phenomena of individual crises, to clarify their causes and results, and indeed to include such an analysis within the ultimate goals of political economic research. Jumping immediately into the concrete processes of crisis does not guarantee analytic success, however. While the previously mentioned text, *The Aspirin Age*, fiercely criticized and dexterously described how politicians, industrialists, and economists alike performed various activities during periods of prosperity and post-crisis depressions and in various and pointed ways (even without knowing the essence of the conditions of crisis) this text says nothing about the cause of crisis itself. Of course, this was not the purpose of that essay, which was to merely narrate the 'crash' and nothing more. The challenges of analysing the actual processes of crises are clearly evident in their analysis, yet they could not persuasively clarify the problem of the fundamental cause of crisis, even when adequate archival materials were at their disposal, such as the League of Nations' *The Course and Phases of the World Economic Depression*.[7] This points to extremely important methodological problems for research in political economy, so before I begin the main discussion of this book, I would like to offer my thoughts on this matter.

It goes without saying that *the capitalist commodity economy*, which became the object of research in political economy, did not begin with *the history of humankind*, but rather appeared at a determinate historical period in the seventeenth and eighteenth centuries. From the perspective of the history of humankind, this is very recent. The *commodity economy* itself, of course, is considerably old, having developed through the ancient and medieval worlds. On occasion, this development manifested phenomena bearing resemblances to crisis, but the commodity economy was not something that simply followed

7 Professor Kuruma Samezō has also criticised the nature of this clarification in relation to the UN's *World Economic Survey*, which offers materials and elucidations on post-crisis depressions.

one path of development. Rather, in pre-capitalist societies the commodity economy developed to various and different degrees of development, but it had yet to reach the point of establishing its own basic social relations. This only came about with the character of the commodity itself, which is an extremely important point. As Marx pointed out, the exchange of commodities originally emerged, 'where communities have their boundaries, at their points of contact with other communities, or with members of the latter'.[8] Commodity exchange, therefore, does not emerge from the interior life of a so-called society, but rather at the boundaries between societies, where it then reacts back osmotically into society's interior life. As a result of this osmotic movement, different societies are brought together into a union, with the characteristic of forming a larger, single society. In other words, the *Gesellschaft*, which is formed as a union between *Gemeinschaft* and *Gemeinschaft*, is that which we call a commodity society. Whether we speak of the ancient or medieval societies, commodity economies by and large enact this osmotic role. At the same time, however, commodity economies frequently formed societies which differed in scope from the original, ancient and medieval societies. This is what I would call *a society on the outside of society*, which did not form a *single society* that replaced the old society. Nonetheless, the formation of this kind of *commodity society* took place by extending itself osmotically to *the interior* of a society, leading to the progressive advance of the productive forces of that society, on the one hand, while more or less destroying the social relations of that society, on the other. In medieval society, for example, those relations included those between the feudal lord and the peasants. Thus, even if exchange relations of commodities extend the scope of society and osmotically penetrate into the interior life of society, this does not necessarily lead to the fact that commodity economies, as in today's capitalist society, have been able to control the fundamental social relation of society as a result of their development. Quite the contrary, many countries disintegrated within this process and were succeeded by new countries, which introduced and digested the results of past historical development through commodity exchange relations. Commodity economies thereby established a wider range and scope. In this way, in seventeenth- and eighteenth-century England, the commodity society came to control a single society for the first time, and *the birth of capitalist society* was realized. Society – as a so-called *Gemeinschaft* – was transformed into a *Gesellschaft*.

8 *Capital*, Vol. 1, p. 182.

This process implies that capitalism itself also has a definite process of development. Put differently, capitalism was born at a historically definite period and within the extremely restricted territory of England, whose social foundations it took hold of as it gradually impinged upon other countries. Especially after the so-called industrial revolution in the late eighteenth century, all of society in England fell under the domination of *the principle of the commodity economy* for the first time. Yet, this does not at all mean that a capitalist commodity economy was *fully* established. Occupying the centre of international commodity exchange in the nineteenth century, England by mid-century was certainly the most archetypical capitalist nation in the world, and yet, despite this, certain strata from the old society – intermediary strata that were neither capitalists, workers, nor capitalist landowners – remained left over. At this stage, however, the social relations of the old society themselves were dominated by the principle of the commodity economy, and took capitalist forms as *legal fictions*. For example, the small, independent farmer is analogously 'considered as his own employer (capitalist), employing himself as a worker, and as his own landowner, using himself as his own farmer. He pays himself wages as a worker, lays claim to profit as a capitalist and pays himself rent as a landowner'.[9] Saying this, however, does not mean that every small farmer was simultaneously a worker, a capitalist, or a capitalist landowner. In fact, at least up to the 1860s, the development of the capitalist commodity economy advanced in the direction of actualising the principles of a commodity economy, all the while simultaneously breaking down the strata of the old society. After the late nineteenth century, however, the same could no longer be said, necessarily. Thus, while the capitalist commodity economy first developed around England, it actualised the era of finance capital when so-called late developing countries, such as the United States and Germany, transformed into capitalist commodity economies. And while the effects of capitalistically breaking down the strata of the old society were not entirely suspended, the development of relations no longer tended to advance in a straightforward manner. This was not merely due to the work of policy, however. On the one hand, the capitalist commodity economy was able to maintain the old social strata, as they already existed, while also using these old strata for the augmentation of capital, on the other. Indeed, it could not help but to use these old strata in this way. Unlike the seventeenth and eighteenth centuries, when capitalism first emerged, or the nineteenth century, when capitalism grew to maturity, capitalism after the end

9 *Capital*, Vol. 3, p. 1015.

of the nineteenth century entered a stage of full maturity, or what we could even call a *period of decline*.

Unless we are able to clarify the essential character of commodity economies, as I have described above, we will not fully understand the historical significance of these *stages of development* of the capitalist economy. While the commodity economy originally appeared as an inter-social trading order from the ancient period, the historical fact of capitalism is that it began by converting the commodity economy into society's internal principles at a definite period. This implies capitalism's terminal features of ending at a certain stage, as well. For us, this means that whenever we illuminate *the general principles of the capitalist commodity economy*, we demand that these extreme aspects be taken into account in our method.[10] A method that seeks to directly clarify general economic *norms* that are common to all forms of human society is out of the question, of course, but there is a problem, whenever we explain the economic laws of a specifically capitalist commodity economy, to think that every aspect of society is completely transformed into a capitalist society simply as a mere consequence of an increasingly developed capitalist commodity economy, for this inevitably obscures the relationship between the general principles of political economy, and the stage of capitalist development after the end of the nineteenth century, or the so-called stage of finance capital. This leads to errors in understanding the essence of the general principles, and therefore, at the same time, in the method of its use.

This is a problem not only for political economy, but for all disciplines that strive to clarify historical processes from the perspective of the social sciences. To clarify a determinate social principle means, on the one hand, to take, as an object of analysis, the society which transforms social forms at a determinate period, and which changes ineluctably into the social forms of another society through a definite process of development. On the other hand, it also means that the general principles of a society, as they are commonly applied to different stages of development, must also be clarified. To put it differently, the social principles certainly clarify the processes of a given society's emergence, growth, and decline, but these processes are not thereby expressed directly. What is clarified as social principles is expressed as if it can make society move and develop eternally. This means that what becomes a principle is something that is repeated, inevitably and necessarily. The historicity of a society's birth,

10 [Trans. Note: Cf., Uno's *Hohoron*, UCZ, vol. 9; also Uno's *'Capital' and Socialism* (1958), UCZ, vol. 10.

growth, and decline becomes hidden in the background, so to speak. Thus, when we provide the exposition of the principles of political economy, as a system that begins with the 'commodity' and ends with 'all classes', questions such as the birth of 'commodities' or the end of 'classes' cannot be answered by the systematic principles itself. When, in *Capital*, Marx develops his systematic analysis, he on occasion explains the necessity of capitalism to transform into another kind of society. This problem, however, cannot be solved by the systematic principles themselves. This, at least, is how I understand it. There is no reason and no way that the principles, in and of themselves, can provide an exposition of a society's birth and death. The theory of the fundamental principles become systematised when the commodity, which appears at the outset of the system as the original '*archē*-commodity', is given within the relations of 'all classes', which is determined only at the end of the theory of the fundamental principles.[11] If the birth of 'commodities' and the end of 'classes' cannot be said to develop out of the systematic theory of the fundamental principles themselves, this is because the relationship between both is one in which the former is given by the latter. In other words, the fundamental principles have to consider capitalist society, which constantly enlarges and develops its social relations, as something that must be tentatively defined in this way. If not, we will not grasp the inevitability and necessity of these economic laws.

Of course, to say that these systematic, fundamental principles are correct and true does not mean that it recognises the eternal existence of capitalism. The principles can never be said to exist apart from history, as if in a vacuum. For political economy, this relation to history is secured in the form of the process of capitalism's development, or rather in the development of a commodity economy itself, which is reflected in a systematic theoretical exposition. This form takes as its starting point simple, individual commodities, and culminates in the manner by which classes embody economic laws, which pass through each and every capitalist society. The concept of simple commodities is something that can be applied to each and every stage of development of the commodity economy, and finally the concept of classes is something that is given its determinations for the first time when a capitalist commodity economy has completely come to dominate a single society. To put matters differently, we can say that the logical *exposition* reflects the *historical stages*

11 [Transl. note: Cf., *Capital*, Vol. 1, *Chapter* 1, 'The Commodity', and Vol. 3, Chapter 52, "Classes", the last chapter of *Capital*.]

of development from the perspective of commodity economies, and yet, at the same time, it does not simply reflect the concrete, historical developmental process itself. *It becomes the merely logical exposition of something which repeats the birth of capitalism over and over again within the reproduction process of capitalist society.* As something that repeats compulsively, it gives us the possibility to demonstrate theoretically what is simply a logical exposition. As I have emphasised earlier, we can say that in capitalist society, a commodity economy itself discloses a concrete, historical process of development because, in capitalist society, this process forms the basic principles within the interior of society, whereas in ancient and medieval societies, they only developed on the surface of society to some extent and in ways that were constantly determined by the interiority of that society, but that were also influencing that interior life to a limited degree. Therefore, in the theory of the fundamental principles of political economy, the exposition of the development from commodity to money, and from money to capital, does not itself disclose a concrete, historical process, nor does it reflect one. No matter the differences between societies, and thus the differences in the processes of their concrete development, the osmotic process of commodity economies that takes place on the surface of society will be the same, and the development from commodity to money, and from money to capital, will take place inexorably. However, the grasping and capturing by capital of the production process that forms the basis of society does not happen in any society, but if it takes place, a capitalist society will be formed without fail. In this sense, *in the fundamental principles, the exposition of the forms of circulation of commodity, money, and capital is followed by that of capital's production process as a definite and specific historical form.* Yet, even when capital's production process develops into the circulation and reproductive processes, and especially when profit is distributed into rent and interest, this alone does not point to the concrete, historical process of the development of capitalism. As a movement that abstracts from this concrete process, this exposition is such that, without the establishment of the preceding relationships, those that come later cannot be developed. At the same time, the determinations for that which comes before are included within the determinations for that which comes afterward. This does not mean, however, that everything is related horizontally and in parallel to each other, nor does it mean that the abstract determinations directly form a process of concrete development. I will speak more about this later, when I define the roles that commercial capital and loan capital play in the phase of crisis, but in theoretical political economy, something like merchant capital, for example, can only be considered through the substantial determinations of commercial capital, which presupposes industrial capital. This reveals how merchant capital occupies an extremely important position in the process of the concrete development of capitalism, exerting an enormous influence on it, but also why it cannot be reflected in theory directly. *Capital must be theoretically exposed as the form of merchant capital or money-lending capital, as something that generates without grasping the production process when money develops into capital.* This form would do nothing more than give us a theoretical exposition, as an abstract determination, that is constantly presupposed formally by industrial capital – which captures the production process – and that shares one aspect with merchant capital and money-lending capital. By contrast, *the process by which capital captures the production process must be exposed, in its pure form, as a process of the development of industrial capital itself.* The same can be said for landed property. When explaining how rent, as a branch of surplus value, exists as profit, the fundamental principles do not directly reflect the process by which actual landed property relations become completed as capitalist landed property relations. Rather, the principles provide an exposition of how the parts of surplus value, which are clarified from the outset as industrial profits to be distributed, are redistributed among property owners by their relation to the means of production, which possesses the peculiar restriction of nature, represented by land, which stands in opposition to capital. Marx's exposition of the so-called first form of differential rent into the second form of differential rent, and especially into absolute rent, represents theoretically and precisely the pure form of the process by which capitalist landed property relations are established. Put differently, the process by which a commodity economy comes to dominate a single society as a capitalist society is exposed from the perspective or aspect of the commodity economy. Concretely speaking, in ancient and medieval society, the commodity economy penetrated the interior of these societies from the outside, often annihilating these societies, and at long last their basic social relations were captured in the seventeenth and eighteenth centuries in England. By the mid-nineteenth century, after three-hundred years of history had been traversed, all of society came under the domination of this principle. In the fundamental principles, this process is logically exposed as the development of the commodity economy. As Marx wrote:

> the physicist either observes physical phenomena where they occur in their most typical form and most free from disturbing influence, or, wherever possible, he makes experiments under conditions that assure the occurrence of the phenomenon in its pure form. In this work I have to examine the capitalist mode of production, and the conditions of production and exchange corresponding to that mode. Up to the present time,

> their classic ground is England. That is the reason why England is used as the chief illustration in the development of my theoretical ideas.[12]

In other words, throughout *Capital*, illustrations were taken from the history of the concrete processes of capitalism's genesis and development in England. Of course, this is not to say that *Capital* realizes the equivalent of experiments in the natural sciences through the theoretically reconstructed world image based on abstractions taken from concrete, historical processes, and that it demonstrates that capitalist social relations must be this way if they emerge purely and completely. 'Intrinsically', as Marx wrote,

> it is not a question of the higher or lower degree of development of the social antagonisms that result from the natural laws of capitalist production. It is a question of these laws themselves, of these tendencies working with iron necessity towards inevitable results. The country that is more developed industrially only shows, to the less developed, the image of its own future.[13]

In this way, the fundamental principles are grasped as something that is repeated continually, in all capitalist societies, with an 'iron necessity'. In Marx's words from the preceding quotation, it is likely that this not only includes what I am calling the inevitability and necessity within the fundamental principles, but also the inevitability of the historical stages of development of capitalism. This necessity forces late-developing countries, for whatever reason, to pass through the historical stages through which the advanced countries have already passed, but at the same time, we must be careful not to assume that the concrete process of capitalist development in late-developing countries will necessarily take the same, concrete path that it took in the advanced countries. The development of capitalism in Germany and America, as countries which eventually came to dominate global capitalism, followed in the footsteps of England, and in fact superseded England in the latter half of the nineteenth century, and while Germany's development repeated, in some respects, the process of development of capitalism in England up to that time, it was hardly a mere repetition. *What the fundamental principles clarify are the drives that constitute what is common to the development of capitalism in all countries.* After the latter half of the nineteenth century, the development of capitalism in Ger-

12 *Capital*, Vol. 1, 90.
13 *Capital*, Vol. 1, 90–91.

many and the United States, which followed in the footsteps of England, imported the outcomes of the industrial revolution in their own period of capitalist emergence, and lagged behind but later surpassed England to become leading countries in world capitalism themselves, and while these late-developing countries repeated certain aspects of the process of development of capitalism in England up to that time, in other aspects it was never simply a mere repetition. We could even perhaps say that what is clarified as a principle is the principle that becomes a powerful driving force that propels that aspect which the development of capitalism in all countries have in common. At the same time, it is the principles of this drive which, in different periods, will develop different features. Capitalism in Germany, which passed through the transitional stage of the emergence of capitalism by importing the outcomes and results of the industrial revolution, was dominated by the same principles as those in England, but the process of capitalist transformation, of transforming into a capitalist society, was very different compared to England. In the end, Germany, along with the United States, pulled England into a new stage of capitalism. Furthermore, these different and various features of the stages of development already exist on a level of analysis that cannot be derived by the principles alone. Not only that, they cannot be reflected, as such, in the theoretical exposition of the principles. Put differently, if it can be said that the process of capitalist emergence in the seventeenth and eighteenth century, as well as of capitalist growth after the end of the eighteenth century in England, is reflected to a certain extent in the theoretical exposition of the fundamental principles, this is because theory itself must be grasped as something that forms what I call *a purely capitalist society* from within the process of the world-historical development of capitalism. This is the reason why the theory of the fundamental principles cannot but proceed from the simple to the complex, and from abstract determinations to concrete ones, which is also why theory reflects, to a certain degree, the process of emergence and growth of capitalism in England, but does not reflect capitalism after the end of the nineteenth century. Already by then, capitalism, as a concrete and historical process, no longer tended in the direction of becoming a purely capitalist society. Capitalism had already entered into a new and definite historical period, as a natural outcome of its own development, but this point falls outside the exposition of the fundamental principles. Principles, as a general economic law that propels capitalist society, must also be used, as I have described earlier, even for the analysis of the stage of so-called finance capital. This does not mean, however, that the era of finance capital is something that is found in the process that develops towards a purely capitalist society, which theory assumes. For research in political economy, which illuminates these kinds of historical processes theoretically, this is an extremely crucial problem of methodology. So long as this problem is left unclarified, we risk becoming overwhelmed by the mistaken view that theory is totally useless.[14]

14 The relationship between theory and praxis should not simply be called a 'dialectical unity of theory and practice' without clarifying this point. For even if we assume that theory can be verified according to praxis, what is the meaning of this praxis? So long as the meaning of theory is not clarified, how can we avoid mistakes and errors? Especially in scholarly research such as the social sciences – in which experiments cannot be carried out – it is not uncommon for experimentation to be treated as praxis, but in these cases both theory and praxis cannot really be understood. For the social sciences, theoretical abstraction is the only thing that can be said to correspond to the experiments in the natural sciences. In my understanding, this kind of abstraction is physically carried out in experiments in the natural sciences. It is in industry that the natural sciences are useful in practice. In the social sciences, however, their practical usefulness is found on the level of political movements. To consider economic theory in terms of its usefulness for individual industrial practices is nothing other than a vulgar error in conceptualising the essence of political economy as a social science. Even political praxis does not demonstrate theory. For example, if the necessity of creating a new society is inferred social scientifically, it is verified not by revolutionary practice. In any case, revolutionary practice is something that takes up complex processes that cannot be completely included in theoretical inference, but as long as these processes are not abstracted, such inferences can never be verified. The least that can be said is that, if one were to undertake a demonstration of the fundamental principles of political economy, this does not mean putting it to work in actuality. The only viable method is to make the theoretical construction as consistent as possible, as an abstraction of the social processes of industrial practice, and to examine the extent to which this construction can be demonstrated accurately – or not. As various economists have already shown, the verification of theory is carried out by a method that abstracts from a wide array of observational and historical materials in order to clarify relationships in terms of fundamental principles. We fall unavoidably into errors on precisely this point if we admit individual experiences directly into the fundamental principles, without having passed them through abstraction. Individual experiences can become theorised only insofar as they are abstracted to the point of their social relations. While an abstraction, theory can be said to be theory insofar as it can grasp these social relations in a systematic manner, and therefore in terms of a whole. This can only be done, however, if theory is something that is abstracted. For example, when we speak of the determinations in which the price of a commodity is an expression of value through money, this determination cannot be said to be in error simply because the value of commodities is not necessarily expressed, as it really is, as price, or even because there exists the fact of monopoly prices. Or, consider how, in our country, where the wages of workers are extremely low, to the point where they cannot purchase necessary means of subsistence to reproduce their labour power; even if this could be demonstrated statistically, for example, this cannot deny the determination by which the value of labour power takes the form of wage labour. In clarifying the economic laws that dominate capitalism, this kind of denial must never be allowed to happen. The thought that the general economic laws can be

For a theory of crisis, unnecessary confusions will invariably arise so long as its exposition is not based on a clarification of the research methods of political economy described above. Indeed, it is important to recognise this point that previous theories of crisis, by and large, have not clarified. In other words, for political economy, the first and most important point is that the phenomena of crisis must be illuminated by the fundamental principles as something that is inevitable to capitalist economies. In looking at the processes of individual, concrete crises, if the determinations based on the fundamental principles are omitted, we would be able to clarify neither the fundamental aspects of these crises, nor their individual, particular aspects. This does not mean, however, that we can analyse individual, concrete processes directly by the determinations of the fundamental principles alone. Our approach requires the mediation of different types of determinations of the world-historical stages of the development of capitalism. Especially with regards to the phenomenon of crisis, while it is a phenomenon peculiar to commodity economies, crisis phenomena in what I call the *capitalist* commodity economy are the general expression of capitalism's immanent contradictions, and so theoretically, it must be clarified after capitalist relations have been determined in their many–

corrected by individual experiences, in accordance with practice, is testimony to an ignorance of how and why theory itself is formed. Of course, theory in the social sciences is never divorced from facts, nor does it exist merely as a fancy, or as a simple hypothesis. Theory is the basic aspect of facts that are grasped theoretically as laws, which are exposed in their necessary interconnections of a movement from definite, abstract determinations to concrete ones, and is something that countless economists have repeatedly abstracted from the process of capitalism's development, which, for over three hundred years, has transformed the entirety of society capitalistically. This is not something that can be easily denied or refuted. On this point, theory is often viewed as something that simply provides an exposition based on logic, or as a negation of that which is opposed to logic. And while the development of fundamental economic laws seem to be derived from the logic of simple concepts themselves, this is never accomplished through a simple deductive method. Indeed, we could say that the history of political economy, which accompanied the development of capitalist economy, points to this question. In our country in recent years, where we confront actual, urgent problems, we cannot cope with them only by the importation of foreign institutions and scholarly research, unlike in the Meiji period. Does this mean that we should ignore the fruits of scholarly work that has developed over this long period of history in the advanced countries, and blindly tackle reality at once? If people think that theory is not helpful simply because the facts of our country are not advancing in the direction of what is assumed in theory, this is because they do not know how to use theory. This kind of error also begins as soon as it is assumed that the general principles of political economy can be used to directly analyse the present situation of our country.

sided aspects in society. Put differently, in the fundamental principles, crisis should be given as the almost final determination of those principles, but that is exactly why it cannot be determined as that which is shared between the various stages of the development of capitalism. The types of appearance of crisis in capitalism's periods of emergence, growth, and decline must also be distinguished. It is only after these different types of determinations are finally allowed to mediate our analysis, will we be able to use our theoretical determinations for the first time, and for the analysis of crises in specific countries and in their concrete processes. For our analysis here, the first level of research involves the determinations of the fundamental principles as they relate to crisis, but before this can be addressed, this level must be distinguished from a second level of research first. In other words, crisis phenomena must be distinguished in terms of their types, and as they appear in differing conditions, with differing features, in the stages of development of capitalism. On the basis of this distinction, we must clarify which types may help in directly bringing out determinations on the level of the fundamental principles. It is hardly enough to look for the common points of crisis phenomena in all historical periods. Rather, unless we assume that the totality of society has come under the sway of capitalism, we will not be able to grasp the determinations of crisis as a peculiar inevitability that is endemic to capitalist methods of production. This point has not been clarified by most theories of crisis, especially the so-called theories of the business cycle. These approaches possess a theory of fundamental principles that cannot go beyond determining capitalism as a mere commodity economy, and even when this is not the case, the peculiar inevitability of crisis is never clarified.

Let us therefore briefly take up the different types of crisis phenomena according to the various stages of capitalist development, and ask, what is the historical period in which crisis phenomena appeared in a typical form?

1 Typical Phenomena of Crises

Originally, crisis always appeared phenomenally as a financial crisis, emerging, to a considerable extent, when payments on loans could not be met, and when loan funds were simultaneously uncollected to a considerable extent. Therefore, insofar as this is the case, crisis is a phenomenon whose birth became possible when capitalist commodity economies spread to some extent, and crises broke out frequently, suddenly, and into the open throughout the seventeenth and eighteenth centuries in Holland, England, and elsewhere. For example, the crisis that broke out in the cities of Holland from 1634 to 1637 –

also known as the so-called tulip crisis – was caused entirely by speculations on tulip bulbs.[15] It is also said that crisis phenomena were visible in England in 1640, 1667 and 1672, when war and civil unrest led to suspensions of payments by financiers with tight relations with royal finances.[16] In the crisis of 1695–96, and especially in the crisis of 1720 in England (known as the South Sea Bubble), crisis resulted from failures of risky investments in stocks of burgeoning industries as well as of trading companies.[17] A partial crisis is also said to have broken out in 1745.[18] For the most part, however, all of these crises were little more than contingent and local phenomena. While a remarkable development of the capitalist commodity economy at this time could already be seen at the commercial level, a general capitalist social basis had not yet been established at the industrial level. Funds formed and accumulated by merchant capital were utilised only to a limited extent in order to expand substantially the scope of industry itself. Invariably, the funds were instead invested in speculative buying and selling of particular commodities, in loans with direct ties to the King's finances, or else in almost no prospects at the industrial level. Moreover, this led to excessive investments and to the appearance of crises as their subsequent failures.[19]

15 See Arthur Spiethoff, 'Krisen', translated by Yoshiyuki Mochizuki, Tokyo: Sanseido, 1936, pp. 121–2.

16 Bouniatian, Mentor (1908), Ch. 1.

17 On the crisis of 1695–6, see Bouniatian (1908), Ch. 2. On the South Sea Bubble in 1720, see Spiethoff (1939), p. 123 ff.

18 Bouniatian describes this crisis in Chapter 3 of his book, cited above.

19 On this point, see Walter Bagehot (1910), Ch. 6, where we can read a fascinating section on the role of new companies in 1695–96 and 1720. Bagehot also has the following to say about the conditions of the time: '[I]n the seventeenth century, a lawyer, a physician, a retired merchant, who had saved some thousands, and who wished to place them safely and profitably, was often greatly embarrassed. Three generations earlier, a man who had accumulated wealth in a profession generally purchased real property, or lent his savings on mortgage. But the number of acres in the kingdom had remained the same; and the value of those acres, though it had greatly increased, had by no means increased so fast as the quantity of capital which was seeking for employment. Many too wished to put their money where they could find it at an hour's notice, and looked about for some species of property which could be more readily transferred than a house or a field. A capitalist might lend on bottomry or on personal security; but, if he did so, he ran a great risk of losing interest and principal. There were a few joint stock companies, among which the East India Company held the foremost place; but the demand for the stock of such companies was far greater than the supply. Indeed, the cry for a new East India Company was chiefly raised by persons who had found difficulty in placing their savings at interest on good security' (1910, pp. 134–5). With these conditions in mind, we can better understand the completely reckless quality of the speculative fever of the late seventeenth and

These excess funds – which I will clarify later as an important factor in considering the phenomena of crisis – should have been used as funds to invest capitalistically, but the situation was such that appropriate channels for investment did not exist. Moreover, even if such channels were found, they did not have a basis in the social reproductive process. Rather, these investments had no choice but to float commercially on the surface of society as merchant activities. It is no surprise, therefore, that crises here were born from contingent factors and resolved at a very local level. This is precisely the nature of crisis in the era of mercantilism. Of course, this character of crisis gradually changed along with the development of capitalism. The tulip crisis, the fiscal financial crisis, and the South Sea Bubble crisis can be said to be exemplary of precisely these changes. *What cannot be said, in any case, is that these crises were based on a fundamental economic law that was regulated by the reproductive process itself that forms the basis of a single society.*

Continuing on from the previous period, namely from the latter half of the eighteenth century to the beginning of the nineteenth century, the phenomenon of crisis was repeated during the period of the so-called industrial revolution, nearing a crisis that we could say is based in the reproduction process itself. On the one hand, crisis phenomena accompanied the capitalist stage of what I call a period of transition; on the other hand, they were also influenced by the events of the Independence of America, the French Revolution, and the specific conditions in England that accompanied the continental war. Therefore, a clear determination for crisis cannot be grasped through the crisis phenomena of this period. It was only after the post-war crisis of 1819, when the so-called business cycles in England took the form of a periodicity, that a typical form of crisis emerged.[20]

---

early eighteenth centuries. As the most extreme example of companies during the South Seas Bubble of 1720, we can even read about 'Undertaking[s] which shall in due time be revealed', but in which 'so tempting was the offer, that 1000 of these subscriptions were paid the same morning, with which the projector went off in the afternoon' (Bagehot, 1910, p. 138).

20 Regarding the question of when the business cycles first began, Spiethoff notes the following: 'It is generally thought that the alternations of the business cycles began at the end of the eighteenth century. Schmoller, moreover, believes that, in the case of England and Prussia, distinctions between upswings and depressions spanned from the end of the seventeenth century to the middle of the eighteenth century. It is clear, however, that these phenomena fall outside the purview of our present problem. The time between good and bad periods each spanned eight to twenty-five years, and stemmed principally from external causes, in other words, from changes in global modes of trade, from the emergence and decline of various trade wars between Holland, France, and England, as

From the 1820s onward, crises erupted consistently and with a periodicity of ten years or so, namely in 1825, 1836, 1847, 1857, and in 1866. Each crisis was determined, of course, by specific circumstances, but crisis was already no

---

well as from epidemics and poor harvests. Indeed, as Bouniatian wrote regarding England, "The meaning of the big crisis of 1793 is that it ushered in a new period of industry." Bouniatian, however, does not point out the alternations of the business cycle and only documents how individual crises, as well as phenomena bearing resemblance to crises, are led by speculative movements and the reactions that follow' (Spiethoff, 1936, p. 148). It goes without saying that Spiethoff would deny the existence of business cycles during this period, but he also writes that, 'Short term upswings and downswings can be recognised after 1790, in regards to western Europe's principal national economies, and especially in regards to those areas that became wrapped up in international trade. Speculative movements and their reactions appeared in short periods through a new mode, pointing to how, according to Clement Juglar, bank of issue reports pointed to clear, short-term, wave-like movements' (ibid). Spiethoff's research develops a theory of crisis without first clarifying what I have originally called the three levels of political economic research. What he does not consider is how to investigate a theory of crisis in terms of the fundamental principles. He does not, therefore, clarify theoretically why the business cycles adopt a cyclical process, and only analyses them as facts given to experience. Of course, Spiethoff is not altogether wrong to say that 'economic alternations between 1790 to 1820' are generally 'born out of war economies, transitional economies, revolutions in frequently demanded changes in foreign trade, or out of conditions of harvests', but when each crisis is looked at individually, what he called 'capitalist cycles of business alternations in the true sense of the word' also emerged out of just so many specific conditions. The problem is why, after the nineteenth and twentieth centuries, crises are repeated periodically. The problem is that, even when we analyze the historical process of business fluctuations from the 1820s to the 1860s, this alone cannot demonstrate the inevitability and periodicity of crisis.

Regarding the years when crises, or phenomena resembling crises, appeared after the latter half of the eighteenth century, Bouniatian provides the following:
1763: speculations after seven years of war, and the crisis in Holland and Hamburg; these influence the London market;
1772: crisis stemming from and following the Paris Peace conference;
1778: speculative investments stemming from the war against American colonies and their bankruptcies;
1783: prosperity following the American War of Independence and financial stringency;
1793: prosperity and crisis appearing under the influence of the industrial revolution;
1797–99: crisis determined by special circumstances of continental war and the suspension of currency convertibility of the English-Dutch Bank;
1810: speculative exports to South American markets, which were opened in order to cope with Napoleon's continental blockade, and crisis as their reactions;
1815: failures of anticipated investments from the restoration of peace;
1819: the same post-war crisis as the crisis of 1815, which concluded the extreme conditions of the end of the eighteenth century.

Regarding this list, Spiethoff also doubts whether all of these events can be considered crises. Indeed, it can be said that this is natural as transitional phenomena.

longer an accidental phenomenon.[21] In all cases, the recurring process was one in which a definite period of prosperity was followed by the appearance of an extreme degree of prosperity, which then fell suddenly into crisis conditions. Then, after a period of crisis, a definite period of depression unfolded before turning, once again, into a new period of prosperity. It could be said, however, that the specific circumstances surrounding the extreme degree of prosperity, which constituted the causes of individual crises, were still accidental. For example, the crisis of 1825 was caused by the prosperity stemming from the independence of Spanish and Portuguese colonies in South America, and the subsequent expansion of markets into those territories. By contrast, the crisis of 1836 was based on the economic prosperity that resulted from an unusual increase in English and American railway construction and an unusual increase in exports to America in the first half of the 1830s; this was ignited by the crisis in America. Performing a major role in the crisis of 1847 was the boom that stemmed from the opening of the market in China and the railway investments across the European continent, which was influenced by the bad harvest of 1845, and which began with the plummeting of grain prices resulting from both excessive speculating on railway stocks and good harvests. Unlike the previous two crises, however, excessive speculations on commodities based on foreign trade did not play the most significant role in the crisis of 1847. The basis of this crisis was rather constituted by the general expansion of English industry during the first half of the 1840s. By the 1850s, factors such as the expansion of market channels with the opening of gold mines in California in the late 1840s and in Australia in the early 1850s, and the economic recovery from the Crimean War of 1853 became important again. At the same time, after 1854, prosperity was not restricted simply to England and America, but extended to all countries in the European continent. The influence of the crisis of 1857, which followed the relatively long boom period beginning in 1852, was therefore as extensive and far-reaching as it was grave and acute. It is also said that America and Hamburg were hit the hardest. Lastly, specific circumstances especially surrounded the crisis of 1866. The so-called cotton starvation, emerging out of the American Civil War in the first half of the 1860s, led to an expansion of British foreign trade to India and Egypt. The cotton industry, then the leading industry, could not escape this influence. However, as free trade across the continent accelerated, general industry experienced a boom after 1862 through an acceleration of free trade across the continent, and it was especially intensified with the reopening of American dealings in 1865 – until payments by a London-based

21 On nineteenth-century crises, see Tugan-Baranowski 1931 [1894].

bill broker were suspended, leading to a sudden fall into a crisis situation. Of course, the crisis was not caused by contingent conditions of bankruptcy of a single bill broker; sooner or later, a fall into a situation of crisis was unavoidable.[22]

After the 1870s, however, the *periodicity* itself of crisis was not so much only changed from what it was before, but the very mode of the cyclical process itself – of prosperity, crisis, and depression – gradually pointed to different features. The depression after the crisis of 1873 turned towards a recovered prosperity at the end of the 1870s, but the prosperity at the beginning of the 1880s was extremely brief, and the turn from prosperity to depression after 1883 was not accompanied, as it was before, by the sudden appearance of crisis phenomena. The turn in 1890 was the same, and when the two-year prosperity between 1898 and 1900 turned towards depression, England was already no longer experiencing industrial crisis in the same way as Germany. The turn towards depression in England in 1907 was influenced by the crisis in America,

---

22 Regarding the outbreak of crisis in May of 1866, Tugan-Baranowski points out a fact of great interest, namely: 'Without exception, all of the previous crises in England broke out in the autumn. This is not a coincidence' (1931 [1894], p. 136). The crisis that year in May, which was sparked off by a bank run by Overend Gurney (the name of the bill broker mentioned above), 'likely would have broken out in the fall of 1866 or 1867, even if the Overend firm had not gone bankrupt in May, for the speculations over the past few years had made an outbreak of crisis unavoidable' (ibid). As for why crises, as a rule, generally broke out in the fall, he writes, 'Most of the commodities in international trade are primarily plants, and for the most part, plant products are reaped in the fall, when not only grains, tobacco and grapes are harvested, but also industrial raw materials such as raw cotton, flax, and hemp. For this reason, prices for the most important foodstuffs are also decided on in the fall season. Moreover, the extent to which speculations hit the mark or not is also understood during this period. In other words, it is during the harvest that failures of optimistic plans are proven by the mercilessness of reality.'

'The foregoing describes the number one cause of the outbreak of crisis in the fall season. In England, other causes move in the same direction. As a rule, England imports raw materials and exports manufactured goods. England especially pays for imported goods directly, in cash, but exports goods by selling on credit, and frequently at extremely long periods. As a result, payments do not return to England in the fall, as precious metals and money flows out of the country; it is only afterward, after a period of time has passed, that it returns to England.'

'Trading firms in England, therefore, need especially large amounts of species around October; at the same time, it is around this time that there is a relative drain on currency. Moreover, it is during the fall season, when the flow of commodities after the harvest intensifies, that domestic firms further demand currency' (Tugan-Baranowski 1931 [1894], pp. 136–7). Of course, while this relation is repeated every year, it does not clarify the cause of crisis in itself. However, these conditions that arise in the fall can explain why so many crises break out in the fall.

and what is especially notable is that the turn towards depression took place without a situation of crisis even presenting itself.[23] The prosperity in 1910 and 1913, in addition, was resolved with the outbreak of World War One.

As I have mentioned before, this period marks a moment in the development of world capitalism in which Germany and America became new dominant capitalist countries, and which differed from the previous period, when England represented manufacturing countries while other countries worked as agrarian countries, more or less. This point is the first thing that makes it difficult to directly adopt the economic cycles in this period for theoretical consideration. While a clarification of the relations of the fundamental principles of political economy, as mentioned above, assumes a so-called purely capitalist society in which capitalist relations are developed across the entirety of society, once Germany and America, in addition to England, came to occupy a dominant position in the world as capitalist countries, we can no longer say that England, as one country alone, approximates such a purely capitalist society. During this period, the economic cycles of England were now overwhelmed by capitalist competitors such as Germany and America, thereby coming to have different features than before. On this point, Tugan-Baranowski writes:

> If we compare recent industrial fluctuations in England with those that came before, we can immediately recognise differences. Already the movements are no longer as abrupt, sharp, or sudden as they were before. Before, sharp spikes punctuated the trajectory of exports, which are now wave-like, with no noticeable spikes. Before, while drastic reductions in exports were followed by even stronger increases, today, exports have gradually declined over the past several years. Hence, while in the past there were fewer years of decline than years of increased exports, today the opposite is true. In addition, periodic industrial fluctuations in England were previously accompanied by disturbances in credit. Once the peak was exceeded, the movement of decline affected the totality of economic organisations as if by a single, violent blow. Now, industrial fluctuations no longer present credit disturbances, English industry no longer moves by rapid leaps and bounds, and conditions of prosperity have shifted directly into total ruin.[24]

23 The trajectory of this historical period is taken up by Tugan-Baranowski (1931 [1894], Vol. 1, Ch. 4, 'Periodic industrial fluctuations from the end of the nineteenth century to the last several decades', and Ch. 5, 'Periodic fluctuations of English industry over the past ten years').

24 Tugan-Baranowski 1931 [1894].

Of course, if these were the only issues, we could say that these were unique to England and that the normal features of capitalism have to be found within the development of world capitalism, now including Germany and the United States. We could also say that it is as if the original process of the cycle is no longer typical in this period. However, in this way, compared to England, the new leading capitalist countries such as Germany and America – and Germany especially – experienced capitalist development differently and relied on the form of joint stock companies very early on in its development of capitalism, thereby disclosing fundamental characteristics of so-called finance capital. On the one hand, this allowed large-scale industry to develop rapidly, without the restrictions of individual capitalist accumulation in late developing countries, therefore making the transformation of every industrial sector into capitalist business increasingly unnecessary. On the other hand, the capital formed by this development was invested not only domestically, but also advanced in the direction of direct investments overseas. This was remarkably different from English capitalism's development in the mid-nineteenth century, which applied capital resources to exports of commodities to foreign markets by means of credit, and which domestically went so far as to transform the agricultural sector capitalistically. On the level of economic policies, the differences between free trade and protective tariffs can point to this difference in the development of capitalism. The development of so-called monopoly organisations can also be seen here, but this development clearly did not tend to transform all aspects of society capitalistically like capitalist society up to the 1860s. Instead, capitalism in this period maintained the original and older social relations, *as they were*, all the while tending in the direction of extracting monopoly profits. This is not to say, however, that the process of breaking down the original and older social relations was suspended; rather, it could be said that, by the late nineteenth century – certainly in Germany, but also even in other countries – capitalist relations no longer tended towards the realisation of something that approximates a purely capitalistic society through a process of development.

Of course, the economic cycles after the end of the nineteenth century do not immediately point to an overall difference from the previous period. We can see global crises after World War One twice, in 1920 and 1929, but in 1937, England and America sank into a condition of crisis without passing through a major boom, while Germany and Japan were expected to avoid the same condition thanks to a huge wartime armaments boom. Ultimately, crisis was resolved after 1939 with World War Two. Here, we should especially pay attention to the following extremely important phenomena: *statist* economic policies, which were adopted by all countries after the great crisis of 1929 and which targeted industrial cycles; and, in addition, the dissolving of the crisis of 1937, like the one in 1913, by means of world war. Moreover, as I mentioned before, the development of colonial industries during World War One, as well as the post-war world agricultural crisis, drove recent capitalist development into such dire straits that any hopes for a resolution were dashed. An appearance of prosperity throughout all industrial sectors and a complete display of their productive powers increasingly became more difficult, and the tendency to move steadily towards so-called chronic depression become more common. Excess facilities of fixed capital and a chronic surplus of labour power appeared at the same time, revealing the peculiar meaning of the unproductive military industry.[25]

Our preceding simple historical observations have showed that in case we intend to theoretically clarify the phenomena of crisis in capitalist society – its general meaning, emergence, and effects – then it should also be clear that we will not be able to reach this goal if we only take up the common aspects of crisis phenomena from the end of the seventeenth and eighteenth centuries up to the present day. Capitalism emerged at a definite historical period, followed by a definite period with a tendency towards the domination of society in all of its aspects and in its entirety, which was then followed by yet another definite period when it was no longer necessary for all aspects of society to be transformed capitalistically. Theoretically, each of these periods must be considered in terms of their own peculiar meanings. During the period of capitalism's emergence in the seventeenth and eighteenth centuries, crisis appeared without regularity, as a phenomena that existed only on what I call the surface

25 On these trends following World War One, see Varga (1940), Vol. 1, Ch. 5, 'Crisis and cycles during periods of capitalism's general crisis'. In section one of this chapter, titled 'The general crisis of capitalism', Varga provides the following figures regarding the relationship between an excess of capital and surplus populations. On the former, he writes, 'While the research from the Brookings Research Institute in America has shown that at least 80% of the productive capacity of American industry was used during the period of America's prosperity (1925–29), this evaluation seems to be overly optimistic to us. In revising the underlying error of this evaluation, it has become clear that, when calculations were made on the basis of a complete cycle, no more than 67.5% of the productive capacity of American industry was used' (Varga 1940, p. 58). Regarding the latter question of surplus populations, he writes that, 'At the end of 1936, the productive levels in England only increased by roughly 15%, producing unemployment for 1,600,000 workers, a ratio of nearly one in seven workers. For the United States, while levels of production at the end of 1936 attained the levels of 1929, nearly ten million unemployed workers existed. This was the case despite the fact that, compared to the pre-war period, there was a steady decline in the natural increase of populations and immigrants' (Varga, 1940, p. 60).

layers of society, precisely because the social basis of capitalism was not established, but at the end of the 18th century, when England occupied the position of the world's factory with the so-called industrial revolution, and when capitalism was able to stand on its own two feet, the phenomena of crisis no longer remained on the surface of society – through money and finance – *but now existed as a phenomenon based in the social reproduction process itself, revealing the character of a definite and fundamental economic law*. This point is clarified by the fact that, while having various and different external causes, crisis phenomena came to possess a definite periodicity and definite cyclical phases that repeat. However, not only do crises become irregular after the 1870s, but after the twentieth century, they became closely connected to war, i.e., phenomenon that are not, in my words, purely economic phenomenon. We could say that this corresponds to how capitalism no longer promoted the capitalist transformation of all aspects of society. Thus, regarding the general determination for the phenomenon of crisis, crisis roughly from the 1820s to the 1860s – i.e., during the period of so-called liberalism and, more concretely speaking, during the period of the growth of capitalism centred in England – must be understood as its typical form.

To put it concretely, even during this period of capitalism, agricultural countries that were more or less late to develop capitalism existed around England, which imported agricultural products from these countries and exported manufactured goods to them. England thereby transformed its society capitalistically in every aspect, and, therefore, if we only take into consideration England, we will not be able to immediately and clearly show what is theoretically supposed to be a capitalist society. This point begs careful consideration, even when considering the phenomena of crisis of this period. Put differently, what especially requires consideration is how the theory of the fundamental principles should take up foreign trade, which plays such an important role in concrete and individual crises. The next section deals with this point.

2 The Theory of Crisis and Foreign Trade

It is in the nature of a commodity economy, it goes without saying, that foreign trade is an important and indispensable factor for the development of capitalist society, not to mention for that of commodity economies. A country that does not engage in foreign trade is a country that will not develop capitalistically. However, just because we can say this does not mean that the theory of political economy, which clarifies the principles of capitalist society, can take up the theory of foreign trade directly. Why this is so is a point that has not been clarified enough. Similarly, in theoretically clarifying the phenomenon of crisis, foreign trade – which, in terms of concrete processes, is an extremely important factor – is abstracted and omitted from the theoretical clarification because foreign trade must be abstracted in the theory of the fundamental principles of political economy. I would now like to address why political economy must necessarily do this for a theory of the fundamental principles of capitalist economy.

As I mentioned earlier, when we clarify the principles that dominate capitalist society, it is natural in the nature of theoretical composition to presuppose a single society which has been wholly transformed into a purely capitalist society. However, such a society never actually exists, even if in actuality it is progressing in that direction. England in the mid-nineteenth-century most clearly approximated a purely capitalist society, but this emphatically does not mean that all of the older social relations were completely dissolved and transformed into capitalist ones. It merely suggests that England tended to move in this direction. However, the progression towards the formation of a purely capitalist society only means that, in fact, England, as an industrial country, realized the capitalist transformation of society – including the capitalist transformation of agriculture – by exporting manufactured goods to, and importing farmed goods from, foreign agricultural countries that were slower to develop capitalistically. Without the social relations that tied England to these late developing countries through trade relations, the transformation of England into a capitalist society definitely would not have taken place. Therefore, even if we can say that England progressed in the direction of a total capitalist transformation through foreign trade, it should not be overlooked that it remains a point that cannot directly give us the actual basis for the theory of the fundamental principles of political economy. If this is not considered, we will not be able to fully understand Marx's statement in *Capital*, that the case of England serves as 'the leading illustration for the theoretical exposition' of the fundamental principles of capitalist society.

Marx – and it need not be explained here – had already established his historical materialist approach before he completed his theoretical system of the fundamental principles of political economy in *Capital*. Marx supposed that an economic process – or what historical materialism calls the base structure, which moves on its own and by its own objective, fundamental laws – can be elucidated scientifically. What allowed him to begin research of political economy is the fact that, in England, the historical development of capitalism at the time was such that the entirety of society moved in the direction of actualising all social relations as commodity relations. While this may seem irrelevant for the matter at hand, in fact it has an extremely close connection with the abstraction of foreign trade at the level of the theory of fundamental principles and, conversely, with that which makes this abstraction possible in the first place.

Simply put, capitalist society is something that uses the same principles for its own society's principles as that which it uses for foreign relations. Of course, as I have mentioned before, the commodity economy emerged from the interstices between societies, the *intermundia*, which is to say that it did not originate from the interior of a given society.[26] This is why it is possible, more or less, for a commodity economy to enter into a society even when its principles do not abide by the principles of a commodity economy, for example in the ancient and medieval periods. This is nothing short of reflexively internalising a heterogeneous and alien trade relation with outside societies to some extent. Of course, due to the osmotic process of a commodity economy, that society will, on the one hand, continue to increase its productive forces of the production process, whose original goal was not designed for commodity production. On the other hand, while transformations in the so-called superstructure that correspond to this production process in politics, religion, etc., will inevitably present themselves, a commodity relationship will remain a heterogeneous and alien thing to this society unless the basic relations of that society are transformed capitalistically by an increase in that society's productive forces. For these societies, the material base structure is, on the one hand, closely coupled with the political and religious superstructure, but on the other hand, the material base structure is something that includes external, foreign, and heterogeneous elements, and that cannot be grasped by a single principle. By contrast, in the case of capitalist society, foreign trade relations are realized qualitatively by the same commodity economy that also realizes the basic relations of that society, thereby providing the ground, we could say, for the establishment of historical materialism.[27]

26 [Transl. note: Here, Uno is referring to *Capital*, Vol. 1, 'The Process of Exchange', where Marx writes: 'The exchange of commodities beings where communities have their boundaries, at their points of contact with other communities, or with members of the latter. However, as soon as products have become commodities in the external relations of a community, they also, by reaction, become commodities in the internal life of the community' (*Capital*, Vol. 1, p. 182).]

27 This point gives rise to the error of thinking that the historical materialist approach is suitable for today's capitalism, but unsuitable for the ancient and medieval periods. For ancient and medieval societies, it goes without saying that while the economic process cannot be separated from the political and religious so-called superstructure and treated as a pure form as it is in *Capital*, it cannot be denied, however, that the material production process of these societies restricts their social life. Actually, the osmotic process of

Different from non-capitalist societies that have a connection with other societies through a commodity economy, but that nevertheless use principles other than those principles, capitalist society upholds a commodity economy as the fundamental principles of its own society. On the one hand, this makes it possible to treat the economic process of this society as something that operates on its own and as a pure form; on the other hand, it means that, even though capitalism develops through relations of foreign commodity exchange, it becomes possible, on the basis of the tendency to transform every level of society capitalistically, to presuppose the transformation of all of society into the capitalist commodity economy. This is because foreign commodity trade relations are no longer heterogeneous or alien to the principles of this society.

Mid-nineteenth-century England, with its relationship between manufactured goods and imported agricultural products, is an example of precisely this point. England, instead of producing agricultural products capitalistically, produced manufactured goods capitalistically. This was done, quite simply, because relations of overseas commodity exchange were capitalistically advantageous. Foreign trade, in other words, is nothing more than a helpful way to accelerate the expansion of the reproduction of capitalist society's social relations, but it does not constitute a separate and additional factor for theoretical considerations. The world market at the time, which consisted of England as a manufacturing country and other, more or less agricultural countries, practically promoted and accelerated the transformation of capitalism in England from the outside. *Theoretically*, however, the world market can be regarded as a domestic market if it is transferred to the interior of a single society, and if all industrial sectors of that society – from manufacturing to agriculture – are capitalistically managed. It seems to me that it is in light of this relationship that we can explain why, in a theory of fundamental principles like *Capital*, foreign trade, while it is theoretically abstracted as a general rule, is also mentioned on occasion.

As I have already discussed above, even when we consider the typical crisis phenomenon that appeared between the 1820s and the 1860s, every crisis was influenced by specific and peculiar overseas relations. However, we only have to look at how crises, by and large, broke out suddenly and with the same periodicity and with the same cyclical phases to understand that foreign trade,

---

commodity economies is something that constantly influences the productive forces of that society and brings about changes to its social relations, and it cannot be said that the relations of domination and submission of this society vanished naturally by themselves.

which has so many differing influences depending on the time, cannot be regarded as the cause of crisis itself. On the contrary, the rise and fall of foreign trade and its processes of development are regulated by, and are bound to, the cyclical processes of the business cycles, and, as such, foreign trade is an index of the development of capitalism in England.[28] Foreign trade plays an enormously important role in the development of capitalism in England, but it cannot determine what I would call the *qualitative* determinations of the process by which English capitalism developed; rather, it can only be described as something that *quantitatively* expands a definite process of the specific development of capitalism in England. This is not to suggest, of course, that the development of capitalism in England could have been realised without foreign trade. The analysis of the actual process of the historical development of capitalism does not allow for such an abstraction of foreign trade. However, within those concrete processes – which are expanded by foreign trade and its diverse and differing influences – there exists the essence of an inner, objective and fundamental economic law of capitalist development. Put differently, this is no different from saying that in England, the realisation of capitalist development at that time was due to foreign trade, but this does not mean that the theoretical

28 The development of English export prices (in units of millions of pounds sterling) from the 1820s to the 1860s can be seen in the following table:

Year	Value in money	Year	Value in money	Year	Value in money	Year	Value in money
1823	35.5	1837	42.1	1851	74	1865	166
1824	38.4	1838	50.1	1852	78	1866	189
1825	38.9	1839	53.2	1853	99	1867	181
1826	31.5	1840	51.4	1854	97	1868	179
1827	37.2	1841	51.5	1855	96	1869	190
1828	36.8	1842	47.4	1856	116	1870	200
1829	35.8	1843	52.3	1857	122		
1830	38.3	1844	58.6	1858	117		
1831	37.2	1845	60.1	1859	130		
1832	36.5	1846	57.8	1860	136		
1833	40.0	1847	58.8	1861	125		
1834	41.6	1848	52.9	1862	124		
1835	47.4	1849	63.6	1863	147		
1836	53.4	1850	71.4	1864	160		

SOURCE: TUGAN-BARANOWSKI, 1931 [1894]

exposition of the inner laws of capitalist development should be supplemented by additional factors such as foreign trade. Periods of prosperity, which precede crisis, are different depending on the relations with different foreign markets (which have an influence, at times, even on phases of crisis), but whatever the case, prosperity always follows a period of depression of a more or less determinate length of time; then, at a certain level of development, a passage from prosperity to crisis takes place in a cyclical process. Ultimately, a zigzag-like development unfolded on the basis of a periodicity more or less of ten years. In addition, the previous period's highest point of prosperity was developed and overtaken by the following period's high point of prosperity. Export trading also increased in tandem with such developments. In English capitalism at the time, the propulsive force of this development was centred around, and represented by, the cotton industry. The English cotton industry, of course, was obviously accelerated and boosted by foreign trade, but the basis of the cotton industry's development itself was established domestically. Foreign trade was in fact determined by the cotton industry's development itself.[29]

29 The following figures show the rise in the total amount of exported cotton goods (in units of millions of pounds sterling).

Year	Value in money	Year	Value in money	Year	Value in money	Year	Value in money
1823	16.3	1837	20.5	1851	30.0	1865	57.2
1824	18.4	1838	24.1	1852	29.8	1866	74.6
1825	18.3	1839	24.5	1853	32.7	1867	70.8
1826	14.0	1840	24.6	1854	31.7	1868	67.6
1827	17.6	1841	23.4	1855	34.7	1869	67.1
1828	17.2	1842	21.6	1856	38.2	1870	71.4
1829	17.5	1843	23.4	1857	39.0		
1830	19.4	1844	25.8	1858	43.2		
1831	17.2	1845	26.1	1859	48.2		
1832	17.3	1846	25.5	1860	52.0		
1833	18.4	1847	23.3	1861	46.8		
1834	20.5	1848	22.6	1862	36.7		
1835	22.1	1849	26.7	1863	46.5		
1836	24.6	1850	28.2	1864	54.8		

By contrast, the quantity of imported raw cotton is as follows (in units of millions of pounds):

Foreign trade at the time revolved around the relationship between the importation of raw materials for domestic industry, and the exportation of manufactured goods that were manufactured by domestic industry. The general relationship between imports of agricultural goods and exports of industrially manufactured goods, based on the conditions of the cotton industry, thus had a completely different meaning compared to trade in the seventeenth and eighteenth centuries, which centred around the woollen industry, and which developed from an export of domestic raw materials to the export of goods that were manufactured from them. That is to say, foreign trade in the mid-nineteenth century was little more than one internal factor in the process of capitalist reproduction. For capitalism in the seventeenth and eighteenth centuries, the dominant type of capital – itself determined by the type of capital accumulation – was merchant capital. By contrast, the dominant type of capital in nineteenth-century capitalism in England was industrial capital, to which the above-mentioned foreign relations correspond. After the 1870s, this correspondence to industrial capital did not disappear, but as the centre of industry shifted to so-called heavy industries based on iron manufacturing, the character of foreign trade gained new and additional factors. The foreign relationship was no longer as simple as importing agricultural goods and exporting manu-

---

Year	Quantity	Year	Quantity	Year	Quantity	Year	Quantity
1823	191	1837	407	1851	757	1865	978
1824	149	1838	507	1852	929	1866	1377
1825	228	1839	389	1853	895	1867	1262
1826	177	1840	592	1854	887	1868	1328
1827	272	1841	487	1855	891	1869	1221
1828	227	1842	531	1856	1023	1870	1339
1829	222	1843	673	1857	969		
1830	263	1844	646	1858	1034		
1831	288	1845	721	1859	1225		
1832	286	1846	467	1860	1390		
1833	303	1847	474	1861	1259		
1834	326	1848	713	1862	523		
1835	363	1849	755	1863	670		
1836	406	1850	663	1864	894		

SOURCE: ELLISON 1886

These figures do not necessarily fluctuate along with the crises of 1825, 1836, 1847, 1857, and 1866. Generally speaking, the depressed levels after crises mostly increased above previous levels of prosperity in the next phase of prosperity.

factured goods, and while this relationship was not eliminated altogether, the basis of foreign trade now turned around the so-called export of capital. Agricultural goods were no longer imported necessarily as raw materials for the export of industrially manufactured goods. Now profits on exported capital even appeared through the importation of agricultural goods. In Germany after the end of the nineteenth century, tariff policies kept foreign grain imports in check while the importation of manufactured goods, which were competitive on the world market, was also restricted by tariff policies. Cartel dumping and the export of capital to so-called spheres of influence now promoted foreign exports, and the important point for capital here is that the accumulation of capital now proceeded on the basis of finance capital and not on that of industrial capital. It is precisely this change in the character of the accumulation of capital that determined the manner by which capitalism by this time no longer moved in the direction of transforming all of industry capitalistically. No longer was the basic relationship found in buying up cheap grain abroad and exporting manufactured goods. The accumulation of capital no longer relied on the disintegration of domestic agriculture, which was promoted, in so-called Liberalism, by the development of the capitalist commodity economy and by the rise of foreign trade, especially. The increase in the accumulation of capital could now be attained by maintaining pre-existing relationships as much as possible – and generally speaking by intensifying labour. So-called monopoly profits become extremely meaningful here. During this period, therefore, foreign trade cannot be taken up as something that simply carries out the replacement of agriculture for industry domestically, as in the case of England up to the 1860s.

As the foregoing discussion has already clarified, the fact that foreign trade must be theoretically abstracted in the theory of the fundamental principles of political economy is related to how the theory of the fundamental principles of political economy takes capitalist society in England, from the 1820s to the 1860s, as the concrete basis of capital's accumulation. This point cannot be overlooked. This abstraction is possible insofar as foreign trade embodied the same principles that were embodied in capitalism on the domestic front. Or, to put matters differently, abstraction is possible insofar as foreign trade is found in the tendency to transform all of society capitalistically and to accelerate this trend. Insofar as foreign trade acts in this capacity, the necessity to consider foreign trade disappears when we theoretically clarify crisis phenomena. This is because foreign trade complicates theoretical inquiry unnecessarily, and creates ambiguities surrounding theory's essential determination.

It goes without saying, however, that it is impossible to ignore foreign trade when analysing a capitalist economy of a given country in concrete terms. In the cases of capitalism in England in the seventeenth and eighteenth century, capitalism in Germany after the end of the nineteenth century, and the capitalist transformations of our own country after the Meiji period, it is simply impossible to analyze these cases by disregarding the problem of foreign trade. Even when we consider capitalism in the period of so-called liberalism in England up to the 1860s, it is impossible to omit foreign trade from our concrete analysis. The same must be said for analysing particular crises, as well as for elucidating the historical types and determinations of crisis phenomena. However, we cannot understand the crises of the 17th and 18th centuries, as well as those after the end of the 19th century, if we do not clarify the role of foreign trade in the typical phenomenon of crisis in the 19th century and how foreign trade can be abstracted in the principles. Uniformly understanding every phenomena of crisis according to the sole definition of foreign trade can never grasp the fundamental peculiarity and historicity of the phenomenon of capitalist crisis.

In short, when we say that foreign trade must be abstracted in clarifying the phenomenon of crisis on the level of the fundamental principles of political economy, this does not simply mean that we are ignoring foreign trade. Generally speaking, it is proper for the fundamental principles to abstract foreign trade insofar as it does not act as an 'external' factor for capitalist relations of a country. We can abstract the process by which all industry is transformed by capitalism and every product is capitalistically produced insofar as products of the home country are replaced with those from non-capitalist foreign industry. In actuality, of course, this was not completely the case, even for England, but what we can say is that England progressed in this sort of direction up to the 1860s. In theoretical considerations, therefore, while crisis phenomena of this period are treated as a basis, it is possible to disregard foreign trade. Put differently, with such a theory, the analysis of foreign trade can be easily added to points that need to be considered on the level of the concrete analysis of this period. In the concrete analyses of the crises of the 17th and 18th centuries and in those after the end of the 19th century, however, we cannot easily introduce foreign trade even if we use that theory. It is necessary to clarify the meanings of foreign trade that are peculiar to different periods separately.

So far, we have clarified the specific period of crisis phenomenon that forms the basis of the theoretical exposition of the theory of crisis, and we have addressed why foreign trade must be abstracted, but all of this describes nothing more than obvious considerations in the exposition of the fundamental principles of political economy. Lastly, however, if crisis phenomena can be clarified by the fundamental principles as something that is inevitable to capitalism, then the problem for the theory of fundamental principles is that of clarifying which stage, within the fundamental principles, crisis can be clarified, and especially how crisis phenomenon is related to commercial capital. In what follows, I would like to describe this problem in simple terms.[30]

3 The Role of Commercial Capital in Relation to the Phenomena of Crisis

In the theory of the fundamental principles of political economy, the clarification of the role of commercial capital first requires that we distinguish it from mere merchant capital. The theory of the fundamental principles of political economy, as we have already clarified, reconstructs, through a theoretical exposition, the process whereby the entirety of society is transformed capitalistically. This exposition, which starts with the commodity form and therefore with the form of merchant capital, M-C-M′, must be exposed. But this form is nothing more than something that remains as one aspect of capital in the production process that forms the basis of capitalist society.[31] It does not provide

30 These problems do not necessarily need to be described in the exposition of the fundamental principles of political economy itself. The exposition itself of the principles clarifies them, but here I would like to describe my own views of the issue by taking it up as a separate theory of crisis.

31 As a moving embodiment of value, capital is originally that which enables the self-valorisation of value within this movement. That is to say, capital appears, first of all, as M-C-M′, namely as that which purchases a commodity by means of money (M) and then sells it at a higher price than the purchase price, thereby realising a difference in money (M′). This movement is then repeated through this movement of alternating forms as value grows larger and larger. Concretely speaking, this always emerges as merchant capital in places where a commodity economy spreads out to some extent. Merchant capital gains surplus value, in the form of profit, from those who sell commodities cheaply and purchase them dearly, and cannot exist in a purely capitalist society, which is constituted by capitalists and workers as the basic members of society. Of course, in actuality, no matter the capitalist society, this kind of purely capitalist society is impossible to achieve. Merchant capital can still exist even in a capitalist society, and in fact is left over, but this is not to say that it becomes determined theoretically as commercial capital. To put matters differently, merchant capital is transformed into commercial capital with the advance of capitalism to a certain degree, but merchant capital itself – as merchant capital – must be treated as something exterior to the capitalist system. At the same time, from the point of view of the movement of industrial capital, the form of M-C-M′ itself is one dimension of this movement, and must be understood as a primitive form of capital. With industrial capital, profits are not made in the circulation process of buying low and selling high, but rather in the production process, where profits are made from surplus value produced in the production process. This, however, is not to say that profits from the circulation process are to be overlooked, for even the surplus value stemming from the production

us with the determinations of merchant capital itself, which has an independent existence. As something whose basic aspects are abstracted, this form can be useful, to be sure, in explaining the determinations of merchant capital. It is the same as when the determinations of commodity and money are helpful in elucidating the functions of commodity and money in societies that preceded capitalism, but which are not helpful in providing the determinations themselves of commodities and money in pre-capitalist societies. In these earlier societies, commodities and money were established by a productive basis that was different from that of capitalism, and thus they cannot be regarded, in any respect, as the same as those of capitalist commodities. For example, the simple aspect of commodities – namely that of having a uniform quality as a value but a total heterogeneity as use-values, and that of realizing the value of the commodity in mutual exchange – is something that is commonly shared in ancient and medieval commodities, just as much as in capitalist commodities, and in this regard, the determination of the theory of the fundamental principles of political economy is something that can explain every commodity. However, as soon as we ask the question 'what is this quality?', and 'by what is this quality determined?', we are not able to equate capitalist commodities with other commodities. In fact, we cannot solve the question of the substantial determination of such a value unless we argue on the basis of the transformation of every aspect of society, as a capitalist society, by a commodity economy. The specific relationship of the price of commodities in ancient and medieval societies should be concretely clarified as the standard criteria of principles acquired in this way. The same can be said regarding capital; it is possible, regarding its formal determinations, to expose that aspect which is common to merchant capital as the form of merchant capital, and that aspect which is common to money-lending capital as the form of money-lending capital (M…M′). This must be done, for otherwise we will not clarify the transformation of money into capital. Additionally, unless capital captures the production process by the form of industrial capital (M-C…P [production]…C′ [another commodity with the increased value]-M′), we will not be able to clarify the fundamental social ground of the valorisation process, which establishes capital as

process is subsumed by the form in which it is bought cheaply and sold dearly. For each industrial capital, the surplus value produced in its own production process does not directly become profit on its own. Rather, it is based on the nature of capital. This is also why the capital invested in the process of M-C is turned into cost price as so-called production costs. Indeed, we will not understand the character of capital properly if we ignore the theoretical implications of the form of merchant capital just because capital comes to assume the form of industrial capital that grasps the production process.

self-expanding capital. Merchant capital, which augments the value of capital by buying cheaply and selling dearly, is something that does not exist at least in the theory of the fundamental principles, and while the historical conditions of its concrete existence must be analyzed, this should rather be analyzed on the level of concrete and historical analysis, guided by the theory of the fundamental principles. By contrast, commercial capital is explained within the fundamental principles as an independent capital, one that is put in charge of the process of the sale and purchase of commodities, or C′-M′·M-C, and especially C′-M′, which is originally carried out by industrial capital itself within its movement process of capital. However, by carrying out the sale and purchase of commodities in a concentrated manner, commercial capital equalizes and economizes the circulation costs in the process of this sale and purchase, economizing it, thereby receiving one part of surplus value that industrial capital earns as profit. Thus, commercial capital is not something whose profits can be gained by a relationship of simply buying low and selling high, as in merchant capital. Theoretically, the ground of commercial profit is also clarified through commercial capital.

To say that commercial capital has attained this position in this way does not mean that old merchant capital has simply been dropped from this position. The process in which industrial capital came to dominate and capture the reproduction process within a single country must be the process in which it came to have the capacity to perform functions, within its own system, that had been previously carried out by merchant capital, and therefore on the basis of money-lending capital. Originally, the function of merchant capital vis-à-vis industrial capital was nothing other than one of supplying the working funds to industrial capital by purchasing products as commodities produced by industrial capital. The industrial capitalist, in selling these products to the merchant, was able to continue a reproductive process without having to wait to realise the values of these products by selling these products, as commodities, to final consumers. (As for these consumers, they are not merely limited to individual consumers, but also extend to productive consumers, namely industrial capitalists.) In other words, production was able to continue unabated even as the products sat in the market as inventoried stock. Assuming that the industrialist himself tries to sell these commodities to the final consumers, to realise these values in money, and to keep reproduction going, he would have to prepare surplus capital exclusively for the production process during this interim period, a surplus capital without which the production process would not be able to continue on unabated. Now, it goes without saying that, in general, for capitalist industrial production, interruptions in the production process are not advantageous. Thus, while merchant capital is outside of the capitalist system, it assumes a role in relation to industrial capital in which it replenishes and reinforces the circulating capital that must take the form of commodities or money. The development of the modern banking system made its appearance precisely by incorporating this relation into the system of industrial capital – without, of course, actually eliminating merchant capital or money-lending capital.[32] Theoretically, therefore, in the process in which the relationship between industrial capitals themselves mutually finance a portion of capital, which they possessed, either in the form of commodities or money through so-called commercial credit, this relationship developed into one in which the banks mediated industrial capitals' mutual financing, and loan capital was formed; on this basis, commercial capital formed as an independent capital. In this way, commercial capital was able to secure a position within the industrial system for the first time.[33]

---

32 The development of the modern banking system does not mean, however, that all of the sources of funds collected by banks are limited to the use of idle money-capital by industrial capitalists. Nor are those who are provided with funds by banks restricted to industrial capitalists. Rather, merchant capital itself sought out and used banks as a means to become liberated from money-lending capital. Only gradually did industrial capital come to use banks institutionally. Moreover, even when industrial capital came to use banks, they continued to be used largely by merchant capital. The abstraction of merchant capital in the exposition of theory, therefore, does not necessarily mean, in actuality, that banks are not used by merchant capital. But to clarify theoretically the function of banks while taking into account merchant capital is to overlook the former's essence. For in actuality, only when the function of banks gradually assumed the crucial position of providing funds to industrial capital could the abstract determinations of banks be given a ground; only then, moreover, could this tendency be explained. Financial theory – which differs from the theory of fundamental principles – must explain, for example, the process by which the financial system of seventeenth- and eighteenth-century England developed into the financial system of the nineteenth century. Financial theory must explain this process, however, on the basis of the determinations established by the theory of fundamental principles, and in accordance with the development of world-historical capitalism. That is to say, if the fundamental determinations of the banks, as they are established by the theory of the fundamental principles, are substituted for an explication of financial theory, the actuality of the banks in mid-nineteenth-century England will be overlooked. Alternatively, it would be impossible to give the essential determination of the banks, if we understand banks as they originally appeared as a mediator of a myriad of diverse funds. Both ways of thinking are deeply erroneous.

33 Theoretically, the essential determination of commercial credit, which carries out the sale and purchase of commodities and defers the payments of these costs until a later date, will also not be grasped unless commercial credit is understood as something that is mutually given by industrial capitalists. To assume that merchants mediate commercial credit is to make its essence impure by introducing that which comes, as it were, from outside the capitalist system; it is also to misunderstand the function of banks. At the same time, commercial capital and merchant capital will be mistaken for each other. Insofar as com-

In taking up the phenomena of crisis of mid-nineteenth-century England as a typical one, not only is the foreign market an extremely important factor

mercial credit is mutually given by industrial capital, the funds cannot exist independently of, or on the exteriority of, industrial capital as loan capital. Actually, the capitalist who sells on credit cannot avoid the tendency to estimate the interest on his funds during this period, say by raising the price, more or less, compared to retail sales on cash, for example, and in actuality, these are phenomena that are born out of the formation of loan capital based on merchant capital. An exposition of commercial credit that presupposes loan capital does not explain commercial credit's basis in industrial capital. This presumption leads to a search for loan capital, more or less, on the outside of the capitalist system, and as a result, the foundation of loan capital itself – which is developed and formed by industrial capital – is easily overlooked, making it impossible to identify its fundamental determinations. In other words, it comes to determine loan capital on the basis of actually given loan capital. This leads to tacitly and surreptitiously determining loan capital on the basis of old money-lending capital. Loan capital, as something that is formed through capitalist relations of production, cannot be explained in this way. While loan capital's essential determination is provided by the way it necessarily emerges between industrial capitals, the theoretical exposition of it must be based on the commercial credit that takes place between industrial capitals themselves. In actuality, for individual industrial capitals, there necessarily comes a period, in the process of M-C...P...C′-M′, when capital, either in the form of commodities or money, cannot be invested in the production process to perform the role of directly augmenting value, but when it must nonetheless be maintained and kept as a given quantity. Not only does this allow for the use of commercial credit for selling on credit; as long as there is this mutually financing relationship, it can be said, following Marx, that, 'interest, as the difference between the credit price and the cash price', is not 'involved in the price of a commodity' except in the special case where 'bills of exchange have a longer term than usual' (*Capital*, Vol. 3, p. 650). The reason for this – as far as I understand it – is that funds do not become independent as loan capital.

Theoretically, loan capital does not develop into commercial credit; rather, commercial credit develops into loan capital, and it is on this basis that bank credit must be understood, which is to say that, if we took the opposite course, then banks would be simply understood as something that modernised money-lending capital, and bank credit would be explained apart from capital's reproductive process. Bank credit will then increasingly be seen as something possessing a mystical power, making it truly impossible to determine the limits of bank credit. This is because credit seems to appear as a power coming from outside the capitalist system. These factors should not be ignored when we consider the analysis of the historical development of actual capitalism, but locating the drives of capitalism's development in these factors cannot grasp the fundamental economic laws of capitalism, and would inevitably make both determined by accidental factors.

Commercial capital not only needs capital to buy products of industrial capital as commodities, but also must invest capital that must be invested in labour power and raw materials for selling these products. For industrial capital, this kind of capital forms as so-called pure circulation costs, which are subtracted from its surplus value or profits. For commercial capital, however, this subtracted amount itself exists as capital and thus demands profits. This point presents some difficult theoretical problems but my understanding is that commercial capital can be clarified on the basis of an economizing of (as I have described above), but also the role of merchant capital – with its character as commercial capital continuously increasing – plays an equally important role. Theoretically, however, merchant capital has to be presupposed as complete commercial capital and understood as something that bears a part of the reproductive process of industrial capital. Put differently, it has to be understood as something that expands this development quantitatively, and never as a factor in the qualitative determination of the inevitability of crisis. In fact, as I will discuss in the pages that follow, the activity of commercial capital expresses the development of the reproductive process in the phase of prosperity in a distorted way, due to the rise in prices stemming from speculative activity in the phase of prosperity, which conceals real price relations. Prices of stored up commodities go up to extreme degrees. In this way, in the theoretical elucidation itself of the theory of crisis, commercial capital has to be theoretically abstracted. We will do the same as a rule, but in the exposition of the cyclical process of prosperity, crisis, and depression, we must point out how commercial capital, along with merchant capital, performs an important role at the same time that it distorts the cyclical process and obscures basic relationships.

The foregoing discussion has presented some basic and preparatory – but also necessary – considerations for the development of a theory of crisis. Lastly, there is a tendency to sometimes dismiss the inevitability of crisis in capitalist society as a simple question of the possibility of crisis. In the next section, I would like to address this point in simple terms.

---

circulation costs that presume loan capital. With merchant capital – which differs from industrial capital's profits insofar as it lacks a rational basis – profits can be said to be made by buying low and selling high. The same cannot be said for commercial capital, to which one of industrial capital's profits are distributed within the interior of the capitalist system. In addition, circulation costs themselves must be capitalised, which is mediated by the independence of capital as loan capital. Put differently, commercial capital, which requires profit on the basis of funds that can be lent as loan capital and which earns interest on loans, are invested in the purchasing and selling of commodities, thereby revealing the ground of commercial profit, and its limits are given by the degree to which this can economize the circulation costs of industrial capital. In this way, the function of commercial capital can be rationally explained, not as something that operates externally like merchant capital, but as something that functions on the basis of capital's reproduction process, and as something that is responsible for one part of that process.

4 The Possibility and Inevitability of Crisis in Capitalist Society

Properly speaking, the basis for what could be called a commodity economy is secured when products of individual producers are mutually exchanged as commodities. What cannot be said to be a commodity economy, however, is when individual producers directly exchange their products for other products of producers, in the form of so-called barter. The exchange of commodities takes place through money and as the circulation of commodities, and when a separation is made between selling and buying. We can speak of a commodity economy, therefore, with the development of a relationship in which, on the one hand, one can purchase the products of what one needs as commodities, whenever one wishes, because one is in possession of money; and when, simultaneously, on the other, a commodity cannot necessarily be sold simply because it has been produced. Even in cases of direct exchange, it is no longer barter if a price is involved in the exchange. Instead, what we have is exchange as the exchange of commodities. The *capitalist* commodity economy, however, commodifies all aspects of society and all of its products – which means that labour power itself cannot avoid becoming commodified, thereby allowing us to speak of a properly capitalist commodity economy – and it develops this relation throughout all aspects of society. Such commodity exchange relations, it goes without saying, form the general basis for crisis in a capitalist society, but this does not mean that it will develop into crisis necessarily. If a commodity cannot be sold, its price can be lowered in order to help sell the commodity, but a lowering of the price of commodities hardly leads, necessarily, to a crisis. However, on the basis of a definite development of the commodity economy, once money becomes something that can buy commodities at any time – thereby taking on a peculiar form of wealth in a commodity economy – the separation of buying and paying emerges. On the one hand, the tendency to hoard money itself is born, while, on the other – and based on this tendency – commodities can be purchased without money, for payments can be made later with money obtained from the sale of other commodities that one has produced. In this case, if one cannot sell one's own commodity at a definite price, one cannot but fail to make these payments. The conditions of crisis are presented very clearly here, when this relationship is generalised throughout society. Here, we can say that this relationship reveals the possibility of crisis that is peculiar to a commodity economy, and that appears on the basis of this separation of buying and selling. How this possibility becomes actualised as an inevitability, however, cannot be said to develop out of the separation of buying and paying alone. The least that can be said is that the situation in which the socially interconnected failures to make payments generally disrupt the reproductive process of commodities, but the separation of buying and paying alone cannot explain the inevitability of crisis. The fact of the matter is that, even in a society which is not completely dominated by a commodity economy, the separations of buying and selling, and of buying and paying, can appear. To put it differently, a commodity economy only takes place in a partial way, merely in the process of exchanging products on the so-called surface of society, while the process of social reproduction continues to operate in forms that are different from it; because of this, it cannot be said to influence the social reproductive process in a disruptive way.

For a capitalist society, of course, the reproduction process itself must pass through the form of the commodity, thereby furthering the development of the possibility of crisis. However, if we only consider the separations of buying and selling, and of buying and paying, simply in relation to commodity products, then it is clear that we will not be able elucidate the factors in which the possibility of crisis turns into an inevitable necessity. For a commodity economy, and especially for a capitalist commodity economy, commodities that are socially in demand and that possess specific use values are produced by individuals on the basis of prices as a standard and are mutually exchanged. In this way, their reproductive process continues and further develops. This is not to say, however, that exchange will necessarily proceed smoothly. Under certain prices, some commodities may be produced over and above the social demand, while others will not be produced enough. Changes in prices, however, allow for adjustments of these gaps. It goes without saying that these adjustments pass through a process in which the production of commodities, whose prices are lowered, decreases, while production increases for commodities whose prices rise. This mechanism is established, in the way peculiar to a commodity economy, through investments of capital in those industries with increasingly larger profits. The capitalist reproduction process has an extremely complex relationship in which, on the one hand, there is an increase of factors tending towards disproportion and imbalance while, on the other, mechanisms are simultaneously established in which these disproportions are evened out. Simply emphasizing the possibility of crisis by referring to the fact that commodities are produced blindly and anarchically overlooks the crucial dimension of the commodification of labour power; as such, it decidedly does not give us the true reason to understand capitalism.[34] Capitalism is not as simple as this.

---

34 It is my understanding that when Marx looks at the reproductive process of capitalist society, he clearly analyses it from a point of view in which the common and sufficient economic rule, as conditions for all societies, is fulfilled through the commodity form. It is from this perspective that Marx clarifies 'The Reproduction and Circulation of the Aggreg-

The establishment of a capitalist commodity economy can only come about with the commodification of that which capital itself cannot produce, namely labour power. Through the commodification of this peculiar commodity a commodity economy becomes able, for the first time, to dominate the entirety of society in a thoroughgoing way. No matter how extensively a commodity economy has expanded, it will not be able to transform the grounding roots of a particular society into a commodity economy if only mere products are exchanged as commodities in the process of circulation. Originally, the commodity does not have a social character to the extent that it could dominate a single society through such relations. As I have discussed earlier, it originated in the interstices between societies, and then destroyed the older society in a process where it osmotically extended to the interior of society. While it can be said that a single society came to be dominated by a commodity economy in this way, *the destruction of the old society reached an extreme point*

ate Social Capital' by means of what he calls the reproduction scheme in *Capital*, Vol. 2, Part 3. Here, Marx clarifies the division of society's annual products into means of production and articles of consumption, and shows how this process, repeated and reproduced annually, is realised as commodity products of capital. Of course, the process of so-called simple reproduction, which annually maintains and repeats the same scale, points to relationships that are extremely simple compared to that of so-called expanded reproduction, which expands this scale. But even in the latter case of expanded reproduction, means of production and articles of consumption are reproduced mutually in accord with social demand, and expressed in price relations of commodities, just as in the case of simple reproduction.

The fact that expanded reproduction, more than simple reproduction, increases the possibility of an imbalance of commodity production does not to deny how capitalism intrinsically possesses mechanisms by which such imbalances can be evened out. Because the schema is expressed mathematically, and, especially in the case of expanded reproduction, because it does represent completely the conditions of production that fluctuate variously, it is tempting to understand the development of the possibility of crisis as something that obstructs the balancing-out of imbalances, but we cannot say this, either. Conversely, if we add these conditions of production to the schemas and further complicate the latter, we still will not have clarified the original purpose of using the schemas. On the one hand, while the schemas take into consideration the production and circulation of materials of everyday life for the workers' consumption, the reproduction of the commodity of labour power, which forms the basis of capitalist economy, cannot be included in the schemas as such. This clearly reveals the theoretical limitations of the reproduction schemas. Therefore, in what follows, I will not especially explain crisis through the schemas. Rather, *the inevitability and necessity of crisis will be explained on the basis of the unique relationship of capitalism in which labour power itself is commodified, and not on the basis of the exposition of the schemas, which presume labour power as a given.* In many of the conventional theories of crisis that have used the reproduction schemas, this most important point, it would not be an exaggeration to say, was all but ignored.

when labour power was commodified, and it is here, for the first time, that the commodity became a form that dominated a single society in its entirety. This single society was not formed, as it is commonly assumed, through the mutual exchange of products as commodities between independent, small producers. Even if each small producer were to purchase his means of labour, such as tools, or his means of production, such as raw materials – all as commodities – even so, the labour here itself depends on his own labour power. The production process is not, therefore, the production of every commodity. Correspondingly, not every product of the production process is entirely destined to be a commodity. At least one part is treated as use value for self-consumption; in other words, tendencies remain left over from the past in which products are not produced exclusively as commodities. Even if so-called surplus labour products are acquired from the production process for this purpose, this is something that is only possible because of one's own labour, and not because it is something whose acquisition is pursued objectively, as in the case of capital. To call the means of production, such as the tools and raw materials of the small producers, "capital" is nothing more than an abuse of the word 'capital', and it becomes impossible to understand capitalism as a commodity economy. With the commodification of labour power – which presupposes, of course, that owners of labour power do not possess their own means of production and thus cannot use their own labour power for themselves – the production process proceeds when the worker works for another. This does not simply mean that products, as commodities, provide use values for others. *For the worker who labours within the production process, the production process itself is such that the worker labours for another, which is to say that the commodity form is something that reaches into the depths of society's foundations.* In this way, the capital which is invested in labour power produces surplus value based on surplus labour. The capital which is invested in means of production is also an indispensable part of the production of surplus value in this way, and thus surplus value is transformed into profits born out of the total capital. (Here, we especially note that the capitalist, who purchases the labour power of others as a commodity, cannot make a distinction between these investments; this is why the form of merchant capital still remains, even for industrial capital.) At the same time, unlike the products of small producers, the products of capital are entirely all commodities. This means that for the worker who sells labour power, as well as for the capitalist who purchases labour power and means of production for the production process and carries out the production process as a capitalist, no part of the product is ever directly produced as use values for themselves, which contrasts with small producers producing with their own labour power. Profits made from capital allow the capitalist to now purchase necessary use values as commodities. Imagining the capitalist as an independent small producer clearly fails to understand capital's production process. In other words, the production process of capital is formed by the commodification of labour power, and simultaneously by having to produce and sell products-as-commodities, which are completely use-values for others. The meaning of the domination of a single society by a commodity economy is found in this relationship.[35]

In a capitalist society, the only commodity that can be said to be the so-called simple commodity – or a commodity that is not a capitalist commodity – is that of labour power. But labour power is not something that is simply produced. *Labour power, which must be reproduced by the means of subsistence that are produced annually by labour, is reproduced as the labour power of the worker.* However, as an absolute labouring population, labour power is little more than something that passes through life and death and that increases naturally, and so on this point, we could say that labour power, along with land, is a given condition that is itself given by the so-called outside of capitalism. But if the determination of labour power is attributed only to the natural increase in the working population, then as *the* factor of production, labour power would have a definite limit, and capital would not be able to utilize it as a source of infinite value augmentation. A similar concession must also be made when capital confronts landed property owners. However, as part of the reproductive process, capital possesses a mechanism by which it can form a labouring population 'capitalistically', namely through the advance of productive forces,

35 Of course, depending on the development of a commodity economy, there are situations in which the independent small producer is unable to use certain products as use values directly. Moreover, at early stages of the development of the commodity economy, there are cases in which the capitalist directly uses the products of capital for him or herself. However, the commodification of products that is based on the commodification of labour power is one that becomes all-encompassing and unavoidable because the commodity relationship extends into the relationship between nature and humankind, which is realized in the labour-production process. At least we can say that it has this tendency. Through labour, human beings acquire everyday materials from nature to reproduce their labour power, thereby allowing them to work upon nature once again in an absolute, metabolic process. *This metabolic process, which is shared in all societies and which is absolutely vital to human life, eventually passed through the form of the commodity, and it is here that the social and historical meaning of capitalist society is found.* The distinguishing factor between capitalist society and other societies is found precisely here. Ignoring this point and focusing instead on individual and contingent moments is no different from the proverbial problem of seeing the tree instead of the forest. It is similar to how some people remark, in opposition to the norms by which the value of a commodity is determined by labour, that the price of antiques is not determined by labour. These people cannot even understand the word capitalism.

which multiplies a labouring population – not absolutely, but relatively. Generally speaking, the advance in the productive forces of labour means reducing the quantities of labour power that use and put into motion a determinate quantity of means of production for capitalists, and a relative diminution of the variable part of capital allocated to purchase labour power, in comparison with the constant capital that is allocated for purchasing means of production. In other words, through a rise in the so-called organic composition of capital, capital is actually always able to create labour power as a surplus population, and to purchase labour power according to capital's own needs. Thus, labour power cannot be adjusted by capitalist mechanisms in the same way that other products of labour can be adjusted; it cannot be increased, by means of capital, in the same way that the production of other products of labour can be increased, for example when their prices rise. Nor can it be decreased by capital in the same way that capital can decrease the production of other products of labour when their prices fall. Instead, the rising organic composition of capital allows for a continual formation of a surplus population, thereby providing a *mechanism that satisfies capital's demand for labour power*. This mechanism is not something purely commodity-economic, as is the mechanism which adjusts other products of labour, yet it is by means of this mechanism that capitalism is able, through the commodification of labour power, to secure its own foundations.[36]

If the reproduction process of capitalist society is considered to be carried out only by commodities, as products of capital, then in the case of an expansion of the scale of reproduction through the separation of purchases

36 This point is explained in greater detail by Marx in *Capital*, Vol. 1, Chapter 23 (Chapter 25 in the English version), 'The General Law of Capitalist Accumulation'. Along with the development of capitalist production methods, the so-called industrial reserve army is formed, including its various forms of existence. This allows capital to become capable of accumulation without being fettered by the limits posed by the natural multiplication of labouring populations. Capital cannot completely escape this restriction, of course, but it can, by its own workings, create a certain space for accumulation and realistically capture the basis for the domination of a single society. Marx said that any particular society always has its own peculiar law of populations, which is why the production of the relative surplus population is precisely the law of population peculiar to capitalism. In a capitalist society, therefore, the so-called population problem always appears through this peculiar form and is never simply a problem of the natural growth of populations. The historical character of capitalism is completely lost when the population problem is considered merely in terms of an insufficiency of foodstuffs to the population. [Transl. note: Uno is referring to Marx's critique of Thomas Malthus's biologically reductionist yet influential theory of population, found in his 1798 publication, 'Essay on the Principle of Population, as it Affects the Future Improvement of Society.']

and payments – which is based on the separation of selling and buying, or to put it differently, on relations of credit – crisis would only be a momentary disruption of the reproductive process when a fall in prices, accompanying the imbalanced development, leads to defaults on payment. If crisis were this kind of disruption, however, it would never appear inevitably and necessarily as something that is repeated with a definite periodicity. Nor would it appear generally in all industrial sectors. It would only appear, as it were, as an isolated, contingent phenomenon. As I have described previously, and as I will again elaborate upon below, the true cause of crisis phenomena is concealed within accumulated, overstocked commodities accumulated in the expectation of a rise in price through the speculations of merchant and commercial capital. The direct cause of crisis is found in the fact that the forecasted price is not realised and defaults on payments arise. Phenomenally speaking, it thus looks like the root of crisis is found in the fact that, while commodities have been produced, they cannot be sold. If crisis was no more than this, crisis would be a method to resolve the shortages and excesses of anarchic production that are shared by commodity economies in general, and it would not be peculiar to the capitalist commodity economy. We cannot explain why crisis appears throughout the entirety of society, bearing an inexorable and definite periodicity at a definite stage of the development of capitalism when capitalist production methods dominate the entirety of society. The problem is not just that, when a commodity that has been produced cannot be sold at a definite price, the surplus value that is contained in the price of the commodity will not be realised as profit, making it impossible for capital to continue the production of the commodity. If this were the case, all that capital would have to do to avoid crisis is produce other commodities. For individual capitals, of course, this is something that may not always be feasible. As I have described earlier, however, socially speaking, in a capitalist society capital adjusts production by passing through fluctuations in price. If crisis appeared merely as a violent solution when difficulties in realising the value or the surplus value of individual capitals arose in a concentrated manner, a different explanation would still be needed to explain why various phenomena appear inevitably and with a periodicity. Conventional theories of crisis – which rely on the reproduction schemes, described above – looked for the causes of crisis in the disproportion between the departments of social production, and pursued the periods in which this imbalance necessarily emerged. In this method, however, the labouring population that is already given and presupposed in the reproduction schemes is ignored, resulting in the unavoidable tendency to reduce away the contradictions of capitalist society to general contradictions of a generic commodity economy. Moreover, it down plays how capitalist society can resolve these imbalances, on its own, through fluctuations of price. This is not to deny, of course, that there is a tendency towards the disproportion between the departments of social production because of the anarchism of commodity economies, and because of the fact that accumulation in the department of the means of production plays an especially important role due to that aspect of the accumulation of capital in a capitalist society, namely, the aspect of so-called production for production's sake. Nor is it to deny the facts that the workers' consumption is dominated and restricted by the law of wages, which has a definite limit, or that, accompanying the advance in production capacities, there is a tendency for the production of the means of consumption to exceed the wage labourers' capacity to consume. Now, from these conditions capitalist society may not be capable of managing its own productive forces, and socially, the violence of crisis may contribute towards the resolution of this problem. As I have already emphasised, however, if crisis is only considered to emerge from these conditions, we will not be able to explain why crisis breaks out inevitably and periodically. Moreover, even if we were to consider the point that the replacement of fixed capital, which plays an extremely important role in modern, large-scale industry, takes place at a definite period, this does not clarify why there is a tendency to concentrate these investments and replacements at a certain point of time.

Turning now to the reproductive process in a capitalist society, and to repeat another point that I have made already, *the commodity of labour power, as that which capital is incapable of producing by itself, occupies an extremely important position equivalent to all other commodities*. Or rather, the position occupied by the commodity of labour power is that which allows all other commodities to exist as commodities. Thus, even if the products within the reproductive process of capital can be produced in a relationship of equilibrium, that is, even if these products had a relationship of buying and selling at fixed prices, *the reproduction process would be affected in a most extreme and fatal way if capital were incapable of purchasing labour power as a commodity in a favourable way*. The peculiar relationship that capital has vis-à-vis the labour power commodity restricts capital from investing in and replacing fixed capital, and thus the tendency for these processes to take place in a concentrated way, at a certain point of time, can also only be explained on the basis of capital's relationship to the labour power commodity.

The foregoing discussion has described how, for capitalist societies – which we understand on the level of the fundamental principles of political economy as a purely capitalist society that is formed by the classes of workers, capitalists, and land owners – the commodity of labour power is the only simple commodity, the one commodity that capital cannot produce directly. While capital can achieve this indirectly by producing a relative surplus population through an increased organic composition, nonetheless, labour power is never one of capital's commodity products. On the one hand, therefore, this special character of the labour power commodity forms the ground, to a certain extent, of the reproduction process (and especially for the expanded reproduction process) by removing restrictions placed on capital's reproduction process by the natural population. On the other hand, it simultaneously acts as the ground upon which the infinite expansion of the reproduction process is limited. *This labour power commodity is such that, for capital, the extent to which capital can favourably use labour power for its own purposes determines whether capital's products can, or cannot, function as capital.* It is because of this character of the labour power commodity that production's expansion and stagnation take on a peculiar form and in a manner that is hard to understand by common sense. For example, while a vast plethora and excess of things and human beings continue to exist, a union between things and humans, through the form of capital, can be impossible. The commodification of labour power forms the fundamental basis of capitalist society, but since labour power is not originally produced as a commodity by capital, yet is transformed into a one, labour power, in this sense, is the fundamental weak point of capitalist society. *The phenomena of crisis, which represents the fundamental contradictions of capitalist society while simultaneously resolving them practically, is grounded precisely in the commodification of labour power.*[37] Differences in the stages of capitalism, which appear within the history of crises, always appear precisely around the development of this fundamental contradiction, and it is only when we realise this that we can understand the definition of these differences for the first time. The differences of capitalism's historical stages of development, which can be distinguished by modes of capital accumulation, depend on the differences of relations in which

37 As for clarifications of crisis offered by commentators of Marx in our country, crisis is tirelessly and repeatedly explained by referring to the contradiction between the social character of production and private character of appropriation in capitalist society. This kind of explanation is probably based on Lenin's description of 'two approaches regarding crisis', when he criticized Sismondi in *Characterisation of Economic Romanticism* [1897: 'The first theory explains crises by the contradiction between production and consumption by the working class; the second explains them by the contradiction between the social character of production and the private character of appropriation'. A true elucidation of crisis will not be possible unless we understand this contradiction in terms of the fundamental contradiction of capitalist society that derives from the commodification of labour power. The contradiction of social production and private appropriation is common in the capitalist commodity economy, and while it can be said that this contradiction reinforces the possibility of crisis, it is not the ground of the inevitability of crisis. [Translator's note: Lenin's text can be found in *Collected Works of V.I. Lenin*, Vol. 2, pp. 129–265, Verso Press, 2019.]

capital can, or cannot, commodify labour power as a commodity beneath all other relations. The theory of crisis theoretically is what I would call the conclusion or *apogée* of the fundamental principles of political economy. Based on the typical phenomenon of crisis discussed earlier, it clarifies the relation by which the contradictions of capitalism break out periodically, on the one hand, and are practically resolved, on the other, a relation which is produced, inevitably and necessarily, around the commodification of labour power under limited conditions, and in tandem with the advancement of capital accumulation. At the same time, here, the phenomenon of crisis is not explained as a contradiction that has no solution for capitalist society, or as that which inevitably leads to the collapse of capitalist society. What has to be explained is how crisis phenomena appear repeatedly while the contradictions of capitalist society are continually resolved practically, beneath new relationships of labour and capital. The definition of crisis phenomena can also be clarified as that which joins phases of prosperity and depression in the so-called business cycles. In this book, therefore, what I seek to clarify is why the cyclical process of prosperity, crisis, and depression appears through a definite periodicity, and also why this cycle is inevitably mediated by crisis.

CHAPTER 1

Prosperity

Once methods of capitalist production come to dominate a single, given society, its development always proceeds through the so-called business cycle, which necessarily repeats three phases of accumulation: prosperity, crisis, and depression. Crisis is one of the phases of this cycle, and it appears inevitably within the process. What must be clarified, above all, is this inevitability of crisis itself. However, if any light is to be shed on the repetition of these three phases, we must first clarify the phase by which our analysis begins. The cause of crisis is found in the accumulation of capital during the period of prosperity; accumulation during the period of prosperity is based on the reorganisation of capital during the period of depression; and the reorganisation during depression, it can be said, stems from the destruction of capital in the wake of crisis. Every phase, therefore, is nothing less than the result of the previous phase. As I will have opportunity to describe and explain in more detail later, and as I already have touched upon in the Introduction, these three phases do not merely repeat the same, identical process. Composed of these three phases, each cycle reveals a period of prosperity that is comparatively more developed than the previous cycle, but it also reveals a period of depression that falls beneath the previous cycle's period of prosperity, thereby taking on a zigzag path of capitalism's ever-expanding process of development. As a whole, this is nothing but a stage in the advance of capital's accumulation.

Generally speaking, the accumulation of capital has two aspects, one that does not accompany changes to the organic composition of capital, which therefore increases the amount of capital quantitatively on the basis of the *same organic composition of capital*; and another aspect of accumulation, in which a rise in the amount of capital brings about *changes in the organic composition of capital*. While the former increases the number of workers in tandem with the accumulation of capital, the same cannot be said for the latter, necessarily. This represents nothing less than the advance of capital's productive powers, as well as the progressive enlargement of capitalist production and the advance of its continued accumulation, but it goes without saying that the former is the simpler and more fundamental of the two. And while it cannot be said that the two aspects appear immediately, as such, within the accumulation process, and in each phase of the business cycle, it can be said generally that the former is represented by periods of prosperity, and the latter by periods of depression. Crisis, then, is a link in a cycle that binds together –

or that rather *converts* – one aspect of accumulation into the other. The positive advance of capitalist accumulation is accumulation during the period of prosperity. Accumulation during the period of depression is its negative advance. Put differently, on the surface of things, it appears that during the period of prosperity, accumulation proceeds without changing the composition of capital. But beneath this surface appearance is something that already connotes a generally higher composition of capital compared to that of the last cycle, which increases the absolute number of workers, advances capitalist accumulation itself, and inevitably brings about crisis. The meaning of the period of depression is found here, for it reorganizes the excessive accumulation of capital, including the destruction of capital that the course of the cycle produces, and prepares for the next cyclical process. Thus, the cyclical process must begin with the period of prosperity.

1 The Accumulation of Capital in the Phase of Prosperity

For the accumulation of individual capitals, it goes without saying that it comes primarily from the profits realised by the sale of commodity products. First, money obtained from the sale of these commodity products recovers expenditures spent on raw materials and other circulating and constant capital, as well as on variable capital, as wages, and allows for a new round of purchasing raw materials and employing workers. Second, money is accumulated as a portion for the amortisation for the portion of fixed capital; and finally, thirdly, a portion of the profits are divided into the capitalist's personal consumption funds and into accumulation funds.[1] Socially, the commodity products of many and various individual capitals are exchanged through the mediation of money, continuing the reproduction process of these capitals, and supplying the necessary means of production and means of subsistence. Unlike a planned economy, in a commodity economy, commodities are unavoidably produced in a state of excess or deficiency. It is safe to say, however, that this excess and deficiency is something that can be adjusted in accordance with changes in the price of commodity products. Here, however, two points of caution need to be made. The first point is that, when it comes to individual capitals, the

1 [Transl. note:] On amortisation funds, Marx writes, 'Even though … a large part of the money that flows back to replace the wear and tear of the fixed capital is transformed back into its natural form annually, or even more frequently, each individual capitalist still needs an amortisation fund for the part of the fixed capital that reaches its term of reproduction only after a period of years, and then has to be replaced entirely' (*Capital*, Vol. 2, 1992, p. 260).]

funds needed for the amortisation of fixed capital must have been previously accumulated in the form of funds, and for a period of time that is more or less definite, which means that these funds can neither be invested in fixed capital immediately, nor be used immediately for the enlargement of actual capitals. As I will discuss later, this is where the function of credit plays a crucial role for the accumulation of capital in the period of prosperity. The accumulation of funds by individual capitals for the physical replacement of fixed capital corresponds to the production and expansion of the fixed capital by other individual capitals. As a result of these accumulated funds, the function of credit acquires a new dimension of activity. The accumulation of capital, of course, is never simply a matter of obtaining and then hoarding larger amounts of money. The accumulation of capital is nothing other than the process by which, in accordance with the annual product, more and more capital is produced, and more and more surplus value is realised and then transformed into capital on the basis of surplus labour. The annual product, as means of production and as articles of consumption, realises the reproduction and accumulation of capital. Thus, for example, if, on the one hand, the funds for the amortisation of the portion of fixed capital is realised in money and accumulated, in this form, for a definite period; then on the other hand, for the capital whose fixed capital has already reached the time of being replaced, these funds must be expended and used for physical replacements of fixed capital. Socially speaking, the renewal of fixed capital becomes possible in this way, irrespective of individual capitals. For example, even when the products of individual capitals are consumed annually as articles of consumption, a part of the amortisation funds on their fixed capital must be produced, in a socially corresponding way, by other capitals, as means of production for the renewal of the fixed capital; otherwise, the capitals will not be able to replace fixed capital during periods of renewal. Even for capital to produce articles of consumption, the replacement of its fixed capital cannot avoid becoming an impossibility, socially, if the value portion of its amortisation funds are consumed away. If this portion of value can be bought and sold as commodities, this is because it makes the replacement of fixed capital possible, which depends on the exchange of products with other industrial sectors. This is to say that, if it is possible for one portion of capital to be accumulated as money and not be used for the replacement of fixed capital, this is because another corresponding portion of capital is already replacing it. This point is clarified by Marx in *Capital*, Volume II, Part 3, 'The Reproduction and Circulation of the Total Social Capital', in the so-called reproduction schemes. In actuality – and differing from the assumptions of the reproduction schemes – the annual reproduction is not something whose settlement is limited to one year, nor is it something in which the accumulation of amortisation funds guarantees an exact annual balance with the actual replacement of fixed capital among capitals. Nevertheless, such relations must be recognised as basic social relations, and actual relations will not be understood unless these basic relations are clarified.

Regarding accumulation funds, basically the same relation can be assumed. Put differently, while on the one hand money is accumulated by individual capitals, on the other hand, the money accumulated as funds are invested into the actual expansion of production by other individual capitals. Within the portion of surplus value, that which has been accumulated out of the annual product must be allotted, socially speaking, for the expansion of production. Therefore, the accumulation of money is viable and possible, even under a certain quantity of circulating money. Such money, which is exchanged as accumulated funds, and which mutually passes from the hands of one capitalist to another, is socially used to expand production with one part of the surplus products. However, even if it can be said that capital expands production with one portion of the annual surplus product, this portion represents nothing other than the means of production and the workers' means of subsistence, understood as articles of consumption. It is here, then, that we need to raise the second problem.

Even if capital can convert one portion of surplus value into capital and realise production on an ever-larger scale, it is nonetheless incapable of producing, on its own, the workers who constitute the foundation of production. Capitalism, whose foundation is established with the commodification of labour power, was able to realise the commodification of labour power during its formative period through the so-called process of the primitive accumulation of capital, when small producers, especially peasants, originally tied directly to means of production, were separated from these means of production. Then, especially with capitalism's period of establishment, the commodification of labour power was secured through the formation of a relative surplus population, as an industrial reserve army, which stemmed from a rise in the organic composition of capital, thereby showing that the conversion of surplus product into capital was not the simple result of a natural increase in the labouring population. The labouring population is not something that naturally increases with the accumulation of capital. The accumulation of capital basically cannot take place without a rise in the organic composition of capital. Or, to put matters differently, generally speaking the accumulation of capital is not simply a matter of distinguishing between phases prosperity, crisis and depression. Rather, as a process of the total development of capitalism, the accumulation of capital as a whole realizes both the rise of the organic composition of capital and the quantitative expansion of capital.

In reality, however, the tendency in capitalism of a rise in the organic composition of capital does not take place incessantly. In actuality, the replacement of fixed capital of individual capitals does not occur as simply as I have supposed in the basic model stated above, where a group of capitals accumulate amortisation funds while another group of capitals reach the renewal period of fixed capital and invest amortisation funds in new plans and equipment simultaneously and in balance. An advance in the accumulation of capital during the period of prosperity already implies a starting-point in the phase of depression, which presupposes lowered prices and the pre-existence of a surplus population, and which provides the foundations for prosperity in the rise of the organic composition of capital by improvements in productive methods. What is revealed here is how the renewal of fixed capital, as it is already invested, cannot take place until a definite period of time has passed. At the same time, in the period of prosperity, the advance of the accumulation of capital takes place on the basis of this general, renewed fixed capital, and in a different situation compared to that of the period of depression, when pressures from lowered prices make improvements to productive methods inevitable. Even if it can be said that capital always pursues its particular goal to gain extra-profit through improvements to production methods, the drive for improvements in production methods differs in periods of prosperity and in periods of depression. The process of improving production methods would be different if its goal is in shortening the working day of productive workers (although existing fixed equipment as means of labour must prevent the incessant improvement, even in such a socialist process). By contrast, under the form of capital, whose goal is profit, the process of making improvements to production methods would never be performed with such an immediate goal of workers in mind. In periods of depression, when the acquisition of profits is difficult, an enormous amount of energy is spent to improve production methods, and because of competition within the same industry, the renewal of fixed capital ultimately cannot but take place by adopting new methods as quickly as possible. By contrast, during periods of prosperity, the fact that the acquisition of profits is assured itself dulls the drive for improvements in production methods. Moreover, in considering the fixed capital portions of individual capitals that have already been renewed (even when, for example, new production methods are discovered or invented at certain, definite periods), this hardly means that the original capital can be replaced immediately with these new discoveries or inventions. No matter the degree to which an additional expansion of production methods is able to make improvements, it cannot avoid its own natural restrictions. So long as the new methods are not confronted with so sharp a decline in prices as to completely scrap themselves, in the period of prosperity the renewed fixed capital tends to continue to be used until it is forced, by crisis and depression, to renew itself by the destructive drop in prices. Moreover, in reality, the actual implementation of improved production methods does not take place immediately, simply because new production methods are discovered or invented. The fall in prices during periods of depression is the crucial trigger for this implementation.

Of course, in considering the starting point of periods of prosperity, the new cycle of accumulation does not begin with improvements carried out uniformly on the production methods of various capitals and in various sectors. No matter where the prices fall in a period of depression, when improvements to production methods are carried out in a given sector, competition will impel the replacement of fixed capital within that sector. (Here, we can ignore, to a certain extent, whether the period of renewal actually comes or not.)[2] In other words, the tendency of renewing fixed capital is concentrated in this period and generally provides the stimulus for the start of the period of prosperity. By the same token, it is here that the production of the means of production, which was forced during the period of depression to undergo drastic contraction, returns to life. The reason is that improvements to production methods, in spite of a decline in prices, nonetheless can recover profits to a certain

2 [Transl. note: For Uno, the problem of the 'renewal time' of fixed capital, as well as its exclusion from the analysis in the fundamental principles, points to the methodological question of his theory of the stages of capitalist development. This problem becomes particularly meaningful in the stage of imperialism, under the dominance of finance capital, when periods of the renewal or replacement of fixed capital tend to be drawn out over time due to the capitalists' *salto mortale* in selling off old fixed capital, which leads to so-called 'chronic depression'. Especially in periods of depression in the stage of imperialism, and in the sector of the heavy industries specifically, with the rise in capital's organic composition, the massive concentration of fixed capital (e.g., steel-making factories) becomes a material and time-bound burden on capital in periods of depression, when it is difficult, if not impossible, to sell-off the fixed capital. Thus, the sell-off time also needs to be emphasised here as a temporal determination of the renewal of fixed capital. (David Harvey has also emphasised this point with his notion of 'spatial fix'.) This should not distract us from the basic point that Uno is making here, however, which is that, for a theory of crisis, the inevitable temporal and spatial restrictions of fixed capital, which are limited by the form of capital – which is itself bound to the necessity to commodify labour power – and to the temporal presence or absence of amortisation funds needed to carry out the replacement of fixed capital (which connects to the central importance of the credit system), are all crucial problems of capitalism's fundamental systemic instability, which pertains to the exposition of the inevitability of crisis in Uno's text.] On credit and crisis based on Uno's *Theory of Crisis*, see Makoto Itoh, *The Basic Theory of Capitalism*, Macmillan (1988); *Political Economy of Money and Finance* (with C. Lapavitsas), Macmillan, (1999).

degree. Through newfound productivity, the period of prosperity develops in such a way that capital is able to generally reduce the value of labour power and secure the basis of reproduction under new relations of production. Even when improvements to production fail to take place in other industrial sectors, these new relations of production influence other sectors that have not yet been improved and inaugurate a period of prosperity.

In the period of prosperity, capital's expansion of the scale of production does not simply come from the conversion of profit into capital. The conversion of profit into capital not only requires the accumulation of a definite amount of funds, but, depending on the conditions of production, it is also possible that the scale of production will not be able to be expanded immediately. Thus, if there is an accumulation of funds that cannot be invested immediately into production, but that are still as yet insufficient as a fund for accumulation, then in the meantime these funds will have to be given some elasticity for their socially mutual utilization. Insofar as they allow for an acceleration of the production and sale of commodities, the social and mutual utilization of these funds performs an extremely important role in the recovery of the reproduction process in the period of prosperity. That the renewal of fixed capital tends to be concentrated at a definite period of time means that its amortisation funds are added to other funds, thereby increasing various powers of mutual utilization. This is a problem of credit, and so, for our consideration of accumulation in the period of prosperity, it is unthinkable to ignore the important role that credit plays in the expansion of capitalist society's scale of reproduction.

2 The Role Performed by Credit

Generally speaking, the movement of industrial capital proceeds through three stages: M (money invested as capital) – C (means of production and labour power as commodities)...P (production)...C′ (commodities endowed with new and more value) – M′ (money with more value). This movement of M – C...P... C′ – M′ represents a process of buying, production, and selling that requires a given amount of time, respectively. However, for capital to maintain production in an uninterrupted way – and the existence of fixed capital especially requires this – the entirety of capital cannot be invested in the production process. Put differently, the total capital is allocated to each stage of the process in definite proportions, so that when one part is allocated to the segment of M – C, another part goes to the production process; when the capital in the production process enters the process of C′ – M′, the capital found in the process of M – C must proceed to production. The production of surplus value, which is the goal of the movement of capital, can only be achieved, however, in the production process, which represents one stage of the various movements. The circulation processes of M – C and C′ – M′ represent nothing more than a necessary but negative stage of the total movement. Marx's so-called circulation capital is found in this process, and whether it exists in the form of money or in the form of commodities, it exists, as far as capital is concerned, in an idle state.[3] Capital tries as much as it can, however, to minimise this amount so that more productive capital can be allotted to the production of surplus value. So, for example, if, in the case in which a cotton spinning manufacturer is unable to turn his cotton thread (as a manufactured good) into cash through an immediate sale, this sale can be made against a three month bill of credit, and when this credit allows him to purchase raw cotton as his raw material, it goes without saying that, for the textile manufacturer who has purchased cotton thread on credit, as well as for the cotton spinning manufacturer who has purchased raw cotton on credit, the circulation capital that allows for the continued production for both parties is made possible, to a certain degree, by the limitations set by the funds of the raw cotton cultivator. In any case, it is through credit that the textile manufacturer, as well as the cotton spinning manufacturer, are able to immediately transform the required circulation capital, which would be required if their funds cannot be available, into productive capital. In other words, credit actually expands the production process by harnessing a definite quantity of social capital. This does not occur, of course, when a fall in prices makes it impossible to expect adequate profits. Rather, it occurs when there is a turn towards a period of prosperity, when the acquisition of higher profits stemming from a recovery of prices is anticipated, when relations of credit are mutually extended between

3 Marx's so-called circulation capital should not be confused with the circulating or fluid capital that is opposed to fixed capital. The distinction between fixed and circulating capital pertains to the capital in the production process, whose value is recovered, with each repetition of the production process, whether partially, as with machinery and other means of labour, or entirely, as with raw materials and labour power. Here, the value of labour power is not simply recovered each time; it is merely recovered from the value newly produced by labour. Perceived from the turn-over of capital, however, labour power can nonetheless be considered, along with the constant circulating capital of raw materials, etc. as circulation capital. By contrast, *circulation capital* is distinguished from the productive capital within the production process, and exists, as Marx points out, in the form of commodities or money. It goes without saying that, in tandem with the movement of capital, circulation capital then converts into productive capital.

every industrial sector for the sale and purchase of their products, and when the production process is expanded as much as possible. So long as mutual payments are secured, it is unthinkable that an individual capital would not take advantage of these various credit opportunities. Certainly, while all of the relations between industrial sectors cannot be said to be tied by these credit relations, and while there must also be increases on payments to workers that cannot make use of credit, nonetheless, it cannot be denied that credit, as something that mediates payments between capitals, plays an important role in the expansion of production. It thus goes without saying that the enlargement of credit uses, in addition to the original forms of circulation capital as money and commodities, preparatory funds reserved for changes in price, as well as amortisation funds for fixed capital and accumulation funds, which we have discussed earlier. As for the amortisation funds or accumulation funds, a basic relationship is considered, by which an accumulation of money corresponds to the renewal of fixed capital and accumulation while this relationship is utilized here for the expansion of various facets of production. Put differently, for a specific, given industry, the production of means of production and articles of consumption required for the renewal and accumulation of fixed capital are boosted in more profitable industries by rising prices. Of course, in reality, the elastic and mutual utilization of funds increases the demand for means of production and articles of consumption and accelerates that production; price fluctuations thus come to meet an increase in demand and an increasing supply.

Here, however, when we think of so-called commercial credit, its meaning is obscured by the fact that it is buried in a process stemming from operations that specialise in the sale and purchase of commodities: the work of merchant capital, which exists in a relation of exteriority to capitalist relations of production, and the work of capitalist commercial capital. In any case, as the foregoing has shown, the original basis of commercial credit stems from how industrial capital itself is able to expand the scale of production by mutually using this commercial credit. If these matters are not given this kind of exposition, its social meaning will never be clarified, and it will be impossible to analyse the functions of commercial capital, let alone merchant capital. In fact, commercial capital stands in for the commercial credit of industrial capital, and functions as that which strengthens and enhances the latter.

Now, once the mutual use of funds as various idle funds, which exist between industrial capitals, passes through the independent institution of banks, the credit relations between individual capitals develop into a credit relation between banks and industrial capital, that is, into bank credit. In addition to bundling up, in a concentrated way, the various idle capitals between individual industrial capitals, banks socialise the credit relations between individual industrial capitals. For example, it is not necessary for an industrial capitalist, who has sold on credit, to make payments with the trade-bills that he has already accepted, for he can have his trade-bills discounted at the bank and immediately obtain the cash that he needs. On the one hand, banks are entrusted to concentrate the idle funds of industrial capitalists; on the other, they lend, at an interest, those funds to the industries that socially demand the expansion of those funds, and that anticipate payments stemming from the movement of prices of products from industry. In the interim period, and with the so-called profit motive generated by the difference in interest between the deposit and the loan, profits are made on bank capital that is invested in the bank's activities. The bank thus mediates the industrial capitalists' idle funds and generally becomes the institution that socially expands capital's reproduction process, and no longer functions as a form of loan capital that treats one's own funds as interest-bearing usury capital.[4] By passing through both

4 In reality, the funds that are collected in banks are not simply the idle funds of industrial capital. Moreover, the lending of these funds is not limited, as I have discussed above, to the commercial credit required for the reproduction process of industrial capital. This is a distinction that is in fact decided upon by the actual operations of the bank, but here we are not prescribing the bank's role strictly in accordance to its existence as a concrete financial institution. Rather, by focusing on the basic function of the bank, we are trying to clarify how, in a capitalist society generally, credit has a role in the discourse of the business cycle. For a so-called theory of finance, the division and form accompanying the bank's concrete developmental process, as a financial institution, must certainly be clarified, but for the theory of the fundamental principles, the basic role of banks actually cannot be grasped if these concrete functions are considered in and of themselves. Similar to other cases, here we are considering, in a purely capitalist society, the role of credit as it accommodates funds between industrial capitals. Therefore, it is safe to think that the lending of funds, as so-called circulation credit, is limited to the mutual utilization of funds required for the sale and purchase of commodities. The essence of such credit, however, cannot be properly clarified by an explanation that claims that circulation credit is merely the lending of money, and not the lending of capital. That which is lent is neither merely money, nor capital, but funds. Generally speaking, these funds are lent as money that has been liberated, as it were, from the function of the means of circulation, as so-called currency, that is required for the sale and purchase of commodities, but they function as capital that is constantly used as a means of circulation by borrowers. Moreover, as I have described earlier, it also goes without saying that we cannot consider the process of mutually using the funds of merchant or commercial capital directly (in the fundamental principles). More concretely speaking, as for the prosperity-phase in the accumulation process, while it can be said that an important role is often played by the making available of funds that fall outside of the idle funds of industrial capital, a consideration of these factors cannot be made here, for it would not only complicate our analysis unnecessarily, it would also miss their basic relations of determinations.

the deposit and the loan, these funds are commodified and given interest as a sort of price. The bank thus becomes a merchant, buying up funds cheaply and selling them dearly. Interest can thus be said to form the value of these funds as commodities, to be paid for their use value as capital and used over a definite period of time, and to be returned thereafter. At the same time, even in cases when these funds cannot be used as capital, they can become bought and sold as commodities similarly at the same price.

In this way, industrial capital – in addition to depositing its idle funds in banks as much as it can while simultaneously using the funds that are concentrated by the banks as the need arises – socially uses the funds that cannot be used directly by individual industrial capitals. This is nothing less than a method by which the scale of production is expanded, capitalistically and socially, to the greatest extent possible. Through the use of credit, industrial capital forms increasingly larger funds and supplies them to banks, which serve as a market for funds, while also using them as much as they can. At the same time, the supply and demand of funds pass through changes in the interest rate, which comes to adjust the funds allocated by the reproduction process. Ultimately, this is based on, and restricted by, the rate of profit, but this does not necessarily mean that a low interest rate means a low profit rate, or that high interest rates mean high profit rates. Quite the contrary, often there are cases in which interest rates rise when profit rates fall, as well as times when a fall in interest rates can be seen when profit rates rise. It is precisely here that the capitalistic, social function of loan capital is exhibited.

On the basis of a fall in general prices and a fall in wages that emerges alongside a fall in profit rates in the period of depression, capital is able to anticipate a revitalisation of industrial activity once an even partial recovery of the profit rate – itself generated by newly improved methods of production – is seen. However, this does not mean that a recovery of the profit rate for all capitals is presented immediately. As I have pointed out earlier, while there is a tendency for the general replacement of fixed capital to take place, by and large, in a concentrated way and at a definite period of time, the fact that improvements in production methods can take place with one part of capital does not mean that another capital can move immediately towards the same improvements. For the majority of capital, improvements to methods of production result from, and are compelled by, competition, and are determined by the extent to which the continued use of fixed capital is regulated by older production methods. But for various industrial sectors, and especially for individual capitals, while this fact leads to the appearance of imbalanced and uneven development, it also, by the same token, hinders this development. Similarly, regarding funds, while its formation is hindered at certain, definite periods of time, there is a concurrent tendency towards the partial growth in the demand for these funds, which is often the reason why, within a situation in which a general recovery in the profit rate cannot be seen, a rise in interest rates takes place. However, when improvements in production methods have taken place within industrial sectors, and when the basis for the recovery of the profit rate is provided for by the general completion of the replacement of fixed capital that is promoted through competition, conversely a fall in the interest rate can be seen at the same time.[5]

Based on new relations of production, industrial capital, as a totality, not only re-opens its activities of reproduction, it continually expands commercial credit, and accelerates the formation of funds, so that even if there is

---

5 In 'Typical Cycles and Alternating Cycles of Business Alternations', Arthur Spiethoff (1873–1957) provides the following chart:

Depression

- Fall (fall in capital investments, the consumption and production of iron, and interest on loans)
- First stage of upswing (cessation of the slow-down of iron production, consumption, and capital investments and the beginnings of a feeble movement of recovery)

Prosperity

- Second stage of upswing (energetic growth of capital investments, especially in stocks. Iron consumption nears the peak of the previous highest point)
- Highest point (rise in interest on loans; surmounting of the peak of the previous highest point in iron consumption)
- Shortage of Capital (*kapital mangel*) (difficulties in procuring capital, that is, a slow-down in investment capital, a sudden rise in interest on loans, stagnation of the stock market, decrease in housing construction, stagnation of iron consumption)

Crisis

- destruction of credit, frequency of failures on payments

Spiethoff's research is not only based on England but primarily on Germany, especially after the 1840s, but it presents several questionable points, notably a total failure to consider the distinctions between different stages of capitalist development before and after the 1870s, as well as a failure to critically examine basic concepts – such as capital – that have already been elucidated in *Capital*. But while his research distinctly lacks overall clarity, I would generally accept his foregoing description – as phenomena accompanying the three stages of depression, prosperity, and crisis – of the fall, the first upswing, the second upswing, the highest point, and a shortage of capital. In my analysis here, Spiethoff's so-called second upswing overlaps with the transitional period from depression to prosperity, in which a recovery of profit rates accompanies low interest rates.

Let us now take a look at Spiethoff's comparison between the alternations of periods of prosperity and depression, on the one hand, and fluctuations in the interest rate, on the other. (Here, the interest rate is taken as the lowest average discount rate of interest of the Bank of England.)

an increased demand for these funds, interest rates will fall as a result of an increase in the supply of these funds. The low position of interest rates, which is born out of the recovery in profit rates, makes it possible, moreover, to accelerate the social use of funds, and it is because of this that the reproduction process of industrial capital enters the process of development with all of its powers, thereby generally bringing about prosperity. Of course, the expansion of the scale of production does not simply depend on these funds; it is rather based on the transformation of profit into capital. In the period of prosperity, however, industrial capital cannot resist using every convenient method. Credit

---

		Pound	Shilling	Pence
Prosperity 1844		2	10	0
1845	highest point	2	13	8
1846	‘	3	6	6
1847	capital shortage	5	3	6
Depression 1848	Fall	3	14	5
1849	‘	2	18	7
1850	First phase of rise	2	10	1
1851	‘	3	0	0
Prosperity 1852	Second phase of rise	2	3	0
1853	‘	3	3	10
1854	High point	5	2	3
1855	‘	4	17	10
1856	‘	6	1	2
1857	Capital shortage/crisis	6	13	3
Depression 1858	Fall	3	4	7
1859	‘	2	14	7
1860	‘	4	3	7
1861	First phase of rise	5	5	4
Prosperity 1862	Second phase of rise	2	10	7
1863	High point	4	8	2
1864	‘	7	8	0
1865	‘	4	15	4
1866	Shortage of capital	6	19	0
Depression 1867	Drop	2	10	9
1868	First phase of rise	2	1	11

To reiterate, in Spiethoff's analysis, the norms for each stage of this period have already been set by the case of Germany. Moreover, we cannot say that his comparison is precise because when he references interest rates through the discounted bills of the Bank of England, this is in fact an average interest rate. Nonetheless, general tendencies can be observed in his analysis.

plays an extremely important role here, and it tends to drive industrial capital into more or less speculative development.

3 Speculative Development and the Rise in Prices

The advance of the accumulation of capital, which first appears in response to rising demand for means of production, comes to see a general rise in prices when it passes through a recovery of the price of means of production. Of course, while this may not always occur depending on the specific circumstances, generally speaking, the price of raw materials, more so than finished goods, shows an unusual rise in price during the period of prosperity compared to its extremely low price during the period of depression. This is why there is a tendency towards an intense absorption of funds, socially collected by banks, with enlarged production and the buying of raw materials. The speculation on buying, in particular, in fact is made with the funds of merchant capital, or else through the social utilization by merchant capital of the funds collected by banks. This does not mean, however, that with industrial capital there is no speculative buying, or that there is not an expansion of speculative production. Even if industrial capital were to mutually share the funds that it forms itself, so long as there exist, among individual industries, differing degrees of anticipation on the acquisition of profits and on rises in prices, the use of these funds will assume a speculative tendency without fail. It is true, of course, that the rise of prices of raw materials and other means of production, in addition to the prices of finished goods, recovers out of the fall in prices during the period of depression, leading to speculation across the totality of industrial sectors and to a general rise of prices. This is also why there is a rise in the mutual utilization of funds available through the mediation of banks. Moreover, as long as the scale of production is constantly enlarging, banks will be able to forecast the formation of new funds and to increase the amount of issued banks notes to a certain degree, thereby bringing about what is commonly called the phenomena of inflation, and thus performing a role in widening speculative tendencies.[6]

---

6 So-called inflation becomes a social problem when governments, incapable of securing funds through its fiscal income, artificially provides these funds by increasing the issuing of paper money and other currencies, thereby leading to an inflation of prices, stemming from a so-called inflation of currency, which affects every level of society in myriad ways. At the same time, during periods of prosperity, there are many cases in which inflation occurs when a rise in price accompanies an inflation of credit. The causes of the rise in price in both cases,

Generally speaking, it goes without saying that a rise in prices brings about a rise in wages, along with a rise in the price of means of subsistence. In the period of prosperity, however, the cause of the rise in wages is not based on this alone. As described earlier, the rise in price for general commodities itself incites a rise in supply, and reaches a definite limit set by the relationship between demand and supply. Of course, for raw materials and semi-finished goods, whose increased production cannot be carried out rapidly, a rise in price continues on for a significantly long time, thereby causing speculative purchasing. But even so, this does not mean that a rise in supply, stemming from an advance in production, cannot take place. This is not the case, however, with the commodity of labour power. As I have already mentioned, capital can produce labour power passively, as it were, by creating a relative surplus population on the basis of a rise in the organic composition of capital; but in response to a rise in the price of labour-power, capital cannot increase the supply of labour-power on its own. The production of labour power is something that can only come about within the worker's individual, everyday life itself; capital can do nothing more except produce means of subsistence as commodities, and to thus reproduce labour power indirectly. For example, let us say that a rise in wages provides workers with a little more leeway in their everyday lives, thus accelerating the natural multiplication of workers by an increase in marriages and a decline in mortality rates. Even if this were so, it would not guarantee an increased supply of labour power in the face of capital's increased demand for labour power in a period of prosperity. The beginning point of the period of prosperity, moreover, is in fact based on the formation of unemployed workers in the period of depression, and along with the accumulation of capital, these workers are mobilised, thereby securing a supply of workers. As long as this is the case, there is no immediate problem, but this alone already reveals the

however, are different and should not be confused with each other. The bank's provision of funds, which stems from an increased issuance of bank notes, originally serves as the ground upon which new funds are formed in relation to the expansion of the production process, whereas recent inflation is caused by an artificial provision of paper money by governments. As recent so-called inflationary policies especially show, the government itself has carried out a policy of raising prices by providing artificial funds during periods of depression, and is, to a certain extent, increasingly adopting a method to merge both ways of providing these funds. In other words, through a rise in prices stemming from an artificial inflation of currency, excess goods are united with a surplus of population, thereby contributing towards the formation of new funds. The significance of this, however, cannot be clarified without an analysis of the causes and effects of the rise in prices and its limits. This cannot be viewed as the same thing as fiscal inflation, nor can fiscal inflation be justified simply by referring to it. Here, an extremely complicated relation must be given its proper theoretical exposition, but suffice it to say that it cannot be explained by inflation.

appearance of a restriction on, and a limit to, this supply. For example, when we consider capital's accumulation that attains a relatively higher growth in its composition of capital by replacing fixed capital, even if it could, by itself, constantly form a working population as a relative surplus population, this process, it must be said, takes place in the transitional period from depression to prosperity, when the surplus population is formed and now a given fact. It cannot be said, therefore, that a surplus population is formed due to an advance of accumulation in the period of prosperity, a rise in demand, and also a rising composition of capital. The surplus population is only gradually mobilised and absorbed, and its wages cannot but rise accordingly. Wages do not rise in the same way as a rise in commodities that have been speculatively purchased; they are in fact concealed behind these speculatively purchased prices of general commodities. Although a rise in wages is considered to be caused by little more than a rise in prices – and this is something that holds true to a great extent – there is something at its root that capital is powerless to increase.

Unlike the rise of general prices, the rise in wages that accompanies an increased demand for labour power substantially works against profit and erodes the rate of profit. This is not because a rise in wages allows the price of commodities to be raised, however. Strictly speaking, the value that is paid out as wages has no relation whatsoever to the value of the commodity formed by labour. The former is paid out to workers, with which they purchase their means of subsistence, which are consumed in the workers' everyday life. For capital, this represents a loss of value. With the purchasing of labour power through a payment of value, however, the labour power that is consumed in the production process is turned into labour, thereby forming new values and allowing capital to recover the previously lost value, and to acquire, as surplus value, the portion that is left over. Put differently, in the production process, the value of wages is not preserved and transferred to new commodities like raw materials and other means of production. Capital is able to acquire and obtain surplus value precisely because the value that is formed by labour is a new value. What is paid to workers as wages represents the value of labour power, whereas the new value is formed by labour, or the use-value of labour power. The fact of the matter is that when labour power is in the hands of the worker, it is something that possesses value as a commodity, but as soon as it passes into the hands of the capitalist, it is already no longer a commodity that possesses value, in and of itself. The capitalist, after all, cannot resell the labour power that was previously purchased as a commodity. The capitalist can only consume it in the production process and realise it as labour that creates value. Because this point has not always been clearly understood, it is commonly thought that a rise in the value of commodities takes place because of a rise in wages, as if the latter was the same thing as a rise in the value of raw materials. But this is far from the truth. A rise in wages reduces the surplus value that is distributed as profit. Simply because profits are the distribution form of capital's surplus value, a rise in wages does not directly correspond to an immediate reduction of individual profits. What is clear, however, is that a rise in wages generally brings about a decline in the average profit rate itself.

In actuality, the speculative rise in prices in the period of prosperity that I have described above frequently conceals a rise in wages, and especially possesses a function that essentially mitigates this rise in wages. Consequently, there is a confusing problem to solve. A general rise in prices that results from speculative buying can only reduce, it goes without saying, the actual increase in the portion of the workers' consumption that stems from a rise in wages, and cannot immediately reduce the profit rate. The maintenance of the profit rate by a rise in price is in fact nothing but an illusion. The inventory of over-stocked commodities cannot realise the prices that have been speculatively envisioned. The profit rate, which cannot but fall as a result of a rise in wages, is nothing more than an assumed high rate of profit that exists beneath such illusory prices. Even if we supposed that these commodities could actually be sold, it would not be possible to maintain prices in the same way that increased wages can be substantially reduced, and therefore a decline in the profit rate would inevitably be exposed. Put differently, speculation in the period of prosperity, which is determined by the forms of over-stocked commodities that cannot be sold, expresses a concealment and distortion of capital's basic relation to labour.[7]

Of course, the speculative rise in prices, which depends on the making available of funds that are concentrated by the work of various financial institutions centred around banks, and especially on the basis of the so-called creation of credit that comprises the imagined funds formed by the enlargement of the scale of production; this speculative rise in prices will certainly hinder a real rise in wages to the bitter end, but because of this, the rise in the demand for these funds – made possible by the actual sale of commodities and by the supply of funds that are formed by the realisation of value – will not be sufficient, and will inevitably lead, in turn, to a progressive rise in the interest rate. Funds will be borrowed, of course, to pay back the principal loans, but will also be borrowed even for making payments on the interest on these loans.

7 It seems to me that this relationship also forms the basis of how, as Marx writes, 'the conditions of the direct exploitation and the conditions of the realisation of this exploitation are not one and the same'. On this point, see Appendix 1, '*Capital* and the Demonstration of the Inevitable Ground of Crisis'.

Then, depending on the selling off of commodities, when these payments can no longer be avoided, the prices that have been speculatively increased now suddenly plummet in the opposite direction, making visible a drastic fall in the profit rate, and making defaults on payments inevitable. It is here that the phenomenon of crisis is born.

CHAPTER 2

Crisis

By making idle funds available to each other, not only is the accumulation of individual industrial capitals accelerated; once the accumulation of industrial capital becomes driven by the so-called creation of credit that anticipates an expansion of the scale of production, the social reproduction process is expanded to the highest degree. This represents the method by which the accumulation process of private, individually separated, and independent capitals is socially advanced as much as possible. At the same time, it always leads to an excessive expansion of production which, through the work of its peculiar method, cannot avoid becoming a self-regulating movement. Such an excessive expansion of production, which overcomes the limitations set by capital's relationship to workers, is regulated by capital through the form of loan capital, which opposes individual capitals and regulates industrial capital. In actuality, since this takes place primarily with speculative purchasing by merchant and commercial capital, the impetus for this self-regulation is provided when merchant and commercial capital fall into bankruptcy, and while commodities that cannot be sold are considered to be the cause of crisis, this is, as I have described above, little more than a distorted expression of industrial capital's excessive accumulation. In the midst of the period of prosperity, indeed, all industrial capital – which in actuality is constantly advanced by merchant and commercial capital's buying – will invariably experience an excessive expansion of production to a greater or lesser degree, thereby causing a general upsetting of the reproduction process. Consequently, while there comes to appear, on the one hand, excessive means of production and means of subsistence in the form of commodities or productive capital, and, on the other, a growing number of unemployed workers, it becomes impossible to combine these two things together for the continuation of reproduction. Thus, so-called excess capital and surplus populations appear simultaneously. In this way, within the stagnation of the reproduction process, capital loses value as capital, making it impossible for capital to continue production with the same relations of production as before. Crisis appears as a rapid process in which capitalist methods of production socially increase productivity, and in which capital, in order to overcome its own limits and to reorganize the reproduction process on an enlarged scale, experiences a drastic loss in the value of capital itself.

1 The Collision between the Profit Rate and the Interest Rate

The process that advances accumulation, which has the goal of acquiring larger and larger profits, is not simply a process of transforming into capital the surplus value obtained through the production process. Moreover, as I have already discussed, nor is the transformation of portions of surplus value into accumulation funds something that can be spent, immediately and directly, in the expansion of individual capital's own production process. Rather, capitalist methods of production cannot avoid using these funds socially for the capitalist expansion of the accumulation of capital. At the same time, this expansion inevitably causes an excessive expansion, and thus the first point that must be clarified is the question of what this excessive expansion means.

1.1 *The Falling Rate of Profit That Accompanies the Advance of the Accumulation of Capital*

Generally speaking, the development of capitalist methods of production – understood as a condition for the advancement of productivity and as a result of this advance in productivity that accompanies the rise in capital's organic composition – is unavoidably accompanied by the tendency of the profit rate to generally fall. Not only is the basis for this general tendency provided for with the advance of accumulation in the period of prosperity, but due to the mobilisation of labour power in the form of the so-called industrial reserve army and an attendant rise in wages, the profit rate cannot avoid declining in a way that differs from the general, tendential fall. In other words, an enlargement of capital produces a fall in the profit rate due to a decrease in the mass of profit, meaning that larger and larger amounts of capital are only able to raise smaller amounts of profit. Thus, this fall of profit rates is totally different from the tendency of the general profit rate to decline that the development of capitalism, as a rule, presents over the long run.[1]

---

1 [Transl. note: For further theoretical context on Uno's comparison between the rate and mass of profit, see of *Capital*, Vol. 3, Part Three, Chapters 13–15. In Chapter 13, Marx writes, 'If we take a given working population, of 2 million for example, and further assume that the length and intensity of the average working day is given, as well as wages, and hence also the relationship between necessary and surplus labour, then the total labour of these 2 million workers always produces the same magnitude of value, and the same thing is true of their surplus labour, as expressed in surplus-value. But as the mass of constant (fixed and circulating capital) set in motion by this labour grows, so there is a fall in the ratio between this magnitude and the value of the constant capital, which grows with its mass, even if not in the same proportion. This ratio falls, and with it the profit rate, even though capital still commands the same mass

For example, let us suppose that, for all industrial sectors, there is a 10% increase in profits on a total capital of 100 million. Now, when there is an increase in capital of 20 million, and if we were to suppose an 8% fall in the profit rate due to a rise in wages, the mass of profit will be reduced from 10 million to 9.6 million. From the perspective of capital, the accumulation of capital of this 20 million thus becomes something meaningless; it becomes excess capital. In any case, it is safe to say that, up to 100 million, even with a decline in the profit rate, the mass of profit would continue to rise to 10 million. But supposing that capital could somehow be increased, and that the only profits that could be made was less than 10 million; if that were so, then capital would inexorably become excess capital. Even if capital could somehow increase its products, the mass of profit would fall against the increase in capital despite increased production by capital, and capital would become, unmistakably, excess capital. This is nothing other than the phenomenal appearance of a peculiar contradiction of the capitalist mode of production, which is based on the particular commodity of labour power. If labour power could be produced directly by capital like any other commodity, we can be certain that this phenomenon would never happen, and yet, despite this, the particular commodity of labour power nonetheless constitutes the basis for the survival of capitalism itself. If things were produced simply by means of other things, then that which we call society would not have come into existence. The labour power of human beings, by working on nature, produces things, things by which labour power is then reproduced in the so-called metabolic process between nature and man, a process that is certainly found in all societies. In capitalist society, however, the process passes through the commodity form and takes place as the production process of capital. It is here where we find capitalism's peculiar difficulty and formal contradiction, its ir/rationality and antagonistic nihil of reason (*muri*).[2]

of living labour as before and absorbs the same mass of surplus labour. If the ratio changes, this is not because the mass of living labour falls but rather because the mass of already objectified labour that it sets in motion rises. The decline is relative, not absolute, and it has in fact nothing whatsoever to do with the absolute amount of the labour and surplus labour set in motion. The fall in the rate of profit does not arise from an absolute decline in the variable component of the total capital but simply from a relative decline, from its decrease in comparison with the constant component' (Marx 1991, p. 323).]

2 [Transl. note: Uno's term *muri*, which is one of his original and unique concepts, connotes several meanings: a fundamental difficulty, a contradiction, an ir/rationality, antagonism and enforcement. All of these meanings are contained in the concept of *muri*, but in Uno's text it always refers to the fundamental contradiction surrounding the labour power commodity, namely that while capital must consume labour power as a commodity to produce surplus value, capital is nonetheless incapable of producing labour power as a commodity directly.

It is precisely on this point that capital, as it takes this form, will be incapable of continuing, despite its efforts, the infinite accumulation that it naturally aspires towards. The valorization process of capital can only take place by transforming into a commodity that which is not, originally speaking, a commodity, namely labour power. It is also because of this contradiction that the desire for the infinite expansion of value cannot avoid turning into its opposite.

Of course, as I have already referred to with some frequency, the commodification of labour power is provided by the basic conditions in which a relative surplus population is formed by the rise in capital's organic composition. In this regard, we can say that capital itself produces labour power, albeit indirectly, and is able to create, by itself, its own foundation. Now, are we to think therefore that, with accumulation in the period of prosperity, the composition of capital *constantly* grows, that a surplus population will be formed while it is simultaneously mobilised and absorbed, and that, through such a method, the general profit rate of capital will fall tendentially while the mass of profit, by virtue of the advance in productivity stemming from the growth of capital, will also progressively grow as well? In fact, the accumulation of capital decidedly does not proceed in this manner. For accumulation in the period of prosperity, as I have already discussed, the tendency is for production on an increasingly expanded scale to proceed with a fixed and given composition, which means that the increase in demand for a definite mass of labour power will inevitably lead to a rise in wages.

However, when we consider excess capital, it is not something that appears necessarily and directly, as such, to individual capitals. Generally speaking, the basis for the general profit rate is attained by distributing the surplus value, first obtained in the production process of individual capitals, as an average between individual capitals in the process of realising this surplus value. Socially, this is nothing but the formation of a general, average rate of profit through the competition of capitals that are pursuing industries with higher profits. In actuality, variations in profit rates remain, not only between differing industries, but also between capitals in the same industrial sector and depending on differing conditions of production, which consequently leaves differences in rates of profit. That profit rates fall because of high wages does not necessarily mean that all profit rates fall in the same way. Then again, even if such a decline, for example, were generalised, individual capitals attempting to avoid such a fall would be incapable of stopping the accumulation of cap-

Rather, capital must pass through this ir/rational *muri* in order for labour power to become a commodity to be consumed. See Kawashima (2005); Nagahara (2008); Walker (2016).

ital. Just because a profit of 10% was obtained in the case of a capital worth 100 million, while only 8% was obtained on a capital worth 120 million, this does not mean that a capital worth 20 million can be set aside and left idle. Even if that 20 million is not invested, a fall in the profit rate would be unavoidable due to a rise in wages and as a consequence of the advance of other capital's accumulation. In any case, it will not be possible to maintain a 10% profit rate. For individual capitals, the profit rate will fall as something given from the outside, irrespective of whether the accumulation of this capital will take place, or not. If 20 million were not added to the total social capital, this would not happen, but this is unrealistic due to the 'private character' of capitalist production. Even in this case, individual capitals would do all they could to compensate for a falling profit rate by increasing the mass of profits stemming from an increase in the magnitude of capital, and by working towards the maintenance of the power to accumulate. Thus, socially speaking, even when capital is always-already falling into a condition of excess, the competition between individual capitals is not able to restrict the excessive accumulation on its own. It is precisely here that the social function of loan capital is fully exhibited. It is concealed to a certain extent, however, by the speculative rise in prices during the period of prosperity, which boosts accumulation to an extreme beneath an assumed (and often imaginary) profit rate, and ultimately, this excess can only be exposed by the relation to loan capital.

1.2 *The Sharp Rise in the Interest Rate at the Highest Point of Prosperity*

The funds that are supplied by banks, let us recall, represent nothing more than funds that were originally turned into idle funds by the work of industrial capital itself. Therefore, with the funds created along with the advance in capital's accumulation in the period of prosperity, there is a rise in the funds accumulated by banks, on the one hand, and an increasing rise in the funds that need to be absorbed for the practical purpose of investments, on the other. This means that during periods when an expansion of the scale of production leads to an anticipation of higher profit rates, a demand for these funds naturally tends to exceed their supply. As I have described earlier, more than anything else, insofar as banks can reliably expect an expansion of industrial capital's reproduction process, banks can increase the issuance of bank notes and form funds on its own. Moreover, just as the funds concentrated in the hands of the banks are decidedly not limited to the idle funds of industrial capital, so too are the users of these funds not limited to industrial capitalists, but are also extended to merchant and commercial capitalists, who, in their demand for these funds, become important users themselves. This point becomes an extremely complicated relationship, but what constitutes the fundamental basis of the credit system is nothing more than the making available of social, capitalistic funds produced in the social reproduction process. This relation fundamentally regulates the extent to which banks are capable of increasing the issuance of bank notes.

It goes without saying that the interest paid on the mutual availability of these funds comes from a portion of the profit of industrial capital. For individual industrial capitals, however, the use of not only their own capital, but also of the funds of others, allows them to pay interest from increased profits, and so long as profits can be left over after paying the interest on borrowed funds, profit rates for individual capitals will rise accordingly. Unlike the profit rate, the interest rate does not have a fixed standard, and because of this, the interest rate moves in completely different directions than the movement of the profit rate. In fact, in the period of prosperity, even when confronted by falling profit rates stemming from a rise in wages, industrial capital puts into action methods to maintain the advance of individual rates of profit as much as possible, even by means of borrowing funds with rising interest rates. On the one hand, this is the case because capital has already been invested in the production process, which cannot refrain from incessantly continuing production. But this is not all. Even with a decreased rate of profit, for example, an increase in the mass of profit, obtained by an increase in capital, can, up to a certain limit, not only pay off interest but also leave an additional profit, thereby compensating for a fall in the profit rate on one's own capital. In this way, however, this relation inevitably points to a decrease in the funds themselves that must be borrowed. Not only are the idle funds of industrial capital decreased; the banks – which supplied funds by increasing the issuance of bank notes on the assumption that the reproduction process will expand – now also face difficulties because the formation of these funds, as far as the reproductive process goes, contributes directly to a decrease in the mass of profits accompanying the fall in profit rates, or else indirectly, to the piling up of overstocked commodities, created by speculative buying, which delays return payments. Consequently, a continuation in the expansion of credit becomes impossible. While a rise in the profit rate initially witnessed a rise in the interest rate, here the opposite is the case: a fall in the profit rate is now accompanied by a rise in the interest rate.

While the source of profit and interest is found in the surplus value produced from within the movement of industrial capital, profit distributes this surplus value directly in relation to capital, whereas interest, which forms one part of profit, does not take a direct relationship to the movement of industrial capital, but rather exists at the outer limits of this movement, where it receives a share of the profits. Whereas profit possesses a substantial standard for distribution, interest simply possesses an external allocation standard. However, when we view the rate of distribution, these relationships are completely reversed. For individual capitals, the profit rate, as a social standard, exists as a general profit rate that is simply created as an average of various and different rates of profit. Unlike the interest rate, therefore, it does not appear directly as a definite, concrete rate, and only as an average of various individual rates of profit. This averaging out of the profit rate is in fact realised socially through the movement of loanable capital, which mediates the idle funds used mutually by industrial capital. Although the formation of the general profit rate is (and must be) theoretically presented as an effect of the competition by industrial capital to seek out more profitable industries, the social regulation of capital in fact necessitates the mediation by loanable capital as an externalised mechanism of the competition between capitals. This is analogous to how the exchange of commodities in general must be socially mediated by money. Actually, the movement of individual capitals takes place within each particular industry, being restricted by specific use values and unable to migrate immediately from one sector to another simply because there exists a more profitable industry. Although an owner of capital may want to invest additional capital in a more profitable industry, this does not mean that this owner can make such an investment directly. Of course, capital itself is not something that is continuously restricted by specific use values, like commodities, for capital is nothing more than a value that creates more value. The self-expansion of value as capital could not take place, however, without being invested in specific industrial sectors under the restriction of particular use values. And just as the value of a commodity can only become realised by being sold to money – which originally emerged as a universally equivalent commodity among all commodities – so, too, does capital socially manifest itself, as capital, by a regulatory mechanism that tests whether or not capitals can operate advantageously even after paying interest. In cases in which individual capitals have already, socially, become excess capital, individual capitals are not only powerless to regulate this excess capital; on the contrary, they exacerbate this tendency. It is precisely in such a relationship, however, that loanable capital appears as something that regulates this excess socially. Unlike the profit rate of industrial capital, the rate of interest to loanable capital does not possess a definite quantitative social relation with surplus value to serve as a substantial standard vis-à-vis a definite magnitude of capital. Based on the movement of industrial capital, but existing without a direct relationship to it, loan capital socially regulates excess capital from outside of industrial capital's accumulation. This is the peculiar, socially regulatory method corresponding to capital's anarchic production. In short, by commodifying its own funds which can be transformed into capital at any time, capital's anarchic production of commodities becomes regulated by the anarchical commodity form itself.

1.3 *The So-called Shortage of Capital*

When, by a rise in wages, the profit rate falls – the tendency of which is concealed, as I have already described, by the prices speculatively envisioned for the accumulation of overstocked commodities – and when interest rates suddenly rises, industrial capital falls into a situation in which it cannot make payments on interest, let alone on principal loans, and is forced to borrow more money to pay off interest. Of course, the expansion of capital's reproduction process in the period of prosperity does not proceed evenly throughout every industrial sector. Rather, it is guided in a speculative way as a result of the uneven rise in prices that is itself based on the uneven development among industrial sectors. Now, the aid provided by the banks, in the form of funds to industrial and commercial investment, becomes a burden which banks cannot accept, neither for falling profit rates resulting from higher wages, nor for the difficulties in selling-off the accumulated stocks of commodities that express the distortion of this fall in profit. While the aid extended to the industrial capitals that have defaulted on payments certainly represents a loss for the banks themselves, the banks naturally do not assume the direct burden of falling profit rates. Interest rates do not fall simply because profit rates fall. In fact, interest rates increasingly rise in such a situation, where industrial capitals progressively experience difficulties paying back loans, and defaults on payments sometimes lead to business liquidations by the banks, even bringing about a concentration of capital. For industrial capitals that have continued, more or less, to speculatively expand and purchase, it is now clear that a fall in the anticipated prices of commodities does not take place along with a fall in wages. Rather, what is exposed is that a sudden rise in wages cannot but reduce the profit rate. In this way, by its own doing, many industrial capitals fall into defaulted payments while becoming saddled with an enormous amount of capital produced in the form of means of production and commodities, incapable of continuing its operations. In actual practice, through the interventions of merchant and commercial capital, the form of this excessive capital appears in an accumulated and unsalable stock of commodities, and thus defaults on payments also often appear in merchant and commercial capital. While this counteracts the reproduction process of industrial capital and leads to a crisis, the basic relationship is found in the opposition between industrial capital and loan capital, which has assisted the rapid expansion of industrial capital.

The essence of the phenomenon of crisis will never be grasped so long as this basic relationship, which is distorted by the superficial facts of reality, is not clarified. Even when we consider speculative expansion, this is not something that takes place groundlessly. This ground is not simply the peculiar form of the development of capitalist methods of production, it is provided by the very material relations with which expansion becomes possible. Increasingly larger and larger means of production and articles of consumption come to be produced, and so long as labour power is given, the means of production and articles of consumption will be able, as capital, to continue the self-expansion of value, thereby producing increasingly more and more means of production and means of consumption, and expanding the scale of production. The ability of banks to create funds through an increased issuance of bank notes is also only possible on this basis. Therefore, at the same time, this possibility is inevitably reversed when the means of production and articles of subsistence, which have already been produced, become excessive when restricted by labour power. Banks also do not simply operate to finance the materials produced by industrial capital.

It is here that the phenomenon, commonly known as the shortage or lack of capital, makes its appearance. This never means a shortage of capital as means of production or commodities. Quite the contrary, the very superfluity and excess of so-called capital goods makes the self-expansion of value, as capital, inoperable. This difficulty, which cannot be expressed by capital directly, is rather indirectly displayed by a depletion of funds in the form of loanable capital. We could say that this points to how capital is not, properly speaking, a mere thing, but a relationship between human beings that passes through things. Here, however, the relationship is such that capital, in taking on the form of a lack of loanable capital, appears as a relationship between things. As long as capital appears as a thing, so, too, will its lack appear as a thing, not in the lack of actual materials of means of production and articles of consumption, but in a lack of funds-as-things. Of course, even funds are not simply things. As an independent existence of the value created by labour, funds differ from means of circulation and do not simply exist within circulation. Rather, as something that is released from circulation, funds stand in opposition to commodities by being able to purchase commodities at any time, but not simply as mere currency and as a thing possessing a definite use value. Rather, we could say that it possesses the quality of what Marx called *money as money* (*Geld als Geld* in German), money as an independent thing of value that stands in opposition to commodities within the circulation process. Moreover, so long as it exists as money and as an independent existence of value in opposition to commodities, there is no necessity for this money as money to exist physically as gold within the social reproduction process. This points precisely to the relation whereby banks are able to extend loans, as funds, by increasing the issuing of bank notes on the assumption that future funds will be created when the reproduction process operates favourably and expands; it is a relation, in other words, in which the lending of bank notes creates, along with the value of the purchased means of production and labour power, the formation of funds as newly formed value. At the same time, these funds cannot be formed without limits and apart from the social reproduction process, no matter an increase in the issuing of bank notes. This is the reason why, during times of crisis, the creation of funds cannot be made simply for the purpose of selling off unsold commodities. Rather, the capitalist commodity economy proceeds through a kind of social restriction by funds that are operated by loanable capital. Insofar as this is all based on the value created by labour in the social reproduction process, it cannot possibly be something that exists apart from the social relation between capitalists and workers. In the production process, if the production of surplus value is no longer able to pay the value of the interest, then the capital, in the form of means of production, will already be lacking the qualification of being capital and thus will no longer function as capital. The means of production and articles of consumption that exist as commodities cannot be sold as commodities. On an international level, these funds as a rule need to exist as physical money (gold), and in the actual process of crisis, the reserves of gold needed for foreign payments restricts the amount of these funds. However, on the domestic level, the amount of gold reserves by no means restricts the amount of funds. This point was greatly confused in England's Peel [Banking] Act of 1844, and is the reason why, during the time of crisis, a suspension of this restriction could not be avoided.[3]

---

3 Regarding the Bank Charter Act 1844, Engels provides a clear account: 'The Bank Act of 1844 divides the Bank of England into an issue department and a banking department. The former receives securities – principally government obligations – amounting to 14 million, and the entire metal hoard, of which not more than one-quarter is to consist of silver, and issues notes to the full amount of the total. In so far as these notes are not in the hands of the public, they are held in the banking department and, together with the small amount of coin required for daily use (about one million), constitute its ever-ready reserve. The issue department gives the public gold for notes and notes for gold; the remaining transactions with the public are carried on by the banking department. Private banks in England and Wales authorised in 1844 to issue their own notes retained this privilege, but their note issue was fixed; if one of these banks ceases to issue its own notes, the Bank of England can increase its unbacked notes by two-thirds of the quota thus made available; in this way its issue was increased by 1892 from £14 to £16½ million (to be exact, £16,450,000)'.

'Thus, for every five pounds in gold which leave the bank treasury, a five-pound note returns to the issue department and is destroyed; for every five sovereigns going into the treasury a new five-pound note comes into circulation. In this manner, Overstone's ideal paper circulation, which strictly follows the laws of metallic circulation, is carried out in prac-

In practice, since the speculative expansion occurs together with speculative purchasing, excess capital appears as an excess of commodities, that is, in a form in which the speculatively anticipated prices cannot be realised, and

---

tice, and by this means, according to the advocates of the Currency Theory, crises are made impossible for all time.'

'But in reality, the separation of the Bank into two independent departments deprived its management of the possibility of freely utilising its entire available means at critical times, so that situations could arise in which the banking department might be on the verge of bankruptcy while the issue department still had intact several millions in gold and, in addition, its entire 14 million in securities. And this could take place so much more easily since there is a period in almost every crisis when heavy exports of gold take place which must be covered in the main by the metal reserve of the bank. But for every five pounds in gold which then go abroad, the domestic circulation is deprived of a five-pound note, so that the quantity of circulating medium is reduced precisely at a time when the largest quantity is most needed. The Bank Act of 1844 thus directly induces the entire commercial world forthwith to hoard a reserve fund of bank-notes at the outbreak of a crisis; in other words, to accelerate and intensify the crisis. By such artificial intensification of demand for money accommodation, that is, for means of payment at the decisive moment, and the simultaneous restriction of the supply the Bank Act drives the rate of interest to a hitherto unknown height during a crisis. Hence, instead of eliminating crises, the Act, on the contrary, intensifies them to a point where either the entire industrial world must go to pieces, or else the Bank Act. Both on October 25, 1847, and on November 12, 1857, the crisis reached such a point; the government then lifted the restriction for the Bank in issuing notes by suspending the Act of 1844, and this sufficed in both cases to overcome the crisis. In 1847, the assurance that bank-notes would again be issued for first-class securities sufficed to bring to light the £4 to £5 million of hoarded notes and put them back into circulation; in 1857, the issue of notes exceeding the legal amount reached almost one million, but this lasted only for a very short time' (Engels, in Marx *Capital*, Vol. 3, 1991, pp. 688–89).

The Peel Banking Act's original consideration of money was guided by the so-called Currency Theory, which was based on the mistaken assumption that the entirety of gold should become money. As Engels writes, however, during times of crisis, while on the one hand this brought profits to banks from high interest rates, it also led to difficulties for the operation of the banks themselves, on the other. That this Act sufficed 'to overcome the crisis' most definitely does not mean that industrial and commercial capital was able to avoid being hit by the crisis and continue their operations. The crisis that was unnecessarily intensified by the Act was merely alleviated. Domestically, even when gold is not held in reserve, so long as securities are guaranteed, banks can meet demand during times of crisis by increasing the issuing of bank notes. Of course, for banks that make loans whose payments are not secured, bankruptcy is unavoidable, even in the case of the Bank of England. Moreover, this point equally reveals how money that is provided for domestic payments must basically be treated as an independently existing thing of value in a way that is similar to gold's relationship to commodities. The biggest error committed by the Peel Banking Act is that it attempted to restrict the demand for domestic funds by actual gold in the same way that it did for foreign payments, and probably also for the securing of foreign payments. This stems from the fact that funds do not necessarily have to exist as gold. Bank notes can be substituted for these funds as an independent existence of value so long as banks can expect to create funds whose pay-money emerges as the sole thing possessing value. Beneath this appearance, however, is the fact that capital, as commodities and as means of production, is already incapable of creating surplus value as profits. Of course, it goes without saying that the capital that exists in the money form cannot create surplus value from the surplus labour of workers so long as it remains in this form. However, in obtaining high interest, loanable capital becomes the sole, existing capital that is capable of increasing itself in the period of crisis, whereas industrial capital, which has now become incapable of functioning as the capital to pay this interest, can no longer be said to be capital. In this way, a concentration of capital at the sacrifice of industrial capital comes into existence. In these times, however, banks themselves often cannot avoid bankruptcy. It is in conditions such as these that the common observation of a shortage of capital is in fact born out of an inability to grasp the true meaning of capital. This is not to say, however, that a shortage of capital has no meaning. This common observation should not miss the true significance of the excess of capital. Actually, an accumulation of excessive, real (industrial) capital appears in a shortage of capital in the form of money (or loanable capital), observable as a shortage of capital.

2 The Excess of Capital and the Surplus of Populations

The excessive accumulation of capital in the period of prosperity finally brings forth an excess of capital, in the form of means of production and means of consumption, and in relation to a population of workers. From the workers' perspective, however, the means of production and means of consumption are not in excess absolutely. For even though a rise in wages in the period of prosperity expands workers' consumption, this increase has a definite limit. Even if means of consumption have been overproduced, the meaning of this excess is not that it is beyond the workers' ability to consume them. In a capitalist society, the rise in workers' wages is limited. It is this fact that simultaneously produces an excess of capital and a surplus of workers.

2.1 *The Rise in Wages and Its Limits*

Generally speaking, in a capitalist society, the wages of workers, as the price of the commodity of labour power, fluctuates around the value determined by the labour time necessary for the reproduction of labour power. In this sense,

ments can be made with certainty. Gold can be money, also so long as it can always, and at any time, purchase commodities.

the commodity of labour power is similar to other commodities in a capitalist society. However, as I have repeatedly mentioned, labour power differs from other commodities insofar as it cannot be produced directly by capital itself. Therefore, even if the value of labour power can be determined by the labour time necessary for the production of labour power, for capital, it is still not a commodity that capital can produce anytime, simply by harnessing this labour time. Its value is determined indirectly by little else than the labour time required for the production of the workers' means of subsistence. These means of subsistence, however, are produced by workers themselves in capital's production process; as products of capital, they are turned into capital, which ensures for the capitalist that labour power will always stand in a relation of separation from the means of production. While economics frequently treats the workers' means of subsistence as capital precisely for this reason, it goes without saying that for the capitalist, production does not take place with means of production and the worker's means of subsistence. Means of subsistence themselves never exist as capital within the production process. In truth, the workers' means of subsistence represents, for the capitalist, commodities that must be sold; for workers, they represent nothing more than commodities that must be bought with money obtained as wages. Workers will not be able to buy these commodities unless they receive these wages. Capitalists, moreover, will not escape a drop in the prices of these commodities if they cannot sell them to workers.

In short, as a product of capital, means of subsistence are no different from capital that has taken on the commodity form, and thus they exist as capital, as things that can be sold as a commodity. So long as labour power is not purchased as a commodity, and so long as wages are not paid to workers, it will be impossible for means of subsistence to be sold as commodities. That both the means of subsistence and means of production exist as excess capital, however, does not merely signify a direct relationship in which, for example, a surplus of foodstuffs stands in relation to the working population. It is an excess that is born out of the advance of capital's accumulation, in which an increased demand for labour power raises wages while decreasing the amount of surplus value as profit, as well as out of an inability to invest advantageously, as capital, the means of production and means of subsistence that are produced on an increasingly larger and larger scale. This is an excess completely specific to capitalist society.

The wages of workers are such that, on the one hand, they are never to fall to the point where the life of workers is threatened by an inability to purchase the means of subsistence required for the reproduction of labour power. (In actuality, the limits imposed on the reproduction of labour power are determined socially, historically, and even to a certain degree physiologically, and are never fixed or definite. Moreover, labour power is never actually supplied exclusively by the dispossessed workers that we theoretically presume here, hence in actuality it is possible that wages fall even below the value of labour power.) On the other hand, however, wages are never to rise so far as to prevent capital, in its accumulation process, from expecting an increase in profit. Wages rather fluctuate within the limits bound up with definite class relations. Unlike other commodities, the supply of labour power cannot be increased simply because an increase in the demand for labour power takes place. Therefore, capitals are forced to coordinate the supply of labour power by the so-called industrial reserve army. At the same time, even if an increase in demand does not necessarily raise the price of labour power above its value, this rise in price is not something that the capitalist can control, either. Of course, while it can be said that individual capitalists will try in all cases to buy as cheaply as possible, their efforts cannot ensure success because a rise in wages – in the advance of accumulation and in the period of prosperity – is unavoidable. This is not all. Even if the profit rate falls because high wages accompany the advance of accumulation – a fact that is actually concealed by a rise in speculative prices – there is still no stopping accumulation's advance.

To say, however, that the rise and fall of wages is determined simply by the opposing relationship between capitalists and workers is undoubtedly insufficient. Properly speaking, capital itself – and especially its accumulation – is nothing more than the transformation into capital of the surplus value that is objectified surplus labour, or the so-called unpaid labour of workers, and thus the capital creating the demand for labour power is in fact nothing but a product of the workers' surplus labour. Put differently, as Marx says, it is, 'at bottom, only the relation between the unpaid and the paid labour of the same working population'.[4] Marx continues:

> If the quantity of unpaid labour supplied by the working class and accumulated by the capitalist class increases so rapidly that its transformation into capital requires an extraordinary addition of paid labour, then wages rise and, all other circumstances remaining equal, the unpaid labour diminishes in proportion. But as soon as this diminution touches the point at which the surplus labour that nourishes capital is no longer supplied in normal quantity, a reaction sets in; a smaller part of revenue is

4 *Capital*, Vol. 1, p. 771.

> capitalised, accumulation slows down, and the rising movement of wages comes up against an obstacle.[5]

In *Capital*, Vol. 1, however, this determination is a matter that develops around the general and basic relationship between capitalists and workers; the 'counter-acting force' described here does not appear directly on the plane of competition between individual capitalists. The counter-acting force rather appears through loanable capital, as a social capital that opposes industrial capital, as well as through the contradiction and collision between falling profit rates and suddenly rising interest rates. This, however, is just a particular expression of 'the relation between the unpaid and the paid labour of the same working population'. The contradiction that takes the shape of this expression would never have come into existence had the workers' labour not passed through the form of capital. It is this particular form, moreover, that gives birth to the phenomenon that so many people cannot make sense of, namely of why the excessive work of workers inevitably leads to a loss of work. Marx's statement that, 'the real limit to capitalist production is capital itself', must also be understood to pivot around this point.[6]

2.2 *The Excess of Capital as an Excess of Commodities*

In this way, when we speak of an excess of the means of production or the means of subsistence that are produced in progressively larger and larger quantities with the expansion of the scale of capitalist production, this is not an excess simply in relation to the working population. Means of production or means of subsistence become excess insofar as they function as capital. Those products would not constitute such an excess if they did not take on the form

5 *Capital*, Vol. 1, p. 771.

6 [Transl. note: *Cf., Capital*, Vol. 1, chapter 25, Section 3, in which Marx writes: "The condemnation of one part of the working class to enforced idleness by the overwork of the other part, and vice versa, becomes a means of enriching the individual capitalists, and accelerates at the same time the production of the industrial reserve army on a scale corresponding with the advance of social accumulation." (*Capital*, p. 789) This points to Marx's discovery of the *law of populations* peculiar to capitalism, which is important in Uno's theoretical exposition because it allows us to grasp how capitalism's fundamental contradiction – of capital's absolute necessity to consume labour power as a commodity (to produce surplus value) and its absolute inability to produce labour power as a commodity directly – is given a prosthetic yet inevitable resolution in the formation of a relative surplus population. "The labouring population therefore produces, along with the accumulation of capital produced by it, the means by which it itself is made relatively superfluous, is turned into a relative surplus population; and it does this to an always increasing extent. This is the law of populations peculiar to the capitalist mode of production …." (*Capital*, Vol. 1, pp. 783–84).

of capital, or if, to put matters differently, workers produced by using their own means of production and consumed their own means of subsistence in everyday life. The fact is that at the height of the period of prosperity, even with a rise in wages, this rise is circumscribed by definite limits. This does not mean that articles of consumption are produced in excess over and above the ability of workers, as human beings, to consume. In actuality, as a result of a rise in speculative prices, this excess appears as an accumulated inventory. These prices do not rise to a great extent on a practical level, but from the perspective of capital, this excess comes into being when investments of progressively larger amounts of capital yield decreasing rather than increasing magnitudes of profit. The same can be said even for means of production. The nature of capital's production process is not something that is developed by shortening the working day corresponding to advances in productivity.

Therefore, the production of the means of production also falls under definite, capitalist restrictions. Similarly, the means of production that have become excess capital would not be found in such an excess if they were used by workers themselves. If these means of production could be produced as something that workers themselves could use – for example, by shortening the working day, or by alleviating their labour – then the production of excess in the form of means of production would have never materialised in the first place. It would then especially be possible to devote increased production for articles of mass consumption, which is impossible to realise capitalistically.[7]

7 In a capitalist society, if the means of subsistence of everyday life, which are historically determined in a given society, are given to workers over and above what is historically determined to be necessary for the reproduction of labour power, then workers might not work the next day as wage labour. Due to the definite limits of wages, workers are compelled to work and to live a wage-worker's everyday life. This, however, presupposes that the means of production exist as capital, and that workers buy back, with wages, means of subsistence as products of capital. In short, it presupposes capitalist methods of production, by which the means of production appear as capital and the means of subsistence are bought back by workers with their wages. There is no way that this could have taken place generally in all human societies. In the aftermath of the developments of the social methods of capitalist production, the method by which workers, for themselves and by themselves, use the means of production directly, can be realized only in a socialist society. But if it is supposed that in socialism, workers are supposed to work like wage labourers because it is thought that they may not work if they are given means of subsistence beyond their daily requirement for reproduction, then we could say that this supposition absolutizes the capitalist social relation. Of course, the fact that over the long course of the historical process, workers have not used the means of production, by themselves and for themselves, to produce and consume products as their own; this fact does not refute the argument for socialism. This is an issue that, in practice, cannot be solved as abstractly as it can be done in theory, but to think of workers only as wage labour, whose daily subsistence cannot be allowed to go beyond the daily require-

This excess of means of production and means of consumption does not mean an excess of means of consumption in relation to means of production; nor does it mean the excess of one part of the means of production in relation to another part. This excess of commodities results from the over-production of commodities caused by the so-called disproportion or imbalance of production sectors. The excess of capital is thus different from the excess of commodities. As I have discussed earlier, capitalism possesses a mechanism that can adjust such disproportions through the movement of price. Of course, within the concrete processes of individual crises, such disproportions undoubtedly play an important role. Indeed, especially when crises are sparked off by frenzied, speculative buying by merchant or commercial capitals, as well as by the latter's bankruptcies, it can often be thought that crisis is born out of such an uneven, imbalanced development. However, even in this case, the basis of crisis does not simply stem from uneven development. Crisis is caused by the limitations of capital itself, which are different from the imbalances of capitalist production. In fact, even if the outbreak of crisis stemmed from bankruptcies born out of such imbalances, crisis cannot be explained by the adjustment of imbalances alone, or by the mere fact of falling prices of certain kinds of com-

ment to reproduce labour power for one day, is a narrow way of thinking that is dominated unconsciously by the ideology of capitalism itself. Of course, while we cannot demonstrate the 'formula' of a socialist society scientifically, this distinction must be clarified, nonetheless. As far as the scope of research in political economy is concerned, insofar as capitalist development itself advances the social productive forces and, with it, the basis of socialist methods of production, the possibility of socialism has to be recognized within the scope of research in political economy. This does not mean that capitalism is consciously oriented towards this goal, or that the transformation to socialism takes place, by itself, naturally and spontaneously – for, to put it differently, capitalism also develops factors that work against the transformation to socialism. Of course, insofar as the areas of political economic research proceed from (i) the principles of political economy to (ii) the stages theory of capitalist development, and finally to (iii) the concrete, historical analyses of contemporary capitalism, this *possibility* turns from being a negative problem into a positive one. Theoretically, we cannot positively prove, on the abstract level of the principles of political economy, the necessity of socialist society. While the assertion that political economy can demonstrate the necessity of socialism can be seen to provide a powerful scientific basis for socialist movements, this argument also risks, depending on the situation, diminishing the significance and meanings of actual practices in socialist movements. The historical process is not as objective as these kinds of scientific analyses make it out to be in their conclusions. Such conclusions, it must be said, are born out of a mechanical understanding of inevitability and necessity, and by a theory that cannot be said to be able to analyze the historical process as something that is, in fact, historical. Of course, this is not to deny that such conclusions are emphasized in socialist movements. I will return to this point in Chapter 5, 'The Inevitability of Crisis in Capitalist Society'.

modities, or even by the fact that the imbalance stemming from the complex combination of production processes upsets the totality. The process in which crisis is followed by depression points to how it cannot be solved by merely adjusting the imbalance between commodities.

Likewise, even when we are speaking of the imbalance between commodities, the problem here is the disproportion or imbalance between commodities as products of capital, and commodities that are not products of capital. This is not merely an imbalance of the kind found in the case of commodities as products of capital. In other words, it is not a disproportion or imbalance that can be adjusted through the movement of price. For this very reason, the emergence of the phenomenon of a general excess of commodities, as that which cannot be thought to abide by the commodity form, becomes possible.[8] While capitalism transforms the entirety of society into a commodity economy by commodifying labour power and by mediating, through the commodity form, the relationship between capitalists and workers as the fundamental relationship of society, there now emerges, from the depths of capitalist society, a point that is left over by capitalism, a point where it is unable to completely transform society into a commodity economy. This point exposes how the commodity form cannot serve as the absolute form for human society. No matter how much human beings are regarded, commodity-economically, as a human resource, workers are human beings, not resources. They are not things, nor can they be produced as mere things. Workers cannot be produced as things by capital itself either, and while workers may be viewed as a resource similar to nature, unlike nature they are not given externally, from the outside. Workers are rather reproduced annually by the means of consumption as products of labour, which, in a capitalist society, are products of capital. It is precisely because of this that capital is able to take a form that dominates a single society. As I have described above, the surplus or lack of a working population itself comes to appear as an internal factor to the development of capitalist production, constituting a contradiction immanent to capitalism. Not simply a contradiction between things, it is a contradiction born out of the form itself that turns human beings into things.

---

8 Marx discusses the relations between 'excess capital' and 'excess commodities', and 'partial excess' and 'total excess', in light of his critique of Ricardo, and in his clarification of the confusions of various theses after Ricardo (see Marx, *Theories of Surplus Value*, 1951, Vol. 2, Part 2, Chapter 3, 'The Accumulation of Capital and Crisis', section 4). Here, Marx remains in his primary consideration of the capitalist commodity economy in its commodity form dimensions, and does not clarify the fundamental cause of crisis directly. [Transl. note: In the Progress Publishers edition of *Theories of Surplus Value*, Part 2, see chapter XVII, numbers 1–15, pp. 470–547.]

If the excess of commodities, as an excess of capital – which in actuality frequently appears in the form of speculatively purchased inventories of commodities, but which can also be understood as such – could be dealt with socially, then it goes without saying that it would not occur as a crisis. However, as a commodity economy, it is already an impossibility to socially manage and sell-off this excess. Capitalism cannot manage and dispose of this excess-portion, exclusively and immediately, as an excess. The excess to be managed is rather expressed in a form in which virtually all commodities become an excess. Capital, therefore, cannot avoid bringing production entirely to a complete standstill. Individual capitals competitively try, as quickly as possible, to sell off these commodities, and here the selling-off of the surplus products itself already proceeds by way of the commodity economy.[9] This phenomenon corresponds to how excess capital is not directly exposed by a fallen profit rate, but indirectly, by defaulted payments caused by a sudden, high interest rate. In this way, the excess of capital appears, simultaneously and inexorably, as an excess of populations. This is neither simply an excess of capital in relation to populations, nor simply an excess of populations in relation to capital. Rather, in the beginning, capitals appear excessive in relation to populations, but later on, populations appear excessive in relation to capital, which implies how, beneath a given relation between capitalists and workers, capital becomes incapable of managing the products it has produced itself, as capital. The origin of this incapacity is found in the fact that the labour power of workers is not allowed to

9 Along with the development of capitalism, foreign investments of capital take place, thereby allowing for handling commodities as excess products to a certain degree. This, however, is completely different from the social management of excess products discussed here, for it takes place as investments that are made in the pursuit of higher profit rates. It is valid, of course, to note here how so-called monopoly capital is formed by the concentration and growth of capital, and in ways that reveal an intensely close connection to the state, and in this regard, it is not impossible to identify certain aspects of a movement towards a kind of social management. Foreign investment takes place, in other words, not only to pursue higher profits, but also to serve as a means by which to circumvent sudden falls in the profit rate. This point, however, requires special research and cannot be theorised here because it pertains to what is called finance capital, as a phenomenon accompanying the developmental stage of recent capitalism, wherein industrial capital is no longer opposed to loanable capital. We should at least be quick to affirm here, however, that even in this case, the contradiction originating from the commodification of labour power and the subsumption of labour is not fundamentally resolved beneath the form of capital. Indeed, it can be said that the source of all of the problems, which have proven to be difficult to resolve in the era of so-called monopoly capitalism, remain as signs of this contradiction. The meaning of the unprecedented development of the military industry should also probably be clarified in relation to this point.

exist, as labour power, unless it is sold and turned into a commodity – unless, that is, it is given the form of capital. Capital becomes an excess, as capital. This is also the reason why capital, as excess capital, is ineluctably expressed in the form of an opposition between industrial capital and loanable capital.

2.3 *'Poverty in the Midst of Affluence'*

In light of the foregoing, an excess of capital and an excess of populations can hardly be said to be incompatible with each other. In the development process of the period of prosperity, money simply appeared as a means for the exchange of commodities, while commodities appeared as the sole thing possessing real value. Commodities, as capital enabling the extraction of surplus labour from workers, were in the hands of the capitalist. Now, however, commodities, instead of serving as a means to acquire more value, become incapable of being sold even as mere commodities. Money suddenly becomes the only thing possessing value, and every commodity desperately tries to transform into money. It is as if a certain outlook presented itself whereby the only form in which capital can exist, as capital, is in the money form of loanable capital. *Strictly speaking, loanable capital, to which just a portion of profit is allotted as interest, now becomes the representative of capital in place of industrial capital. This is an inverted expression of the detonation of contradictions immanent to capitalist methods of production.* The functioning of vast sums of capital, in the form of commodities and means of production, is blocked or stagnates, so long as they are in these forms. Not only capital's accumulation but also its reproduction process itself fall into stagnancy. Workers are laid off, their labour time is reduced, or their wages are cut, and the money, needed by workers to purchase articles of consumption which they themselves have produced, does not come their way. All the while the means of consumption grow even to the point of becoming superabundant, yet the workers themselves, who have produced them, cannot consume them. This is a phenomenon that corresponds with the impossibility of uniting the now excessive means of production, as capital, with labour power.

Thus, when we speak of workers labouring in the production process, it goes without saying that they can work only by the sale of their labour power commodity; the wages they obtain in this sale is no more than a helpful means towards the reproduction of their labour power, and a means through which they can buy back the means of consumption that they themselves have produced. If the reproduction process comes to a standstill and wages are not obtained, or if the only wages that can be obtained are smaller than before, then it is clear that the means of consumption, as products of capital, will not be capable of being sold. Workers can sell their labour power as a commodity only while certain magnitudes of surplus value are being produced. Completely different from general commodities, labour power is a commodity that is not useful as a use value for its owners, and while this is what makes it a commodity in the first place, if labour power is not sold, not only is it unusable as such, but its use value is also lost. If the commodities, which workers must constantly buy back, are not produced along with other means of production with a certain profit, then workers will not be able to consume the commodities that they themselves have produced. Capitalist production is one that specifically achieves a general and basic economic process, whereby human beings labour upon nature and obtain means of subsistence to means of production through a particular form; this means that capitalist production is bound up with the restrictions and limits of surplus production. In capitalist production, because the original relationship between human beings and nature is subsumed within the form of capital, workers cannot directly consume the things that they themselves have produced. If the production of surplus value cannot be expected in the next reproduction process, they will not be able to make one portion of the products of past production their own. While labour power may become commodified, it is never exchanged, like the commodity in general, as a thing possessing a specific use value. It is on the basis of this relationship that there appears, simultaneously, an excess of capital, and an excess or surplus of populations.

In this way, just when capitalist production exhibits its productive forces to its fullest extent, it will become, within a given and fixed relationship, unable to handle its products. It will bring forth so-called overproduction, on the one hand, and too many human beings to obtain the necessary level of means of subsistence for the reproduction of labour power, on the other. Overproduction is not an excess over and beyond the needs and desires of this multitude of human beings. Rather, means of subsistence become excessive while the workers' needs and desires, which are already restricted to an extreme degree, go unsatisfied. This excess has not the slightest relation to the workers' needs, and thus we find here what is called poverty in the midst of affluence. Not only this, however. We also find that, despite the workers' intentions to produce their own means of subsistence, production already is no longer capable of continuing on. The means of production are no longer useful as such. Just because workers produced too much means of subsistence, as well as means of production required to produce them, they have become incapable of consuming the means of consumption that they have already produced. Furthermore, workers have also become unable to produce new means of consumption and means of production with the labour power to be reproduced. In other words, the demand for products is decreased precisely because products have been produced excessively. Common sense then tells us that these products cannot be bought because there is a shortage of money. This, however, is not merely a matter of supply exceeding demand. This is not an issue to be solved if commodities can be sold off even at reduced prices. The issue is that the reproduction process itself has become paralyzed because capitalist production is unable to continue with the given and definite relationship between capitalists and workers. While this does not signal an absolute deadlock for the reproduction process, it does reveal a condition in which capital cannot strike out anew unless it destroys and reorganizes its own value relation.

3 The Destruction of the Value of Capital

When capitalist production, in terms of individual capitals, makes use of loanable capital to expand to the fullest extent – and I have already described how, practically speaking, this use of loanable capital is unavoidable – capital exercises its productive powers to such an extent that it cannot carry on in terms of the given value relations. Commodities continue to be produced, but they come to be unsold. Commodity prices cannot avoid falling, but the fall in prices is not one by which the reproduction process restores a balance and commences again. Originally, the excess of commodities in the period of crisis is nothing more than one aspect of the excess of capital, and excess capital is not born out of an excess of commodities. If the overall phenomenon of an excess of commodities exists, this is because it is born out of excess capital. Since this is an excess of commodities that is caused by capital's inability to continue the reproduction process, even banks cannot provide relief through the creation of credit. If finance cannot be continued for commodities that cannot be sold, this is because reproduction itself cannot be continued. Even if reproduction can be continued by means of credit, it cannot so easily change the capitalist productions that are unable to pay for interest, to ones that are able to pay interest. In actuality, as I have made frequent reference to already, the intervention of merchant and commercial capital adds more complex relations to the speculative expansion of industrial capital by the use of loanable capital. Nonetheless, the basic relationship is found at the point where industrial capital is incapable of continuing the reproduction process advantageously and favourably. An accumulated inventory of commodities, formed by merchant speculations, does nothing else except conceal and enlarge this relationship. The fall in commodity prices that appears in crisis does not merely represent a loss here, only to be gained elsewhere. This kind of relationship is included in the problem, but this in itself is not enough, for the problem is the loss of the value of capital, born out of the stagnancy and chaos of the reproduction process itself, of which a fall in commodity prices is but one of its factors.

The destruction of capital value resulting from crisis does not mean, therefore, a mere loss of value in commodities resulting from the imbalance of the reproduction process and the inability to sell commodities. Rather, it means that a loss of the value of capital itself (in the form of commodity capital and productive capital) takes place, together with a fall in commodity prices, and as a result of the stagnancy of the reproduction process. For when the reproduction process stagnates, and when the production process also stagnates, partially or entirely, it goes without saying that the means of production are not going be of any use as means of production. When the reproduction process is going well, the means of production will come into use once again, and because of this, its use value will contribute to the production of new use values, thereby transferring this value to new products. The value of capital, therefore, is not simply lost. Similarly, in terms of use value, when we look at fixed capital such as machinery, insofar as it contributes towards the formation of new use values, its value can be transferred to new products. While it can be said that the only thing that will decrease here is its own use value, as long as it continues to be in use, its use value will be preserved *free of charge*, thus allowing capital to benefit from this use, free of charge, within the labour process. With the interruption of the reproduction process, however, if costs to maintain the means of labour power are not covered, a rapid loss of the value and use value of these means of labour comes about. This is not a problem exclusively for means of labour such as machinery; the same can be said for raw materials and other circulating capital portions. For all of the materials that do not decompose when they are transformed into new products, once they fall into disuse in the production process there is no stopping the loss of use value. This is exactly what the destruction of capital means. And despite the fact that the unemployment of workers does not, in itself, represent the slightest loss for capital, capital will simply cease to be capital even if it does not destroy its own value. As I have discussed before, however, the truth of the matter is that it is the workers' unemployment or semi-unemployment, as an effect of the cessation of the production process, that destroys capital value along with use value. The workers' labour process itself is that which preserves and augments capital's value, thereby qualifying capital as capital; if capital does not increase its value, it will lose its value.

Originally, capital is a value in the form of a moving body, which would suggest that it would lose its value, along with its use value, should its movement be interrupted. In fact, however, this movement itself is always mediated by human labour. This insight is completely lost when capital is understood as if it only existed like merchant capital, where the movement of capital mediates the transformation of commodities into money, and money into commodities, simple processes which do not add any new values – and which, even if it did so, would not amount to much except for incidental additions related to things such as storage or transportation. In the production process of capital, since labour is carried out as the consumption by capital of labour power as a commodity – in other words, as the labour performed by other people – this essential point is liable to be forgotten. Crisis exposes this point in all of its nakedness. Capital is only capable of becoming a moving body of value through a production process conducted by the labour of human beings, thus allowing capital to proceed as a self-expanding value that simultaneously preserves its value. Similarly, the movement of commodities and money, in the form of so-called circulation capital, is also mediated, albeit indirectly, by the labour in the production process. If the labour process is interrupted, the movement of the circulation process also cannot avoid stagnating. The interruption of the labour process therefore cannot but destroy the value, as well as the use value, of capital.

Of course, the destruction of capital value that takes place in the wake of a fall in commodity prices does not occur uniformly in all industries. The prices for raw materials and semi-manufactured goods, which have exhibited sharp increases in the period of prosperity, now do the opposite, exhibiting a sharp fall. Lagging behind the expansion of production, industrial sectors such as these realise expansion for the first time by the heightened rise of prices during the period of prosperity, in which an acute increase in the mass of production tends to induce a sharp fall in prices. In times of crisis, a drastic destruction of capital value cannot be avoided. However, just as the differences in the prices of products in these industrial sectors cannot be said to have sparked off the development of the period of prosperity, in the period of crisis, the extraordinary influence of prices, in and of themselves, cannot recover capital's reproduction process. Crisis, caused by the relation between capital and labour, appears as the manifestation of a contradiction internal to capital itself and is not something that merely results from the imbalance of prices. An excess of capital and an excess of populations are born on the basis of a definite social productive force. This result shows how capital advances to such a degree that it can no longer manage its own productive force with the existing relationships between capitalists and workers. To put matters differently, while capital is able, by the productive forces, to progressively produce more and more means of production and means of consumption, if it does not change the labour time necessary for the reproduction of labour power, it will not be able to re-obtain profits and expand reproduction. In the period of crisis, the differing conditions of various industrial sectors, and the relationships between large capitals and small capitals, not to mention those between industrial capital and financial institutions such as banks, all bring about bankruptcies as well as concentrations of capital, and while the imbalance between capitals forms a basis for balance, this forms, to a certain degree, a factor in the recovery of the reproduction process. However, all of these things alone cannot bring about a new relationship between capitalists and workers. Indeed, following the period of crisis, the phase of depression emerges as a preparatory process that develops this new social relationship.

CHAPTER 3

Depression

Thrown into disorder by the crisis, the social reproduction process spends several years in a period of depression, preparing for recovery by a process that disposes of excess capital. According to Spiethoff, the depression after the crisis of 1825 lasted six years, until 1831; the depression after the 1836 crisis extended to 1842, also six years; the depression after the 1847 crisis spanned four years, until 1851; and the depression after the 1857 crisis lasted until 1861 before entering a new period of prosperity. The disposal of excess capital that is carried out in these definite periods is not a simple matter, however. By lowering production costs through improvements and upgrades to production methods, the clearance of excess capital takes place by creating new relations between capitalists and workers. This is the sole reason why periods of depression exhibit a considerable duration of many years. It is a process that proceeds by way of the tough competition between individual capitals, and by the sacrifices of workers. It is also a phase where loanable capital plays a special role.

1 The Stagnation of the Reproduction Process

In a period of depression that constitutes the opposite of the period of prosperity, a fall in commodity prices resulting from crisis brings about a complete end to speculative activities, and in the wake of the destruction resulting from the crisis, the reproduction process continues to contract. This hardly means, of course, that individual capitals undergo these reductions uniformly. Industries, in which large increases in prices occurred in periods of prosperity, will be forced to make even bigger reductions and contractions in the period of depression, but this does not necessarily mean that these contractions and reductions can be carried off easily. Rather, the opposite is true. This point sheds light on why, in the heavy-chemical industries such as iron works (where large-scale operations eventually developed along with the development of capitalism), monopolistic organisations of cartels and trusts (or the so-called combined industries producing both raw materials and semi-manufactured goods) together tend to grow. In any case, in the period of depression, the contraction of the reproduction process of individual industries and individual capitals assumes different shapes and forms, precisely because of the diverse resiliency and resistance among capitals. Generally speaking, however, along with the stagnation of the reproduction process, the growing amount of idle capital cannot but push down the profit rate, and even for capitals that can boast of favourable conditions and an impressive resiliency, the fall in prices makes the contraction of production unavoidable. Even if it has become technologically possible to improve production methods, or to introduce entirely new production methods, this does not mean that the existing production facilities can be so easily sacrificed and replaced. Quite the contrary, the facilities that were expanded and enlarged during the period of prosperity will be used for as long as possible, and not be replaced, because the fall in the price of manufactured goods – despite a fall in the price of raw materials or wages – will have created difficulties for effective management. The loss of its capital value is unavoidable, and important methods by which to get through the depression are carried out: the slashing of wages due to rising unemployment or semi-unemployment, or else the intensification of labour and the cutting back on means of production.

In competition wars, large capitals that exist under favourable conditions buy up and concentrate smaller capitals existing under less favourable conditions, so as to make their management more advantageous. Despite this, however, the reproduction process does not move in the direction of a general expansion. For in periods of depression, competition wars appear in the form of protecting one's own capital at the expense of other capitals, and while the essential problem is expressed in a distorted form, this distortion itself puts into action a process of preparing for the development of new social relations. Without questioning how an excess of capital came about in the first place, individual capitalists single-mindedly seek to relieve his or her burden on the backs of others. As Marx writes,

> As long as everything goes well, competition acts, as is always the case when the general rate of profit is settled, as a practical freemasonry of the capitalist class, so that they all share in the common booty in proportion to the size of the portion that each puts in. But as soon as it is no longer a question of division of profit, but rather of loss, each seeks as far as he can to restrict his own share of this loss and pass it on to someone else. For the class as a whole, the loss is unavoidable. But how much each individual member has to bear, the extent to which he has to participate in it, now becomes a question of strength and cunning, and competition now becomes a struggle of enemy brothers.[1]

1 Marx, *Capital*, Vol. 3 (1991), pp. 361–62.

In periods of prosperity, in the competitive quest for higher profits that ultimately produces an average profit, the competition between individual capitals also reveals differences in their mutual 'strength and cunning', which is why it is possible to think that capitalists can get their profits through skill and ability. Ignoring these differences would not be a good idea, of course, but these differences themselves cannot explain why capitalists who are inferior in 'strength and cunning' are still able to make profits – albeit in lesser quantities. Individual profit rates may differ from each other, but the point is that the profit that is obtained generally never comes from 'strength and cunning'. Similarly, with regards to the losses incurred during periods of depression, 'strength and cunning' also cannot be said to give birth to the losses themselves, for what they are doing with their 'strength and cunning' is merely drawing attention to their individual differences. Thus, even if an excess of commodities can be considered a relative matter, once it becomes a general excess, it is not something that can be cleared away by the differences between individual capitals in shouldering losses. Be that as it may, in contrast to competition in periods of prosperity, in which everyone competes for the acquisition of higher profits, competition in periods of depression are inevitably intensified as a struggle over the sharing of losses that threaten the very existence of capital.

The fall in the profit rate that we have seen, however, is now accompanied by a fall in interest rates. In periods of prosperity, speculative activities dramatically increase the demand for funds to the point where it cannot even be covered by a rise in the supply of loanable funds; by contrast, in the period of depression, an increase in the supply of funds – and especially the supply of newly created funds – is already not only incapable of being increased, it is clearly reduced, but because demand has declined, a fall in the interest rate cannot be avoided. While it was possible in periods of prosperity to transform money capital into loanable funds due to the expansion of commercial credit and a heightened velocity of circulation, money capital in periods of depression, when the velocity of circulation is greatly reduced, remains stuck as mere means of circulation. Even if money were made into funds, this would happen, in this case, within the crucible of a reproduction process in stagnation, and thus it cannot be viewed in the same way as the creation of new funds accompanying a revitalised process of reproduction. Moreover, financial institutions such as banks, far from fabricating credit by anticipating the creation of funds, cannot avoid reducing interest rates because there is plenty of loanable funds as 'unemployed' capital that cannot be lent out. This signifies that the stagnancy of accumulation, as a lack in opportunities for capital to invest, has become an accumulation stuck in the money form.

The fall in prices of raw materials and other means of production; the slashing of wages; the intensification of labour and the cutting back on means of production; and the drop in interest rates of loan capital; all of these things, in and of themselves, however, do not bring about the recovery of capital's reproduction process. Not only is there also a fall in the price of products, but so long as the relationship between capitalists and workers – which constitutes the basic cause of excess capital exposed in crisis – is not transformed into a new relationship by the aforementioned reactions, recovery will not yet take place. Even in these circumstances, however, the slashing of wages is something that begs special consideration. Of course, the slashing of wages is also born out of the stagnation of the reproduction process, and while wages alone are not decreased, the commodity of labour power differs from other commodities, for its supply does not decrease simply because a demand for it decreases. Just because labour power cannot be sold as a commodity hardly means that workers do not have to live; the fall in wages is thus particularly intense and invariably dragged out. It is as if it corresponds, in an inverse way, to the rise in wages during the period of prosperity.[2]

2 If, in the period of prosperity, the actual rise in the wages of workers were hindered by a rise in prices stemming from the speculative buying of merchant or commercial capital, or else from industrial capital's merchant capital-like speculations; then it could be said, conversely, that the actual fall in wages would be ameliorated, to a certain degree, by the fall in prices in the period of depression. This would only come about, however, when wages had already fallen due to the depression, or when wages cannot be obtained due to unemployment. We should notice that the movement of wages is, in reality, deeply influenced by such mercantile speculations. However, what should not be lost sight of is how the fundamental cause of crisis is found in the very methods of capitalist production based upon the commodification of labour power. What should be considered, therefore, is how these phenomena of merchant capital-like speculations point to the concealment of the fundamental cause of crisis.

In clarifying the general laws of capitalism on the level of fundamental principles, the workers' wages, as the value of labour power transformed into price form, are presupposed to revolve around a certain standard of living, though in actuality, of course, we know that wages differ, depending on various industries and regions. Even in theoretical considerations, we must also recognise how, in light of each phase of the business cycle, wages rise above the value of labour power in a certain phase, only to fall below the value of labour power in another phase. That the value of labour power can be assumed, in a general inquiry, to be based on a certain standard of living is not to deny the possibility of these fluctuations. Although the actually existing differences in wages among industries or regions can be ignored in basic, theoretical considerations and in accordance with the historical tendency in capitalist development to dissolve them, the rise and fall of wages stemming from fluctuations in the business cycle are not subject to such a historical tendency to dissolve them. Thus, in the basic theory, the value of labour power should be understood to be paid through the rise and fall in wages that takes place within the whole business cycle. Of course, when we speak of a rise in wages during periods of prosperity, this corresponds to its obstruction or

2 Inaugurating New Accumulation through Improvements to the Production Process

By the mere improvement to methods of labour – not to mention by the adoption of new machinery – capital is able to bring forth a fountain of 'super' or 'special' profit by lowering cost prices. While capitalist management is always

its fall during periods of depression. While the effect of this correspondence is one of amelioration, this in no way means that the standard of living of workers is the same. Insofar as the value of labour power, as that which forms the standard for wages, is never only determined biologically but by standards of living that are determined historically and socially, it is not something that excludes fluctuations and changes. For this very reason, the way in which workers' everyday lives are impacted by the slashing of their wages, or by unemployment during periods of depression, cannot be treated lightly. At the same time, however, in theoretically presupposing a capitalist society, and in abstracting away the existence of so-called independent producers such as peasants and handicraft workers, it would be wrong to understand unemployed workers as if they were all necessarily starving. While individual, concrete cases of unemployment reveal tragic and miserable conditions that are often accompanied by severe social instability, it should be presupposed generally that the unemployed population, as a weight on the employed population, is able to continue to survive. This relationship is revealed with so-called part time work, in which employment does not pay for the value of labour power for one full day, but rather for one part of that day, thus cutting back on labour time – and exhibiting one of the important means by which wages are cut.

Looking at mid-nineteenth-century England, Marx defined three forms of the relative surplus population as a so-called industrial reserve army: the floating, the latent, and the stagnant, to which he also added the sphere of pauperism. The surplus population, born by crisis and depression, bases itself on this general industrial reserve army, and even within the sphere of paupers, there are those who possess the ability to labour whose 'quantity ... increases with every crisis of trade, and diminishes with every revival.' (*Capital*, Vol. 1, p. 797). Marx, moreover, speaks of the floating population as the part of the labouring population, that is, in accordance with the fluctuations of the business cycle of modern large-scale industry, which is at times absorbed and at other times expelled. However, another factor to this surplus population is the way in which floating populations are formed when the absorption of younger workers expel older workers, thus pointing to a relation in which this expelled working population is thrown on top of the medium and small industrial workers who exist as a stagnant population. This latter population, along with the latent surplus population that springs from the agricultural sector, plays a role in which it is recruited in response to the increased demand for labour power in large-scale industry during periods of prosperity. The population that large-scale industry creates as a surplus, therefore, does not terminate, immediately or completely, as a mass of unemployed workers, and it is this relation, we should be quick to add, that generally makes the slashing of wages, during periods of depression, possible. 'The industrial reserve army, during the periods of stagnation and average prosperity, weighs down the active army of workers; during the periods of over-production and feverish activity, it puts a curb on their pretensions. The relative surplus-population is therefore the background against which the law of demand and supply of labour does it work' (*Capital*, Vol. 1, p. 792).

competing for this special profit, this practice is an especially important means of competition during times of depression. Hardly a simple problem of 'strength and cunning' in the process of buying and selling, this is a matter that unfolds in the production process, constituting a positive factor that includes the reconfiguration of the worker-capitalist relation, and that therefore differs from competition in the period of prosperity.

It is a general rule for all capitals, however, that this special profit is not something that can be obtained by improvements to production methods that are carried off with relative ease, or that do not require the replacement of fixed capital – for example, through new methods of cutting back on means of production, or through the use of new raw materials that are easily obtained. Competition in periods of depression inexorably moves in the direction of making improvements to production methods that other capitals cannot easily achieve, and of adopting new methods for one's own fixed capital that were not possible before. This possibility is brought about by both the destruction of capital in the period of crisis, and by the renewal period for portions of fixed capital, which passes through competition in the period of depression. Of course, divergent conditions stemming from individual capitals never make this a uniform process. Moreover, there will be differences in the period when new production methods are adopted, as well as differences, for example, that depend on the degree to which mechanisation has already taken place in a single industry. Nevertheless, the socially decisive timing for a generalisation of the improvements made to production methods stemming from investments of new fixed capital is ultimately given by the case of key industries.[3]

---

3 In *The History of Crisis in England*, Tugan-Baranowski writes the following: 'From a certain perspective, the crisis of 1825 actually had a good effect on English industry. According to a testimony taken from a parliamentary committee in 1833, the manufacturer Smith noted that after the crisis steam machinery gradually came to be used in factories nationwide. Similarly, in the blast furnace industry, important improvements were implemented, and according to the manufacturer Teal, the costs of producing iron were lowered dramatically. In the face of declining profits from fallen prices, manufacturers researched various means to lower costs of production. In this way, a defining characteristic of the years following the 1825 crisis was the rapid progress of technology'.

Of course, in periods of depression, improvements to production methods are not generalised immediately, but must first pass through a certain period of competition. If improvements to production methods are carried out during periods of depression, this is precisely because its impetus is found here, in this period of competition.

As I have mentioned in the text above, the period in which mechanisation takes place, and the period in which improvements are made to machinery, differ among industries. For example, in the cotton industries of the 1820s to the mid 1840s, an increase in productivity due to mechanisation took place first in the cotton spinning process, and then in the cot-

The improvement of production methods, it goes without saying, advances productivity per unit of labour, pointing to what Marx called the production of relative surplus value. The organic composition of capital thus grows by increasing the constant part of capital, invested in raw materials and other means of production, in relation to the variable part of capital that is invested in labour power. Improvements that take place during periods of depression thus proceed as an accumulation of capital in which, on the one hand, a relatively small number of workers come to be mobilised out of the already existing surplus population of unemployed workers; on the other hand, the value of capital, as the means of labour used originally by individual capitals, is destroyed, more or less. The accumulation of capital here is thus not simply an increase in the demand for workers, nor is it simply an additional investment to the original capital, nor does it serve merely as a basis for the development of society in general by advancing the productivity of labour so as to lighten labour. The accumulation of capital rather proceeds by way of an inverted form, peculiar to capitalism, which in this case points especially to how, in periods when workers already exist in superfluity, restrictions on workers are further carried out by the adoption of methods that further produce relative surplus populations; and to how, at times when the destruction of capital is ongoing, new methods are adopted that accelerate the destruction of capital value. This is a special form of the development of production methods that has, as its goal, the making of profit. During the time when profits are made, the unemployed population continues to decline, but the stimulus to improve production methods that will form new surplus populations is rather blunted. Capital comes to possess such supplementary ways to accumulate. This is a tendency that is confirmed by the maintenance and continuation of existing fixed capital, in the form of machinery and other means of labour. It is safe to say that, for capitalism, the advancement of social productivity in general cannot become actualized without these inverted forms and relationships.

In this way, accumulation in the period of depression proceeds as a competition between the older capital and new capital. While the period in which the renewal of fixed capital of individual capitals varies – which necessarily implies differences in the time when new improvements are implemented – competition in the period of depression pushes more or less towards renewal on the basis of the destruction of capital value from the period of crisis. Of

---

ton weaving process. Not only was there an increase in productivity due to improvements in machinery; improvements to machinery subsequently proceeded in the direction of advancing the machinery's operating speed (Thomas Ellison, *The Cotton Trade of Great Britain* 1886, p. 69).

course, this process is resisted as long as capitals operating by older production methods are still able to use their fixed capital. And if the burden on capitals during periods of depression is exacerbated by the falling of prices stemming from the special profits obtained by new production methods, this is because the improvement of fixed capital cannot take place immediately. A significant period of time is thus required for the generalisation of improvements to production methods to sink in. In the movement towards the concentration of large capitals, this period is shortened as much as possible as a general, though not unconditional, tendency. Moreover, these improvements certainly do not take place uniformly in all industrial sectors. However, once this generalisation of improvements to production methods is achieved within the key industries and impacts the formation of a new standard of prices to transform the production relations (which signifies lowered prices, not just as a result of crisis but as a renewed standard of prices to establish new relations between workers and capitalists[4]) – the fundamental cause of the stagnation of the reproductive process is removed, providing the basis for a new development of productive forces. This does not mean an immediate turn towards prosperity, but its beginnings become visible. Especially with regards to improvements to production methods, once improvements to fixed capital are promoted with greater

4 This point can be seen in the following table (taken from Ellison's analysis mentioned above), which shows a fall in the average price of manufactured cotton goods in each period of prosperity following the prosperity period of 1822–25. Keeping in mind that the prices here are those of England's exported manufactured cotton goods, and that these prices are influenced by the price of imported raw cotton and various other factors, the pattern that emerges is a continual fall in price below the previous period's price. This can be considered as an effect of the advance in productivity.

	1822–25	1832–36	1843–47	1852–57	1862–66
Cotton thread (per pounds)	23.33 pence	16.086	12.01	10.995	23.682
Cotton weave (per yards)	10.373 pence	6.222	3.97	3.405	5.218

The rise in price in 1862–66 was caused by the dramatic rise, after 1861, in the price of raw cotton that resulted from the American Civil War. The fluctuations of these prices were also likely influenced by the discovery of gold mines of the 1850s. The extent of this influence, however, is beyond the scope of this analysis. Generally speaking, however, the important points to be gleaned here are that the rise in price stemming from speculations in the period of prosperity are buried and concealed by the fall in prices resulting from advances in productivity; and that prices in each period of prosperity falls below the price of the

frequency and speed, the basis is created for the recovery of the production of means of production and means of consumption as well.

3 The Turn towards Prosperity

Along with a new start of accumulation, the beginnings of a resuscitated reproduction process come into sight. Yet, despite this, prices move under freshly lowered standards, and a recovery to the previous prices is far from a sure thing. By the same token, this process does not immediately bring about activity for the totality of the reproduction process, for it must, on the one hand, dispose of the capitals that continue to resist change due to a continued reliance on older methods while implementing, on the other, new production relations for capitals that exist in a multiplicity of conditions and situations depending on the industry. In other words, it is not immediately possible to get out of the period of depression. Of course, the increased demand for means of production will still allow for the operation of those production facilities whose use has not been completely exhausted, thereby presenting a situation in which certain capitals will be left to suffocate beneath the weight of the depression while other capitals will have already begun new developments. What we often see here is an intermediary boom and its reactions, pointing to the period that Spiethoff called the first stage of upswing.[5] Here, in a situation in which a gen-

previous period of prosperity. As an additional note, the following shows the fluctuations of the annual average price of exported cotton thread between 1825 and 1858 (ibid.).

1825	**23.57**	1834	16.35	1843	12.30	1852	10.98
1826	19.86	1835	16.46	1844	12.11	1853	11.22
1827	18.96	1836	**16.66**	1845	12.07	1854	10.91
1828	17.08	1837	16.13	1846	11.68	1855	10.44
1829	15.53	1838	15.56	1847	**11.89**	1856	10.61
1830	15.35	1839	15.57	1848	10.47	1857	**11.81**
1831	14.95	1840	14.39	1849	10.76	1858	10.49
1832	14.98	1841	14.15	1850	11.66		
1833	15.98	1842	13.57	1851	11.06		

5 Regarding the period of depression, Spiethoff describes the following: 'Depression begins with an inversion of all the phenomena of prosperity: a decrease in capital investments, a fall in indirect consumption (iron), a fall in capital profits and loan interest, a slowing down of production and plummeting prices. This is the first stage, and it would be appropriate to

eral recovery of the profit rate has not yet taken place, interest rates on loanable capital indicate a certain rise.

That there is, during this period, a partial recovery in the profit rate and a certain upturn in interest rates does not simply point to a turn to a period of prosperity. Capital is finally able to generalise new production relations and a recovered profit rate only with the reorganisation of the previous social relations, and when they are forced to advance toward the replacement of fixed capital in a competitively disadvantageous position. Capital thus commences the accumulation process on the road to prosperity. Generally speaking, however, capital is not able to immediately allocate its profits to the expanded scale of production. Industrial capital must first activate its accumulation funds and expand commercial credit, and on the level of its relations of supply and demand for funds concentrated in the banks, it presents the phenomenon of a tendency even to force down interest rates. The rise in interest rates in Spiethoff's so-called first stage of upswing is thus presented in a situation in which the recovery of commodity production, developing under new production relations, is reversed and decreased, forming a sluggish financial situation. As Marx also discussed, the healthy development of the movement of capital brings about, 'the relative independence of commercial credit from bank credit, resting on the fluidity of returns, short terms of credit and operations predominantly conducted with one's own capital.'[6] Capital thus becomes overloaded by loanable capital. Small capitals, insofar as they cannot themselves come up with and use these funds, especially entrust the creation of funds to financial institutions such as banks. The longer this situation continues, however, an increase in the demand for means of production no longer turns around the simple renewal of fixed capital. Along with additional investments of accumulation funds that expand the scale of production, the production of means of production is now freshly intensified, and as the advance of accumulation increases under the given composition of capital, the demand for labour power and the production of means of production rises as well. No longer concerned at this point whether improvements to production methods have taken place or not, all industries – including not only the production sectors of means of

call it a stage of decline. In the second stage, the movement and direction of a few phenomena change: the downward decline stops, and there is a turn towards a slight upward movement. In other words, the production of indirect consumption materials, as well as consumption, point to this reversal, and capital investments become brisk. The transitional stage of the upswing begins here. This first stage of upswing, however, is merely an isolated upswing. In the bigger scheme of things, it is unambiguously a depression' (Spiethoff, 1936, pp. 9–10).

6 *Capital*, Vol. 3, p. 627.

production but also the production sectors of means of consumption – become enlarged. The turn from the period of depression to the period of prosperity, or what Spiethoff called the second stage of upswing, finally takes place.

The movement from depression to prosperity, therefore, is not simply the mere repetition of a periodic process. Capital sets out on a new cycle, with productive forces that are larger than before, and while fewer workers are mobilised in relation to the quantity of capital, in absolute terms they are employed in greater numbers. In this way, as the general profit rate marches on its way towards a tendential decline, the rate of surplus value rises, and the production of larger and larger profits is realised by larger and larger capitals. In this way, the recovery of the accumulation of capital proceeds with an enlarged scale of production. Periodic cycles thus always surpass the highest point of the previous cycle, and progress like waves, undulating with highs and lows.

CHAPTER 4

The Turnover Period of the Business Cycle

Capitalist methods of production are grounded upon the historical fact that the direct producers have lost their means of production and are compelled to sell their labour power as a commodity in order to obtain articles necessary to maintain an everyday subsistence. The means of production are given the form of capital because of this fact, which is also a fact of how the capitalist him or herself, in possessing these means of production, must adopt the form of capital and carry out production on the basis of purchasing, as a commodity, the labour power of direct producers. However, even though the separation between the means of production and direct producers initially took place in the case of peasants who have lost their land, this in itself did not immediately establish capitalist production methods. The development of a specifically capitalist method of production was only realised, concretely speaking, after passing through a long process, spanning the seventeenth and eighteenth centuries in Western Europe, and culminating in the so-called industrial revolution of the late eighteenth century and in the establishment of mechanised large-scale industry. Only then was capitalist production first able to secure an autonomous social basis. Moreover, this simultaneously marks the moment when fixed capital, as an investment of capital in the means of labour within the production process, is given an especially important position in comparison to the circulating capital invested in labour power and raw materials, among others. Now, insofar as land is a sort of means of production and that it is possible for peasants, separated from the land, to become workers selling their labour power to owners of land, it is conceivable that owners of land become capitalists in relation to workers. Capitalism, however, was not established in this way. Land itself is not a product of labour, and thus it could not, on its own, become capital possessing value. Capitalism became established only gradually, when the means of production, and especially the means of labour (which themselves possess value as products of labour) took over an important place in the production process. It was not established because its means of production derived from the land as nature. In fact, when we consider the particularly capitalistic development of methods of production in terms of the forms of cooperation and the division of labour constituting the basis of manufacture and mechanised large-scale industry, the mere form of cooperation alone cannot be said to have allowed the establishment of capitalism to dominate a whole era of history.[1] Even when manufacture comes to be based on the division of labour – which Marx depicts in the so-called period of original manufacture spanning the middle of the sixteenth century to the last third of the eighteenth century – this itself was still not able to dominate the entirety of society from its depths and establish capitalism. As Marx writes, 'The collective worker, formed out of the combination of a number of individual specialized workers, is the item of machinery specifically characteristic of the manufacturing period'.[2] Thus, tools, as instruments of labour, never were able to occupy the position that machinery would later command in the period of mechanised large-scale industry. This period rather corresponded to the period of capital's primitive accumulation, when merchant capital was the dominant form of capital. By contrast, with the appearance of machinery as instruments of labour, society eventually came under the domination of industrial capital in its entirety. With industrial capital's advance in productivity, moreover, not only were other methods of production within the same industry pushed out; it became possible for industrial capital itself to create, under certain limits, the labour power required for capital, albeit not in absolute terms but in terms that were relative to capital. Of course, this kind of domination would never have been secured had it not presupposed, as its basis, a productive labour force already formed from the period of capital's primitive accumulation. Capital presupposes, and is based on, a naturally given working population that passes through the historical process of becoming propertyless, which constantly imposes a definite limit. Within these limits, however, and with the appearance of instruments

1 Even in *Capital*, inasmuch as it clarifies a theory of the general principles of the capitalist economy, my understanding is that the main point of addressing the three developmental stages of cooperation, division of labour, and mechanised large-scale industry, is that it clarifies three factors of capitalist production specifically. In other words, the important point is that cooperation forms the precondition of the division of labour while simultaneously constituting the basic factor for the latter; these two aspects in turn form the basic factor for mechanised large-scale industry. Each factor, however, develops from the abstract to the concrete, as a development towards richer historical determinations. An understanding of the period of manufacture necessarily implies such a development. Therefore, when we say, 'that period' in relation to the periods of manufacture and mechanised large-scale industry, the meanings implied in the expression 'that period' are necessarily different. If this is ignored, the significance of merchant capital, at the beginning period of capitalism's development between the sixteenth and eighteenth centuries, will be lost. And while there is no difference between the two (as far as the period of development of the specific capitalist method of production is concerned), the former cannot be said to have dominated a single society in its entirety. This domination was only established when the latter – that is, mechanised large-scale industry – realised the period of industrial capital.

2 *Capital*, Vol. 1, p. 468.

of labour such as machinery, capital has already developed a force as if it can continually sweep away and eliminate these limits.

As a moving body of value, capital in its essence has no other objective than to become self-expanding value. On this point, while it can be said that interest-bearing capital is the purest form of capital, interest-bearing capital itself is not capable of this self-expansion of value, even as loanable capital. Regardless of whether funds lent out as loanable capital are allocated for the sale and purchase of commodities, or for investments in the production process, unless these funds can become realised as larger values, it is unlikely that payments on interest will take place with any certainty. Loans made for the simple purpose of consumption – such as loans to feudal lords by merchants or pawnshops – merely rely on other incomes or assets. In this regard, interest-bearing capital does not present the fundamental form of capital. The general and primordial formula of capital is rather found in the form of merchant capital (M-C-M′), because the formula of money lending capital (M…M′) stems from, and first develops on the basis of, merchant capital. Money lending for consumption must be understood as an incidental matter. Even if loans for funds were allotted for the sale and purchase of commodities, however, this may still represent nothing more than a way to obtain surplus value by buying commodities low and selling them high, and it may not augment new values. Capital, understood socially and not individually, is emphatically not able to dominate society in its entirety through these forms. Capital can only effectively attain the goal of self-expanding value by obtaining surplus value, which can only come about when means of production and labour power are purchased as commodities and then consumed in a production process, where products possessing new and larger values are produced. In this way, in a capitalist society, the social reproduction process bases itself on the establishment of the formula of industrial capital (M-C…P…C′-M′), and by re-forming the formulas of merchant capital (M-C-M′) and money-lending capital (M…M′) in terms of commercial capital and loanable capital, respectively. To recapitulate, industrial capital was only able to develop once mechanised large-scale industry made its appearance after modern industry had passed through the industrial revolution in the latter half of the eighteenth century.

Thus, capital will fail to establish itself socially, as a moving body of value whose sole purpose is to become self-expanding value, unless it produces new values with some sort of use value. Even the interest on loanable capital can be paid, for the first time and with any certainty, only on this basis. The general idea of capital as an automatically interest-bearing force must appear, therefore, as an overall expression of capitalist social relations based on such loanable capital. Of course, it goes without saying that capital does not give birth to interest out of thin air. In reality, with the self-expansion of value stemming from investments of capital in the production process, surplus value is only produced by the variable capital invested in labour power, and most decidedly not by the constant capital that is invested in machinery, raw materials, or other means of production. The idea that machinery or raw materials (falsely) appear to be able to augment value either stems from a confusion, whereby the relationship of distributing profits among capitalists, which is an expression of distributing profits out of the production of surplus value equally to constant and variable capital, is mistaken for the relations of production between workers and capitalists; or else, it simply stems from an error in thinking its relationship to the fixed period of time when new machinery is adopted, which gives capital a special profit with the production of relative surplus value by workers labouring under the specifically advanced productivity of labour. In any case, machinery and raw materials never do more than transfer to new products the values that are already given and determined by the labour time required for their own production. On the one hand, the fact that relative surplus value, obtained by new machinery, disappears when new machinery becomes generalised, testifies to this. On the other hand, generally speaking, capital cannot produce new products by variable capital alone. As I have described earlier, capitalism was not established by the separation of producers from the land alone. Capitalism was established when the means of production – not as nature represented by land but as products of labour – were once again separated from workers as direct producers, thereby creating a relation in which it became impossible for workers to produce anything without these means of production that had come to play an important role in the production process. Moreover, no sooner did the development of the instruments of labour, such as machinery, push out the means of production of individual, direct producers and establish the necessity of capitalism's peculiarly social form of production, than a labouring population had become a relative surplus population. Capitalism cannot be established without entering into a relationship whereby workers themselves are, in a sense, produced by capital itself. Let me reiterate this point, as it is so important.

As I have already noted above, for capital – whose sole purpose is the attainment of self-expanding value – the significance of fixed capital, such as the machinery accompanying the development of modern industry after the industrial revolution, does not simply mean that capital, in having to invest in progressively larger and larger fixed capitals, simply increases the portion of capital that does not itself augment value. The significance of fixed capital is also that it creates an important restriction on capital, for during the period when capital has been invested in fixed capital, it cannot switch over to newly invented machinery. That more advantageous and profitable operations exist elsewhere hardly means that capital can simply move over to those operations. Even if production is running under unprofitable conditions, once capital invests in considerably large portions of fixed capital in addition to the circulating capital for raw material and labour power, it cannot immediately move on to other, more profitable production – at least without sacrificing the presently existing value in fixed capital. We could thus say that the restriction that fixed capital signifies for capital enables and corresponds to the way the adoption of new machinery leads to special profits through the production of relative surplus value. In other words, on the one hand, while capital promotes improvements to methods of production by the availability of special profits, on the other hand, once improvements to methods of production are realised, capital becomes shackled to them, at least for a definite period of time.

In a capitalist society, the restrictions imposed on individual capitals, as effects of the fixity of capital invested in the production process, is alleviated by constant investments of newly accumulated capital, and by the transformation of the idle funds, born out of the reproduction process, into loanable capital. The constant improvements to the methods of production thus proceed, as it were, in an incremental and supplementary way, such that the portion of fixed capital functions as capital in a double sense. On the one hand, it contributes to the production process as instruments of labour, but on the other, even though it takes part in an incremental way by virtue of the transformation of fixed capital's amortisation funds into loanable capital, fixed capital, once invested as a whole, basically presents an unavoidable restriction on the mobility of capital. Fixed capital thus exerts a tremendous influence on the accumulation of capital, as well as on the supposedly ceaseless improvements made to methods of production.

Marx also drew attention to this point with the following observation:

> To the same extent as the value and durability of the fixed capital applied develops with the development of the capitalist mode of production, so also does the life of industry and industrial capital in each particular investment develop, extending to several years, say an average of ten years. If the development of fixed capital extends this life, on the one hand, it is cut short on the other by the constant revolutionising of the means of production, which also increases steadily with the development of the capitalist mode of production. This also leads to changes in the means of production; they constantly have to be replaced, because of their moral depreciation, long before they are physically exhausted. We can assume that, for the most important branches of large-scale industry,

> this life cycle is now on average a ten-year one. The precise figure is not important here. The result is that the cycle of related turnovers, extending over a number of years, within which the capital is confined by its fixed component, is one of the material foundations for the periodic cycle in which business passes through successive periods of stagnation, moderate activity, over-excitement and crisis. The periods for which capital is invested certainly differ greatly, and do not coincide in time. But a crisis is always the starting-point of a large volume of new investments. It is also, therefore, if we consider the society as a whole, more or less a new material basis for the next turnover cycle.[3]

If the replacement of fixed capital has a certain duration, and if, in the period of depression, one part of capital is already improving its methods of production and investing in new fixed capital while another part of capital is put in a disadvantageous position in continuing to use the conventional fixed capital; then the ongoing competition to escape from this disadvantageous position, as I have described earlier, will prolong the duration of the period of depression. Of course, as Marx writes, this competition is such that, for the capitals in a disadvantageous position, the replacement of its fixed capital is enforced insofar as it has 'to be replaced, because of [its] moral depreciation, long before [it is] physically exhausted'. This is not to say, however, that new methods of production bring about replacements immediately, for it is decided by the degree to which the originally existing capital will continue to resist new investments. While the period of the replacement of fixed capital does not immediately determine the time frame for the period of depression, it must nonetheless be recognised as one of the factors of this resistance against new investments. Moreover, it cannot be forgotten that changes to the capital relation, which are based on the destruction of capital, cannot help but accompany the depression following crisis; thus, when capital becomes concentrated with a fall in prices, the resistance to new investments, depending on the situation, will become exacerbated even more. Even if this doesn't occur, while the operations that endure the destruction of capital value as a result of a contracted scale of operations must be prompted, on the one hand, to reduce the renewal period due to competition, they also have, on the other hand, a capacity and power to resist this competition. In any case, improvements to methods of production generally do not bring about the replacement of fixed capital immediately.

3 *Capital*, Vol. 2, p. 264.

In this way, the period of prosperity begins with a general replacement of fixed capital in the principal industries; this replacement stems from competition, which shortens the duration to replace the fixed capital, as well as from the adoption of newly improved methods. Also, when we consider the expansion of scale in terms of accumulation in the period of prosperity, of course we can say that improved methods will be adopted, but these improved methods are themselves based on this *general* replacement, and cannot substitute or be confused for the latter. Moreover, as I have already described, accumulation in the period of prosperity, which obtains considerable profits, does not experience the stimuli and pressures to improve production methods, unlike in the period of depression. In the period of prosperity, the expansion of production tends to be based on already existing and given methods.

Thus, when competition appears in the next period of depression, the time frame for these kinds of investments will differ, and insofar as capital creates these differences to a greater or lesser extent in the methods of production themselves, it goes without saying that the capacities and powers to resist competitive pressure to replace them will also differ. The time frame for general improvements is thus elastic, but even so, it bears such an enormous weight upon the general renewal of fixed capital in the transitional period to prosperity that the mere prolongation of the period of prosperity is enough to shorten periods of depression. Conversely, the shorter the period of prosperity becomes, the longer does the period of depression become extended. In this way, the cycle, as a whole, takes on a definite periodicity, and even if it cannot be said that the period for the renewal of fixed capital alone determines the periodic cycle, it clearly dominates it.

As Marx also states, insofar as the portion of fixed capital's 'value- and durability' increases in accordance with the development of capitalist methods of production, the enlargement of fixed capital has to be factored in as a condition of how the accumulation of capital passes through the process of industrial cycles. This corresponds exactly to the fact that, with the establishment of modern industry, workers are completely turned into propertyless workers, and that the commodification of labour power is completed by the creation of the industrial reserve army. In this way, capitalism, which emerged in western European countries in the seventeenth and eighteenth centuries, and which inaugurated a distinct historical period in human history with its development in England, finally established its foundations through the industrial revolution by the 1820s, and began to exhibit the particular process of development that is unique to capitalism. It is thus hardly a coincidence that the commodification of labour power, on the one hand, and the transformation of means of production into fixed capital, on the other hand, were realized together.

In the early stages of capitalism's development, the process of changing capital's composition by making improvements to methods of production was still a sluggish one and the accumulation of capital that accompanied the production process also went forward only gradually, with an increase in the demand for workers corresponding to this accumulation. Even so, it is crucial to understand that the demand for workers stemming from capital accumulation did not correspond to a natural increase in the population of workers. Hence, capital had to rely on the violent process of so-called primitive accumulation to create the necessary labouring population through artificial means. Various polices of mercantilism clearly point to this. In passing through the industrial revolution, however, capital was able to form, in addition to modern industry, an industrial reserve army, by which the enlargement of the scale of production, in accordance with capital's rapid accumulation, became easier. So-called liberalism was realized as mercantilist policies became unnecessary; at the same time, however, the development of capital could not avoid having to pass through the cyclical process of prosperity, crisis, and depression. In such a process, capital became incapable of incessantly improving on the methods of production and of constantly creating a requisite working population due to the transformation of means of production into fixed capital. Thus, the accumulation of capital takes the peculiar form in which the accumulation of capital that proceeds *without changes to the composition of capital* appears as the general basis for the development of phases of prosperity, while capital accumulation *with changes made to the composition of capital* takes place in the phases of depression.[4]

4 Regarding this point, Marx writes the following: 'This peculiar cyclical path of modern industry, which occurs in no earlier period of human history, was also impossible when capitalist production was in its infancy. The composition of capital at that time underwent only very gradual changes. By and large, therefore, the proportional growth in the demand for labour has corresponded to the accumulation of capital. Even though the advance of accumulation was slow in comparison with that of the modern epoch, it came up against a natural barrier in the shape of the exploitable working population; this barrier could only be swept away by the violent means we shall discuss later. The expansion by fits and starts of the scale of production is the precondition for its equally sudden contraction; the latter again evokes the former, but the former is impossible without disposable human material, without an increase in the number of workers, which must occur independently of the absolute growth of the population. This increase is effected by the simple process that constantly 'sets free' a part of the working class; by methods which lessen the number of workers employed in proportion to the increasing production. Modern industry's whole form of motion therefore depends on the constant transformation of a part of the working population into unemployed or semi-employed 'hands'. The superficiality of political economy shows itself in the fact that it views the expansion and contraction of credit as the cause of the periodic alternations in the indus-

Of course, there is no reason to think that this process of development repeats eternally and unchanged. In the development of capitalism, not only did its central industry of cotton manufacturing, as so-called light industry, shift to iron manufacturing and so-called heavy industries; the 'value and dur-

---

trial cycle, whereas it is a mere symptom of them. Just as the heavenly bodies always repeat a certain movement, once they have been flung into it, so also does social production, once it has been flung into this movement of alternate expansion and contraction. Effects become causes in their turn, and the various vicissitudes of the whole process, which always reproduces its own conditions, take on the form of periodicity. When this periodicity has once become consolidated, even political economy sees that the production of a relative surplus population – i.e., a population surplus in relation to capital's average requirements for valorization – is a necessary condition for modern industry.' (*Capital*, Vol. 1, pp. 785–86).

What I have described in this text above roughly follows Marx's explanation, but if I were to compare what I have described with his, I can immediately discern two or three points of difference. I cannot address the reasons for these differences here, but to take up the *first* point, when Marx writes that 'the methods', by which the demand for an 'increase in the number of workers' accompanying the scale of production's 'expansion by fits and starts', are tantamount to 'the simple process that constantly 'sets free' a part of the labourers', the inevitability of the turn from prosperity to crisis is not clarified. The existence of fixed capital is overlooked. And, as I have quoted before, Marx also recognises that, 'the starting point of crisis is always new major investments'. Furthermore, this investment takes place with a 'life cycle' that 'can be supposed to take, on average, ten years'. The *second* point is that when Marx writes that the 'superficiality' of Political Economy is shown 'in the fact that it looks upon the expansion and contraction of credit, which is a mere symptom of the periodic changes of the industrial cycle, as their cause', he is clearly criticising Political Economy, but even so, while Marx himself recognises the connection between credit and industrial cycles, he does not adequately recognise how this connection is socially regulated by the form of loanable capital. As for myself, I also certainly do not think that the 'the expansion and contraction of credit' alone can explain the alternations of the industrial cycle; but I do not think it is fine to consider them 'mere symptoms', either. As I have already stated in the preceding chapters, it seems to me that the industrial cycles and credit possesses a much tighter connection than the way it is presented by Marx. *Lastly*, the final point: When Marx writes that social production, is bound to 'always repeat this … definite motion … as soon as it is once thrown into this movement of alternate expansion and contraction', I agree that this proposition holds as a theory in the fundamental principles of political economy. At the same time, this also has to be understood as a theory that implies obvious changes in accordance with the development of the stages of capitalism. Since it is unclear whether Marx definitively intended to locate *Capital* at a level of research that is akin to my so-called fundamental principles, whenever *Capital* is (mistakenly) considered to be directly applicable to the stages of capitalist development, criticisms are also inevitably raised that the theory goes against real facts. Although it is not a mistake to address the fundamental principles as that which 'constantly … repeats', and, at least, as that which discloses laws, what requires clear understanding is that the principles may appear with different features in its earliest stages or in the final stages of capitalist development. What this indicates is the specific character of economic laws as abstract, fundamental principles. It is precisely through this specificity that we are given the possibility to grasp the laws of the historical process itself.

ability' of their fixed capital portions could also not avoid changes. Accompanying capitalism's global development, joint stock companies accelerated capital's social accumulation and so-called finance capital realised the stage of imperialism, thereby pointing to new aspects of the process of industrial cycles. Especially in relation to increases in the quantity of fixed capital, while it hindered the drive to make the turn from depression to prosperity, on the other hand, it not only adopted the form of joint stock companies but also made the adoption of new methods of production easier, without necessarily even experiencing the stimulus to improve methods resulting from fallen profit rates in periods of depression. Moreover, for the capitals possessing monopolistic power, the opposite case also becomes possible, namely of *not* adopting improvements, for the sake of profits, over a certain period of time. It is impossible to enter into further discussions of these points here. I will stop by simply pointing out the facts. Brought forth by this historical period, these transformations – it goes without saying – most certainly do not at all deny the inevitability of crisis in capitalist society.

CHAPTER 5

The Inevitability of Crisis in Capitalist Society

The phenomenon of crisis represents nothing other than capitalism's peculiar form of actually resolving the fundamental contradictions immanent to capitalist society. These fundamental contradictions, however, are not fundamentally resolved by the phenomenon of crisis. Rather, the phenomenon of crisis appears as a method of resolving and even extending contradictions, possessing a repetitive quality that discloses its essential law of inevitability. In one sense, this inevitability possesses an operation that appears like a natural law, with a power that cannot be removed by anyone, even by political power. But in another sense, it appears concretely, as an archetypical form, at a definite stage of the development of capitalist society. Clearly, it is most definitely not a mere *mechanical* inevitability; rather, it reveals an *historical* inevitability. It thus goes without saying that the fundamental contradictions of capitalist society, which constitute the ground of the phenomenon of crisis, make capitalism historical, with a definite historical process, which simply means that its birth, at the same time as its termination, can be predicted and anticipated. However, on this point, while these same contradictions provide the drive towards transforming capitalist society into a different social form, the phenomenon of crisis itself does not point to this resolution. Put differently, crisis does not directly signify the inevitable destruction of capitalist society. Herein are found the limits in clarifying the inevitability of crisis in the theory of the principles of political economy. Even though I may repeat myself to a certain degree, I would like to elaborate upon this point here, in this final chapter.

1 Mechanical Inevitability and Historical Inevitability

The inevitability of crisis, which is clarified in the principles of political economy, actually appeared concretely – and only approximately – during the fifty years from the 1820s to the 1860s, a period representing just one-sixth of the three hundred year long history of capitalism. Not only does this suggest, as I have already pointed out, that the inevitability of crisis is never merely a mechanical one; it simultaneously clarifies why crisis, which always appears concretely in differing forms depending on the historical development of each historical period, should not be understood as a generic concept shared by these differing forms. I have already discussed this point to a certain extent in the Introduction, but since it is such an important problem for political economy as a social science, it is not pointless to give it further consideration here.

First and foremost, it is not possible to abstract the concepts of political economy – for example the concepts of the commodity, or money, or even capital – by abstracting them from what is shared in common by various, similar phenomena. This may be fine for common sense, but for science, conceptions are abstracted in the opposite way. The concept of the commodity, for example, must be abstracted only after passing through the analyses of how a capitalist society brings about the domination of a commodity economy. Put differently, even the simple concept of the commodity, as it developed to the point of dominating the entirety of society and its conditioning factors, cannot be grasped historically, concretely speaking, unless the commodity is grasped as an abstraction of the specifically *capitalist* commodity, which is able to dominate an entire society. It is because the theoretical development of the pure form of the commodity itself is enabled by the analysis of the commodity in a historical stage that it develops towards the realisation of a purely capitalist society in terms of a concrete, historical process. The simple notion of the commodity, comprising value and use value, already implies such a development. Of course, such a simple determination shares commonalities with commodities that are born out of extremely primitive exchanges of products, and thus, even with commodities stemming from so-called simple commodity economies (in which so-called independent small producers produce for the purpose of selling products as commodities), this production is not yet based entirely on the production of commodities by means of commodities. Hence, a similar notion of the commodity seems obtainable, also as a simple generic concept, but such a simple, generic concept of the commodity neglects the significance of the commodity form that dominates society entirely in capitalism. As a result, the inevitable and necessary ground of the law of the commodity economy is not clearly demonstrated, for the demonstration of how the value of a commodity is determined by the labour necessary for its production unavoidably becomes trivialised in cases of small commodity production. Unless this demonstration is shown in terms of the capitalist commodity economy, and in terms of how commodities are produced by means of commodities, a logically consistent demonstration of the labour theory of value will be impossible to achieve. This is the reason why many economists, unlike Marx, have not been able to grasp the contradictory opposition between value and use value with real precision.[1]

1 I myself, however, am not fully persuaded by and have doubts about the way Marx proceeds directly in developing the labour theory of value in *Capital*, Vol. 1, Ch. 1, 'The Commodity'. Yet,

Similarly, the reason why most economists cannot clarify the forms of money and capital derives from their tendency to grasp the commodity, money,

---

despite this, Marx developed the theory of the forms of value out of the contradictory opposition between value and use value, which then provided for the correct definition of money, and for the ineluctable theoretical deduction of capital. At least this is how I understand the matter, and I should note that the differences between myself and most other economists begin no sooner than right here, on this point. Grasping the commodity as a generic and common concept induces, even unconsciously, a generalisation of the production of commodities as a generic concept, thereby obstructing our understanding of the historical character and necessity of the development of capitalist production relations that produce commodities by means of commodities. In my understanding, only when the notion of the commodity is abstracted from these various production relations completely, does it first become possible to grasp the contradictory opposition between value and use value as an abstraction that develops inexorably to the point that it takes a form that subsumes capitalist production relations. While we often use the phrase 'commodity production' out of convenience, strictly speaking there is no such thing as commodity production as a general relation of production. Moreover, this rigour and exactitude is lost whenever the term 'simple commodity' is linked to production relations of all kinds. This term should rather be understood to mean the mere sale and purchase of commodities. As a reminder, even in a purely capitalist society, the only commodity that cannot be produced by means of commodities is labour power. Of course, insofar as workers sell labour power as a commodity, and receive wages with which to purchase their everyday necessities as commodities, workers are able to reproduce labour power. It would be an overstated analogy, however, to say that labour power is therefore produced as a commodity, and by means of commodities. While it cannot be said that a capitalist society does not exhibit such aspects, the real fact of the matter is that labour power is something that can only be reproduced within the everyday life of workers. Unlike capitalists, workers purchase means of subsistence not merely in order to produce labour power as a commodity. It would not be too much to say that, insofar as there exists an aspect in capitalist society that enforces this kind of relationship, a reversed phase appears in contemporary society, precisely where pressure is put on the everyday life of workers. This reversed phase cannot be understood unless it is understood that labour power becomes a commodity only insofar as labour power is reproduced, as the human life of workers in their everyday life, by placing workers in a relationship in which the sale of their labour power as a commodity is unavoidable, and in which labour power becomes a commodity for the first time when it is presented in exchange. In this regard, the commodity labour power seems to appear as something that possesses a certain shared aspect with extremely primitive products that become commodities through exchange. That these kinds of primitive relations survive and remain in capitalist commodity economies warrants particular emphasis, as it shows that a capitalist economy is ultimately one form of the social life of human beings. Propertyless workers, constantly placed in a position in which they are treated capitalistically as a mere thing, most emphatically do not remain as mere things; this point reveals the ground on which the myriad problems of capitalist society are found, which is also the ground upon which a transformation of this society into a different society cannot avoid taking place. That a commodity economy completes itself, by itself, by the commodification of labour power, is also the very reason why it cannot make itself eternal. In this sense, an understanding of the peculiarity of the commodification of labour power constitutes the central pivot around which political economy turns.

and capital as simple, generic and common concepts, lining them up from the outset on the same plane. Marx's principles of political economy, which begin with the commodity and which construct a theoretical system out of the unfolding contradictions of the commodity, would simply never materialise if it relied on such a generic and common-sensical method. With such misconceptions and common-sensical methods, it becomes absolutely impossible to distinguish capitalism, as one particular historical society, from the societies of the medieval and ancient societies, and as a result, the word capitalism is allowed to continue to be used without ever really knowing what it means. Even though capitalism unleashes a spectrum of problems into our very everyday lives, an understanding of its causes, as well as its ground, risks being lost completely.

With the concept of crisis, which differs from the concept of the commodity, the concrete phenomena of crisis are almost entirely limited to the period of capitalism. However, as I have already described in the Introduction – and echoing the critique of how commodities are understood in a commonsensical way – the scientific analysis of the phenomenon of crisis will be robbed of real scientific analysis if our understanding of the concept of crisis is abstracted from the common and shared points of crises that have spanned every period of capitalism. Just as the notions obtained by the analysis of capitalist society enabled the concept of the commodity to withstand scientific critique – thereby also becoming useful for the analysis of commodity economies of the medieval and classical periods – the same can be said for the concept of crisis. Thus, if the phenomena of crisis are considered in isolation, it will be impossible to clarify why crisis appeared as a contingent phenomenon in relation to various circumstances throughout the seventeenth and eighteenth centuries. At the same time, if the reasons for why crisis inevitably and necessarily breaks out into the open in a capitalist society are not clarified, it will equally be impossible to grasp the meaning of crisis of these earlier periods. The same can even be said for the phenomenon of crisis after the end of the nineteenth century. Merely stating that crisis breaks out from a simple, generalised defaulting of payments hardly helps us in the analysis of actual reality. Unless the phenomenon of crisis is clarified as something that inevitably could not have *not* broken out in a society in which a capitalist commodity economy proceeded in a pure way, i.e., with all members of society constituted by capitalists, workers, and landowners, we will not be able to understand the process by which crises in the seventeenth and eighteenth centuries came to possess a periodicity along with the development of capitalism. The crises of the seventeenth and eighteenth centuries thus have to be grasped in terms of how they exhibited a peculiarity that was born out of the fact that the development of capitalism, and therefore its composition of society, had yet to develop these social relations. Even for a purely capitalist society, however, in which the inevitability of crisis can be clarified as an economic law of motion, this society in fact came into being, and was formed, historically. In other words, even in the case of mid-nineteenth-century England, a purely capitalist society existed as no more than an approximate tendency. After the end of the nineteenth century, however, a purely capitalist society remained unrealised, and was rather *reversed*. Therefore, without recourse to the scientific suppositions obtained by the analysis of the concrete and practical processes of this reversed turn, we will not be able to understand all of the problems accompanying the development of capitalism after the end of the nineteenth century. Unless this point is clarified, we may fail to properly understand recent tendencies that have turned depression into a so-called chronic problem, or that make it possible to turn crises into wars.

In this way, the analysis of the phenomenon of crisis in every period of capitalism becomes possible, for the first time, by grasping the inevitability of crisis as a principle in a purely capitalist society. This does not mean, however, that the crises of every period can be clarified by the theory of the fundamental principles directly. As I have pointed out earlier, if we restrict our view to only one aspect of the character of the laws of motion that cause crisis, it would appear originally as an operation resembling a law of nature, as if capitalism could be grasped as a form which, while incessantly resolving its fundamental contradictions in reality by passing them through crisis, develops eternally and forever. If, however, the theoretical notion of crisis is adapted straight away to historical realities (and even if an understanding of crises of the seventeenth and eighteenth centuries – as periods in which capitalism still had yet to develop – are not problematised), then changes in capitalism after the end of the nineteenth century would be understood *either* as simple effects of circumstantial changes that neglect the inevitability of cyclical crisis, as if crisis did not originally exist in capitalism, which risks an indifference to the historical character of the stage of capitalist development that forms the terminal phase; *or else*, on the contrary, as little more than a simple supposition that such an inevitable economic law itself does not exist. In either case, the significance and role of economic law in the social sciences cannot be identified.

Admittedly, a purely capitalist society is a theoretically constructed world image. That the society presupposed by this theoretical construction can be grasped, however, does not mean that its laws are to be treated as a simple presupposition. As this purely capitalist society itself is originally presupposed on the actual basis for the tendency of capitalism's concrete development, it is not, therefore, a simple presupposition. This society, of course, is never actually realised. It is, as it were, an experimental device of the social sciences. In the Introduction, let us recall, I quoted Marx's words about how, in the natural sciences and in cases where experimentation is possible, it is possible to grasp the laws of natural processes as they appear in the purest, most certain of situations. This does not mean that these experimental cases, which demonstrate the laws, represent particular exceptions. Natural laws remain true and actual even though they have been grasped through experimental devices. In fact, unless this is done, the laws will not be grasped. Since such experimental devices cannot be made for social phenomena, we have to select an approximation of a purely capitalist society, and choose its period and place in which a development towards such a pure society takes place. Capitalism, as a historical process, certainly bears this kind of period and place. The scientific and theoretical system of the principles of political economy, which abstracts concepts from the analysis of this concrete society, is nothing other than that which reconstructs capitalist society in a pure form.

Even when we analyse capitalist society in its earliest stages of development, the principles of capitalism can be abstracted and grasped to some extent. In fact, many economists have worked in this way. In those cases, however, while it is possible to grasp some general and relatively simple concepts – albeit not in logically consistent ways – the same cannot be said for the more complex concepts that characterize capitalism. Commodities and money aside, when it comes to the concept of capital, our understanding often tends to become extremely one dimensional. Phenomena such as crisis become impossible to grasp. In the systematic exposition of the principles of political economy, more complex forms appear later on, and their laws of motion become impossible to grasp unless they are based on a world in which capitalism has advanced to a definite stage of development and dominated the entirety of society. But this is not all. If these complex concepts are not shown, it will also be impossible to completely determine the simplest of concepts as well. Put differently, with the theoretical clarification of crisis, the whole system of principles that begins with the commodity is given a clear and proper exposition for the first time.

By virtue of their abstract and simple determinations, relatively simple concepts can be applied more widely, to so speak. By contrast, the period and place in which more complex concepts can be adapted straight away are restricted. This absolutely does not mean a denial of their economic laws, however. This point, which has been misunderstood in ways that I have already described, leads not only to distortions or denials of the essence of the economic laws themselves, but also to the impossibility of adapting these simple concepts widely and in a straight forward fashion. Even for commodities, once they are in social relations to be produced, sold and reproduced capitalistically, their concepts cannot be applied so widely and in a straight forward way. These concepts must also be grasped and abstracted from the reproductive relations of a purely capitalist society. The only way to clarify the essence of the laws of historical phenomena such as capitalism is by relying on this method. Unless this point is clarified, the essence of the laws will be understood mechanically, leading either to errors that conclude that different results are born simply from changes in circumstance, or else to a way of thinking that denies the actual facts as if they were accidental phenomena, or further, that erroneously expects that the future will bring about the phenomenon in accord with the law itself.[2]

The inevitability of crisis can thus be grasped under the conditions outlined above. From the point of view of its working as an economic law, while it possesses a quality of repetition that has a power not unlike that of a law of nature that appears impossible to alter by anyone, in its aspects as an historical process, its approximate phenomenon also cannot avoid being restricted to a definite historical period. Nevertheless, what makes this historical process

2 The last theoretical topic in our system of principles of political economy is that of joint stock capital, in which capital itself is commodified. By the time joint stock capital appears concretely as a dominant form, however, it is already impossible to speak of an advance in the continual tendency towards a purely capitalist society. The reason is that, by mid-nineteenth century English capitalism – which comes closest to approximating a purely capitalist society – had already transformed into the era of so-called finance capital. In this regard, for the theoretical system of principles of political economy, joint stock capital, as the final concept *in extremis*, corresponds with the theory's initial, starting concept of the commodity.

As I have pointed out above, the essence of the economic laws of political economy cannot be understood so long as they are explained as phenomenon that are transformed merely due to changed circumstances. The changes in capitalism after the end of the nineteenth century cannot be removed or ignored, simply for the sake of realizing the original economic laws again. The transformation of the circumstances is itself based on the inevitable development of capitalism. The era of finance capital was not realized because it is something that was not originally supposed to have become realised. Rather, it became actualized because *capital itself commodifies*, and because capital cannot but appear as joint stock capital. The era of finance capital was realised with the spread of joint stock capital in industry, and with this, a reversion back to the era of industrial capital became impossible. The process of this turn [to the era of finance capital] is carried forth by the workings of the law of commodity economies. It is precisely here that capitalist relations, which have obviously allowed us to grasp this law, have already brought about a turn in capitalism, moving in a direction that prevents us from seeing this law again. While it is not erroneous to explain how different relations developed because of changed conditions, error will be inevitable if, in explaining these changes, we suggest that it is possible to return to some original condition.

inevitable is the working of this law itself, which, like a law of nature, is carried through by the historical process. This point allows political economy to grasp, in terms of fundamental principles, the movement itself of society's so-called base structure, as a method specific to political economy that grasps the law of the economic process of capitalism. In order to analyze the historical process scientifically and not as a mere experiential fact, the repetitive laws found in it must be grasped, but not simply as a *merely* repetitive motion. Insofar as the economic law of cyclical crises has a certain level of abstraction concerning the so-called base structure, it therefore also possesses a quality of repetition that can only become realised in an approximate way in relation to a certain historical period. Herein lies the difference between the inevitability of crisis and the inevitability of the collapse of capitalism itself.

2 The Inevitability of Crisis and the Inevitability of Collapse

The fact that the phenomenon of crisis appears as an expression of the actual resolution of capitalism's fundamental contradictions signifies how capitalism, as a manifestation of the contradiction between what Marx called the forces of production and the relations of production, has no longer become the most optimal method of production. A turn towards a new social form is thus possible, pointing to the possible arrival of a period in which, 'the changes in the economic foundation lead sooner or later to the transformation of the whole immense superstructure.'[3] Insofar as capitalism is an historical process, its establishment is simultaneously nothing but a process towards its ruination. This emphatically does not mean, however, that capitalism will collapse with crisis. Crisis, while appearing out of the same ground from which the inevitability and necessity of capitalism's collapse appears, nonetheless expresses the process which repeatedly, and in actuality, resolves the contradictions that constitute this very ground, and which forms progressively larger and larger contradictions. Only in this way can the theory of the fundamental principles of political economy, whose object is the abstract essence of the economic process of the base structure, grasp this point.

As I have clarified in the previous section, this suggests nothing more than grasping capitalist relations of production as they dominate an entire society

3 Marx, 'Preface to *A Contribution to the Critique of Political Economy*', International Publishers, 1989, p. 21.

at a given stage of development, and clarifying the structure of capitalist society as a fully formed society while simultaneously grasping, in its background, so to speak, capitalism's periods of emergence and decline and their attendant processes. As I have also already described, the clarification of crisis by the theory of the fundamental principles, and therefore by the theory of crisis, as that which actually resolves capitalism's contradictions, does not mean that crisis fundamentally sublates these contradictions. However, while the clarification of crisis does not seek to assert the eternity of capitalism, the clarification of the economic laws by the fundamental principles cannot avoid adopting a method that affirms precisely this aspect. This is the peculiar method by which the historical process is grasped theoretically. Regarding the dialectic of this method, Marx also writes that, "it includes, within the positive understanding of that which exists, a simultaneous recognition of its negation, of its inevitable demise. It grasps every actual form in fluid motion. That is, it also sees it from its transient side. It does not let itself be impressed by anything. Its essence is critical and revolutionary."[4]

In terms of the theory of the fundamental principles, while the elucidation of the phenomenon of crisis must certainly be understood as that which includes the recognition of the 'inevitable demise' of capitalism, this cannot lead immediately to the demonstration of this 'inevitable demise'. Just as capitalism itself is not merely an economic process, the collapse of capitalism does not appear as the mere collapse of the economic process. As I have repeatedly described, nearly two hundred years were needed before capitalism's economic process could appear as the highest approximation of a purely economic process. Yet, even in mid-nineteenth-century England, society was only able to approximate this abstract conception, but not simply as an economic process. That it was an approximation testifies precisely to this fact. It goes without saying that for the period of capitalism's emergence in the seventeenth and eighteenth centuries, as well as for the period of capitalism's decline after the end of the nineteenth century, the economic process was more closely connected to legal and political superstructures. Capitalism's emergence and decline cannot be clarified merely as an inevitability of the economic process. The same can be said even for mid-nineteenth-century England. Still, in the period of so-called liberalism, the base structure, as an economic process, appears in the purest form, though it can never be separated completely from the superstructure. At the same time,

4 Marx, 'Afterward to the Second German Edition', *Capital*, Vol. 1, p. 103, translation modified. The translator thanks Professor John Noyes for this modification.

however, the economic process, even as an approximation, points concretely to how it can move on its own, enabling theoretical explication of its independent motion. The superstructure, by contrast, must always be studied in accordance with changes in the economic process, forming a definite and certain system that corresponds to economic changes.

While I have been unable to demonstrate this point in relation to every field of study, this kind of inference can minimally be made simply by observing changes, for example, in economic policy during capitalism's periods of emergence, growth, and decline. And while it is impossible to separate the periods of emergence and decline from their attendant political processes, this is not to suggest that the economic process is determined arbitrarily by the political. Quite the contrary, the political is given a definite character precisely because it corresponds to the economic process, accelerating or repressing the latter. For this reason, at a certain stage of the development of capitalism, mercantile policies were abandoned, thereby giving way to the realisation of a period of liberalism. Similarly, the basis of imperialist policy represented nothing more than the shift, in the economic process, towards a period of finance capital. And while political power is directly economic power in the period of capitalism's emergence, a reversed shift occurs in the period of capitalism's decline, which turns economic power directly into political power. While in either case the appearance of the economic laws in the principles of political economy, grasped in a purely capitalist society based on the liberal period of capitalism, of course cannot appear straightforwardly, nonetheless, in terms of the actual process, the political's influence on economic processes is always nothing but the influence of the political as it is determined by the economic process through which it constantly passes. Policies never proceed in isolation from the economic process. If such a policy did proceed in this way, it would surely be corrected by other policies. When political and legal matters carry out new developments, this always takes place by passing through, and corresponding with, economic processes; they never move by themselves, unlike the economic process. It is therefore impossible to carry out an analysis of concrete processes of capitalism's period of emergence, its period of decline, and further, its period of growth during the archetypical period of liberalism, without referring to the criteria of the economic laws clarified in the principles of political economy, while also taking into consideration how these periods begin with capitalism at a given period, and then form a process that enlarges, in a different form, contradictions that deviate from such a world of the fundamental principles. The development of capitalism cannot be regarded as a process that develops evenly towards the realisation of a purely capitalist society. Similarly, if we were to impute a similar meaning to the notion of the inevitability of collapse, this points to little else than how capitalism must have an end, just as equally as it had to have had a beginning. The principles of political economy cannot identify the inevitability of collapse in a particular country at a particular time, nor can it demonstrate the period of decline of capitalism as a general process toward the process of inevitable collapse. Actually, it is impossible to conclude that, just because capitalism has entered a period of decline, the inevitability of collapse will take place due to economic processes and in the same way that the inevitability of crisis is clarified by the principles of political economy.

Now, it goes without saying that for individual countries, the processes of the emergence of capitalism, of its growth, and further, of its decline, all appear as specific processes. Generally speaking, it can be said that the processes experienced by countries that have seen the development of capitalism earlier will basically be repeated, more or less, as an identical process, in countries where the transformation into capitalism comes later, showing how the fundamental principles are carried out after passing through the historical process. It also points to a whole panoply of differing conditions endemic to the period when this transformation to capitalism takes place. The same can be said for the processes of collapse; whatever the case, these processes are specific. Not only that, however. Even if we can recognise the inevitability of collapse – in the sense that capitalism must have its end just as it had to have a beginning – this does not mean that collapse will necessarily occur in advanced capitalist countries. Collapse is not something that appears in a country as if it obeyed the necessity of a natural law, unlike the inevitability of crisis. In world history, once capitalist development enters a period of decline in the era of finance capital, and depending on historical circumstances, the process of the capitalist transformation of society in a particular country itself becomes a process of collapse. On this point, however, while the period of capitalism's emergence discloses its time in radically different ways from country to country, and while, therefore, its features cannot but differ from each other, when it comes to the process of collapse, those features, as well as their timing, can be expected to gradually approach and come closer to each other.

As I have already pointed out, in this period of collapse in the so-called era of imperialism, crisis phenomena are transformed from typical crisis, and the contradictions of capitalist methods of production become manifested in tendencies towards so-called chronic depression and war. The transformation into chronic depression and the inevitability of wars, however, are not things that can be demonstrated by deploying the same abstractions involved in demonstrating the inevitability of crisis. This is not to say that these things do not disclose a complete absence of periodicity, but they do not abide by a periodicity in the same way that crisis does. They are not like crisis, which absolutely cannot be avoided. At the same time, however, even if they could be averted momentarily, the contradictions behind them would remain fundamentally unresolved and would manifest themselves as even larger contradictions, and thus, in the final instance, they still would not be able to be averted. In this way, it can be said that the economic process operates in a most decisive way. For revolutionary processes of transforming capitalist methods of production into a different social form, it becomes a much more concrete process that cannot be predicted by theoretical analysis alone. Of course, the analyses of concrete conjunctures and situations of individual countries can clarify revolutionary situations to a certain extent, but how these situations will proceed concretely depends on the development of organised class movements. It is not something that can be cleared up or understood simply by resorting to the inevitability of collapse.

Although the inevitability of crisis is an historical inevitability and decidedly not a natural, mechanical inevitability, in a purely capitalist society, or else in what comes closest to approximating this society (as in the case of mid-nineteenth-century England), once the actions of discrete individuals become regulated socially by passing through the commodity form, crisis will appear with an inevitability that cannot be removed by the work of political power, let alone by individuals, for political power itself cannot but become liberalistic, precisely because of the economic process. Such an inevitability of crisis should not, therefore, be identified with the inevitability of the actual process of the collapse of capitalism. As I have stated earlier, the argument for the inevitability of collapse due to the historical emergence of capitalism cannot clarify concretely the inevitability of its actual process. The least that can be said is that it cannot be demonstrated to the same degree as that of the inevitability of crisis. Unlike the inevitability of crisis, the inevitability of collapse cannot be demonstrated by the abstract theory of the principles of political economy. Confusing the two and viewing them both as one and the same thing obfuscates the limits and the different levels of research in political economy. This is not a proper way to explicate either the ground upon which capitalism can dominate a single society, or the meaning of manifestations of economic contradictions in the process for social revolution. Even when Marx epigrammatically wrote, with regards to the end of capitalism, that, 'The knell of capitalist private property sounds. The expropriators are expropriated', he wrote of how, in constant correspondence with capital's process of centralisation, there 'grows the revolt of the working class, a class always increasing in numbers, and disciplined, united, organised by the very mechanism of the process of capitalist production itself'.[5] While this is based on the enlargement of the contradictions of the economic process, the economic contradictions in themselves are not sufficient to transform capitalism into a different social form.[6]

---

5 *Capital*, Vol. 1, p. 929.

6 It is likely that there are objections to my interpretation of this point, but it seems to me natural that the transformation of the mechanism of a capitalist society cannot be explained positively by the theoretical elucidation of this mechanism alone. In fact, we should note that in *Capital*, in the chapter on 'The Historical Tendency of Capitalist Accumulation' – including statements in Part 8 on 'so-called Primitive Accumulation' in the final chapter of Volume 1, as well as in the chapter on 'The Theory of Modern Colonialism' – Marx himself also wrote the following words, which probably concern these statements: 'At the end of this chapter, I present some comments on the historical tendency of capitalist accumulation, and the last words I write point to how private capitalist property must be converted into collective social property. In the last portion of that Part (chapter), the fact that no proof was provided in any way to back up this assertion itself was nothing but a summary conclusion of an extended line of development that was shown in the preceding chapters on capitalist production' (Marx-Engels *zenshū*, Vol. 23, p. 157, Otsuki shoten edition, Vol. 19, p. 116, translation modified based on the original German text in Sakisaka's private collection). There is nothing whatsoever in political economy that can prove this argument about a conversion. Moreover, although with regards to the conversion to a socialist society that is mentioned in *Capital*, my own understanding is that this is a general idea to resolve the fundamental contradictions existing in a capitalist society. This general idea is in no way a positive demonstration. While it is not clear how Marx understood the relationship between the level of the theory of the principles of political economy and the level of concrete analysis of economic processes – a relationship that must, in my view, be further broken down between the typical notions of stages of capitalist development in world history and more concrete analyses of the present situation – Marx's statement that the joint stock system 'represents an abolition of capitalist private industry on the basis of the capitalist system itself', for instance, may be a result of neglecting the distinction between what I call the principles of political economy and the theory of typical stages of capitalist development. Marx, of course, writes that, "the transformation into the form of shares still remains trapped within the capitalist barriers; instead of overcoming the opposition between the character of wealth as something social, and private wealth, this transformation only develops this opposition in a new form." (*Capital*, Vol. 3, p. 571). How this 'new form' is to be explicated is left unclear by Marx. Perhaps, this comes from the fact that Marx was not able to see and analyse the era of finance capital, but even if he had been able to do so, it is unthinkable that the principles of political economy could have been developed without presupposing a purely capitalist society. Put differently, even if Marx had written *Capital* in the era of finance capital – the era in which we, ourselves, live – it can hardly be imagined that he would have relied on a method other than the one that explained the fundamental principles of capitalism, which tie individuals together commodity-economically between capitalists, workers, and landowners. The most likely thing that can be said is that Marx would have concluded Volume 3 with an explanation of finance capital in the same way that he explained 'primitive accumulation' at the end of Volume 1. My own thoughts on this matter, to be blunt, is that, simultaneously with the recognition of finance capital, we become capable of clarifying at what level of abstraction the theoretical world of the principles of political economy has to be exhibited. Clearly, it is here that the three-step method

3 The Theory of Crisis and the Analyses of Crises

In my understanding, the inevitability of crisis that is endemic to capitalist society can and must be demonstrated, as I have described in these pages, in terms of the theory of the fundamental principles of economy, which clarify the general economic laws of capitalism. This does not mean, however, that discrete, concrete processes of crisis can be elucidated directly by these principles. Rather, the analyses of these individual and discrete processes must be based upon, and guided by, these principles as a frame of reference. Even in such a case, however, these crises need to be determined historically in accordance with the stage of capitalism in which they appear, which means that it is wrongheaded to think that they can be analysed with the aid of these principles alone. By no means is this point limited to the phenomenon of crisis. Generally speaking, the concrete processes of a given country, as they exist in different stages, cannot be elucidated directly by these principles alone. The goal of such an analysis will not be fully achieved unless it is clarified how each concrete process is mediated by a specific historical process. Of course, in a case such as Lenin's *Development of Capitalism in Russia* – the purpose of which was to clarify the working out of the general law of capitalism in Russia – it can be said that his analysis, which relied only on fundamental principles, was adequate to the task. Such a method, however, cannot clarify the specificities of individual, particular countries. The reason is that, once we consider the specific processes of other, individual, particular countries, it is not seldom the case that their features are widely different from the theoretical image of the fundamental

---

of political economy must enter the picture; it is here where the theory of crisis can, and must, be explained in terms of the fundamental principles. Around the years Marx wrote his *Critique of Political Economy* (in the Preface, section three, 'The method of political economy'), he planned to explain crisis, along with the world market, after having first clarified public finance (by the state) and international trade, but it is not clear to me how long Marx held fast to this framework, or why he necessarily had to do so. While a crisis of the world market, as a concrete process, is no different from a total explosion of every capitalist contradiction, can we really say that we have theoretically proven its inevitability so long as it is not clarified in terms of the theoretical world of the fundamental principles? Unless this is done, it seems to me that it will not be possible to clarify what Marx showed in *Capital*, Vol. 3, Ch. 15, namely that crisis is based upon the fundamental contradiction of the capitalist method of production. Various concrete factors, which contribute to the promotion of actual crises greatly, *but not necessarily*, are misunderstood and misrecognized as causes of the inevitability of crisis based on the fundamental contradiction of capitalism. In the past, this point has not been clarified, leading to debates among economists who rely on Marx's theories. Obviously, I cannot say whether my thoughts are correct or not, but as far as I am concerned, a debate that does not clarify this point will not be able to advance the theory of crisis properly.

principles because of singularly specific conditions. For example, in the pre-war analysis of capitalism in Japan, the issue of the historical character of the exploitation of peasants, in the form of farm rent, required a mediating level of research to clarify why these specific forms of exploitation of peasants became so difficult to dissolve broadly among the so-called late-developing capitalist countries which, in the theory of stages of development, is typically found in the situation in Germany. These historical circumstances and situations cannot be analysed directly by the theory of rent in the principles of political economy.

For something like the phenomenon of crisis, which appears in actuality with various, concrete aspects, it also goes without saying that there are even cases in which it is impossible to adequately analyse the concrete process as the analysis of a single country. It is also further inadequate to take up the phenomenon of crisis in a single country and analyze it merely on the basis of the theory of the fundamental principles. The purpose of analysing crisis can never be reached without clarifying the period in which this country transforms into capitalism, and without making clear at what stage of the development, and under what relationships with foreign countries, it falls into crisis. These concrete circumstances and situations cannot be clarified directly by the entirety of the theory of the fundamental principles, let alone by the theory of crisis. For the most part, conventional political economic analyses of concrete economic phenomena – which are not limited to the phenomena of crisis – have not only left unclear such methodological discretions of applying basic principles too directly, but have also left unclear and incomplete, on the opposite side, that which can be fully elucidated within the fundamental principles of political economy, such as the theory of crisis.

APPENDIX 1

Problematic Points in the Theory of Crisis in *Das Kapital*

In the *Introduction to a Critique of Political Economy*, which is appended to the existing edition of *A Critique of Political Economy*, Marx indicates an arrangement of separate volumes for the discipline of political economy, one that concludes with a final volume on 'crisis' and 'the world market'.[1] Obviously, this arrangement points to the general features indicated by Marx, in his 'Plan' of study, in which the present *Critique of Political Economy* and *Capital* represents just one part of the beginning of that plan.[2] According to Marx's original plan, therefore, a theory of crisis was generally recognised as something that would be found outside the bounds of *Capital*.[3] As I will describe later, while I do not believe that a theory of crisis was developed in a completed form in *Capital*, I also do not believe that the reason for its incompleteness is that it exists outside of *Capital*. It is precisely in *Capital* that we can discover something like the fundamental determinations of a theory of crisis. The problem to consider, however, is why *Capital* was finished without developing the fundamental determinations for a theory of crisis in a complete form. It is on this point that I would like to offer my frank and candid thoughts.

1 [Originally published in *Shakaikagaku Kenkyū* (University of Tokyo), vol. 3, no. 3 (June 1952).

2 In our country, while the six-point, overall plan of Marx's total system of a critique of political economy – of which *Capital* represents one part – has already been problematised numerously, I would like to especially point out Professor Kōichiro Suzuki's essay, 'On the Plan of *Capital*', in the December 1948 volume of *Shisō*., in which six various plans were presented. Another plan of Marx's, which has never been published, is also appended to the Japanese translation of *A Critique of Political Economy* in the third supplementary volume of the selected works of Marx and Engels (published by Otsuki Shoten). Finally, it is necessary to refer – despite its lack of clarity in the matter – to the recently published text by V. Burshinkski and J. Preis, which was recently introduced in T. Teramura, titled, 'Preparations for the publication of a scientific edition of *Theories of Surplus Value* in the Soviet Union', in *Keizaigaku Zasshi* (Osaka University of Commerce), 25, no. 4.

3 In Professor Kuruma Samezō's essay, 'On the Confirmation of Marx's Theory of Crisis', he also considers the relationship between Marx's plan in the *Critique of Political Economy* and *Capital*, and writes that, 'It is obvious that Marx's theory of crisis was left in an unfinished state along with his system for a critique of political economy' (*Studies in Crisis Theory*, Okuryūkan (1949), p. 95).

1

Since I have already published a general consideration of Marx's plan for the parts of political economy, I do not feel it is necessary to review that text again.[4] Instead, I would like to consider Marx's plan in relation to a theory of crisis. On this point, however, we already have Professor Kuruma's extremely careful considerations (in the text mentioned above). Therefore, what I would like to do first is to compare my understanding of the problem with Professor Kuruma's views.

Professor Kuruma scrupulously examines how 'wage labour' and 'landed property', which are arranged within Marx's original 'plan,' are related to the theoretical exposition in *Capital*. What he finds is that a 'proper analysis' regarding 'wage labour' and 'landed property' in the Plan is considered outside its scope in *Capital*. Similarly, regarding crisis, Kuruma writes that, "it is a fact that several descriptions related to the problem of crisis are found therein (in *Capital*), but the theorisation of the problem stops at the level of a theoretical depiction of so-called capital in general – or else in, 'the internal organisation of capitalist production methods understood as an ideal average' – and we are left without ever seeing a proper theory of crisis."[5] On this point, while I, at least, am not clear about what Professor Kuruma means by a "proper theory of crisis", his reasoning evidently stems from discussions related to landed property that are found in three of Marx's letters to Engels. Let us refer to and take up Professor Kuruma's points:

1. In a letter dated 2 April 1858, Marx writes, "1. Capital. First section: Capital in general (Throughout this section, wages are invariably assumed to be at their minimum. Movements in wages themselves and the rise and fall of that minimum will be considered under wage labour. Further, landed property is assumed to be zero, i.e. landed property, as a special economic relation is of no relevance as yet)".[6]
2. Next, on 18 June 1862, Marx writes, "another thing I have at last been able to sort out is the shitty rent business (which, however, I shall not so much as allude to in this part)" [that is, as Kuruma emphasises, in the part called capital in general].[7]

4 See my essay, 'On the Method of Political Economy', *Shakai Kagaku Kenkyū* (University of Tokyo), vol. 2, no. 1, included in my *Studies in the Theory of Value*, republished in *UKC*, Vol. 3.

5 Kuruma 1936, p. 94.

6 [Transl. note: *MECW*, Vol. 40, p. 296.]

7 [Transl. note: *MECW*, Vol. 41, p. 380.]

3. However, approximately one and a half months later, dated 2 August, Marx writes, "[In my last letter I wrote this way, but] I now propose, after all, to include in this volume [i.e., capital in general] an extra chapter on the theory of rent, i.e., by way of "illustration" to an earlier thesis of mine".[8]

Based on these passages, Professor Kuruma concludes with the following:

> Between 18 June 1862 to 2 August of the same year, Marx therefore altered his original plan, 'to include in this volume [i.e., capital in general] an extra chapter on the theory of rent'. This emphatically did not mean, however, that he imagined immediately including [in capital in general] the entire contents of 'landed property' as one of the six major volumes of his original plan [i.e., 1. Capital,[9] 2. Landed property, 3. Wage labour, 4. The state, 5. Foreign Trade, 6. World market]. Rather, it was necessary to be 'included' only to the extent that it served the theory of rent, and only 'by way of "illustration" to an earlier thesis of mine', and only to the extent that the theory of rent served it.[10]

The doubt that immediately struck me when I read Professor Kuruma's interpretation is whether the part on rent in the current edition of *Capital* can be said "to be 'included'" only "by way of 'illustration' to an earlier thesis of mine", as Marx thought here.

For, even if it can be said that Marx's discussions of rent (as well as for wages) in *Capital* do develop an 'earlier thesis' of his, I do not believe at all that this was 'included' only as an 'illustration'. Professor Kuruma himself also writes that, "Indeed, in Volume Three of *Capital* we see included as a topic, 'The transformation of surplus profit into rent', where we find a highly detailed analysis of rent. Moreover, it is an unmistakable fact that in Volume One we find significantly involved research on wages."[11] Professor Kuruma compares these analyses with Marx's "original plan for a critique of political economy, in which 'landed property' and 'wage labour' constitute one part," and then immediately wonders:

> Are the discussions of 'landed property' and 'wage labour', which Marx planned as one part of his original plan for a critique of political economy,

8 [Transl. note: *MECW*, Vol. 41, p. 394.]

9 The term 'capital' here is not precisely the same as 'capital in general', but I will not address this point here.

10 Kuruma 1936, pp. 90–1.

11 Kuruma 1936, p. 86.

> given substance here? In other words, are these analyses in *Capital* themselves relevant for Marx's earlier understanding of the proper analysis of 'landed property' and 'wage labour'?[12]

I myself have no qualms with Professor Kuruma's view that these discussions in the original plan differ from the way they are developed in *Capital*. But while I agree with Professor Kuruma that, "these discussions are only intended to consider landed property and wage labour, which are necessary to clarify the general character of capital", I believe these discussions and analyses are too important to be considered simply "an 'illustration' to an earlier thesis." Rather, I think that, with respect to wage labour, these discussions represent something that determines the fundamental relationship between capitalists and workers. Similarly, regarding ground rent, I believe they represent something that fundamentally determines the relationship between capitalists and land owners. My understanding is that wage labour, as "one part of the originally planned critique of political economy" is precisely what "belongs to the special study of 'wage labour'."[13]

The determinations of wage labour and ground rent, as they are given theoretical exposition in *Capital*, cannot be understood as something specific to any of the stages of capitalist development. This is because England in the mid-nineteenth century points to the highest approximation of typical relations of capitalist production. For this reason, England – not only in the nineteenth-century but also in the seventeenth and eighteenth centuries (which typically point to capitalism's process of emergence) – offers most of the illustrations or examples in *Capital*. This, however, does not mean that these determinations are "an exposition of all these forms."[14] Rather, they serve to provide general, fundamental determinations that pass through various, specific forms. For ground rent as well – and this is completely my own understanding, one that may differ from Marx's intentions – the specific forms of ground rent do not simply present a difference from feudal rent as a difference of a general determination; rather, it seems to me that these forms must also be clarified according to the types accompanying each stage of capitalist development from the seventeenth and eighteenth centuries onward. Of course, this is something that must be understood in terms of the countries representing capitalism's world-historical development; it must not, therefore, directly analyse a specific coun-

12 Ibid.

13 *Capital*, Vol. 1, p. 683.

14 Ibid.

try's rent concretely.[15] Put differently, the concrete analysis of land owners in seventeenth-century England must consider its concrete conditions.

Now, while it goes without saying that when it comes to wage labour, as something that provides for the fundamental determinations of capitalist methods of production, the fact that the theoretical clarification of landed property follows the 'topical' exposition, as it is led by capital, shows that it itself is able to clarify the exposition of capitalist forms of landed property. Without these fundamental determinations, the economic analysis of the processes in which seventeenth- and eighteenth-century landed property transformed into nineteenth-century landed property will invariably be insufficient. Landed property, in and of itself, cannot develop its capitalist forms. Capitalism, moreover, does not merely modernise and privatise landed property; rather, in the process in which ground rent is established as capitalist ground rent, it also establishes capitalist landed property. While this represents nothing other than a process of the so-called theoretical exposition, in which the more fundamental capitalist relationship of distributing surplus value as profits develops a special relationship in relation to land as means of produc-

15 On this precise point, a document to support a most influential counter argument exists. In the Preface to *Capital*, Vol. 3, Engels describes this point in the following way: 'In the seventies Marx engaged in entirely new special studies for this part on ground rent. For years he had studied the Russian originals of statistical reports inevitable after the 'reform' of 1861 in Russia and other publications on landownership, had taken extracts from these originals, placed at his disposal in admirably complete form by his Russian friends, and had intended to use them for a new version of his part. Owing to the variety of forms both of landownership and of exploitation of agricultural producers in Russia, this country was to play the same role in the part dealing with ground rent that England played in Book I, in connection with industrial wage labour. He was unfortunately denied the opportunity of carrying out this plan' (*Capital*, Vol. 3, p. 96–97). In the early 1870s, Marx himself also wrote, 'In the volume dealing with landed property, Russia's forms were taken up in great detail' (*MECW*, Vol. 44). This, however, never materialised. It is not clear, moreover, how Marx intended to use this knowledge. (See Engels's letter to Danielson in *MECW*) In my understanding of this point, I do not think, as Engels did, that the period following the Russian reform serves in the same manner with regard to ground rent as the examples from England serve Marx's discussion of wage labour in Volume 1 of *Capital*. Of course, saying only this is not a real problem, but the reason why it was even possible for England to provide examples of fundamental determinations of wage labour in England is because it also represented the world-historical stage of development of capitalism. I have doubts, therefore, whether the examples from Russia possess the same meaning. In any case, as for myself – and despite Engels's words and even Marx's own intentions on this point – I do not have compelling reasons to follow Marx and Engels's words on this matter, either because it is questionable whether the Russian case in fact points to enough examples to demonstrate the general determinations of a text such as *Capital*, or because the unclear points of my own thinking have not been clarified enough.

tion and especially against the private ownership of land itself, it simultaneously cannot but reflect the historical process, as well. As one of the internal factors of capitalism's economic process, landed property becomes capitalist landed property, and is not something whose form corresponding to capitalism is given as an external factor. This is a different matter than, say, economic policy or public finance, for it points to a relationship that naturally must enter into the categories of the fundamental principles, of the kind found in *Capital*.

No matter whether or not Marx intended to include these discussions of 'wage labour' or 'landed property' in his original plan for *Capital* (and which is raised in the *Introduction* to *A Critique of Political Economy*, or in other texts), if the determinations of wages and rent were lacking, do you think the theoretical system of *Capital* could ever have come about? If this can be granted for wages and rent, then with regard to crisis it would seem difficult to say, following Professor Kuruma, that it is something that must remain within "problems of the various gradations of logical descriptions of so-called 'capital in general', or of the internal organisation of capitalist production methods accompanying an ideal average". Of course, the Professor would probably say that these matters in fact appear in *Capital*, but actually what the Professor has done is simply rationalise the fact of *Capital* on the basis of Marx's Plan in *The Critique of Political Economy*. What remains unquestioned is the argument of whether or not the inevitability of crisis can be positively elucidated by a theory of fundamental principles of the kind found in *Capital*. Instead, he writes, "Marx's theory of crisis, as well as his systematic critique of political economy, remains incomplete."[16] Yet, like wage labour or capitalist landed property, there is no reason to think that the fundamental determinations of crisis should not be developed according to the fundamental principles in *Capital*. On the contrary, is it not impossible to clarify crisis as the peculiar phenomenon of capitalism unless crisis is treated in precisely this way? Thus, the problem is why Marx has not given a theory of crisis its unquestionably proper exposition in *Capital*. This, at least, is what I think.

2

From the point of view that the fundamental determinations of a theory of crisis in *Capital* are presented in *Capital*, Volume 3, Part 3, 'The Law of the Tendency of the Rate of Profit to Fall', I endeavoured to explain this some years

16 Kuruma, 1936, p. 95.

ago, especially by considering Chapter 15 of Part 3, 'Exposition of the Internal Contradictions of the Law'.[17] However, my study fell into the most esoteric and abstruse problems because I did whatever I could to base my analysis on the methodology of *Capital*. Even now, while I do think that the excess capital approach found in that chapter does point to basic determinations of Marx's theory of crisis, I do not believe that this alone can adequately elucidate the sudden outbreak of crisis itself. For, while it may be true, in terms of the total capital, that the sudden fall in the profit rate stemming from excess capital and that only takes place on the condition that investments of additional capital replace the original capital, this is not possible in terms of *individual capitals*. To give a simple example, let us assume that an original capital of 100 is used for social production, and when 20 additional capitals are added, the profit rate falls from 10% to 8% as a result of a rise in workers' wages. Despite capital's increase there is an absolute decrease in the quantity of profit, from 10 to 9.6. In this case, from the perspective of the total capital, the 20 added capitals are meaningless. If, with the addition of 20 additional capitals, the profit is equal to the original profit, then it follows that 'one part of the original capital will be expelled from its place'. For individual capitals, however, it could not be said that any added capital would be meaningless if, for example, there was a fall in the profit rate to 8%. They would not necessarily make the effort to maintain the same rate of profit of 10% through the expulsion of 'one part of the original capital'. This is because the profit rate can now be realised at 8%, even if the original profit rate cannot be realised. For this to then burst out as a crisis, there must be an 'unavoidable inability to make payments on interest and ground rent that is set by a determinate profit rate'.[18] This opposition between the profit rate and interest rate, in terms of the logical ordering of *Capital*, could not theoretically develop a theory of crisis. Marx explained the average profit in Part 2, and continued with the law of the tendency of the profit rate to fall; in Part 4, he theorises commercial capital, and develops interest-bearing capital in Part 5. I also have doubts as to the logical ordering itself of these parts, but this notwithstanding, I cannot help feeling that the purely theoretical exposition of loanable capital is hindered in Part 5, on interest-bearing capital.

In Part 5 of Volume 3, and particularly in Chapter 30, 'Money Capital and Real Capital', Marx frequently strives to delineate a pure form of commercial credit, but when it comes to its connection to crisis, he does not carry out this task.[19]

17 See my 'The Inevitability of Crisis in Capitalistic Society', *Kaizō*, February 1935, reprinted in *Studies of Capital*, Vol. 3.

18 *UKC*, Vol. 3, p. 139.

19 I have encountered extremely difficult problems in explicating this point, and for the same

Instead, he treats credit relations themselves as something external to the theoretical consideration of crisis. For example, after Marx theorises the point at which the expansion of the reproduction process, stemming from credit, transitions to crisis conditions, he writes the following:

> Let us conceive the whole society as composed simply of industrial capitalists and wage-labourers. Let us also leave aside those changes in price which prevent large portions of the total capital from being replaced in their average proportions, and which, in the overall context of the reproduction process as a whole, particularly as developed by credit, must recurrently bring about a situation of general stagnation. Let us likewise ignore the fraudulent businesses and speculative dealings that the credit system fosters. In this case, a crisis would be explicable only in terms of a disproportion in production between different branches and a disproportion between the consumption of the capitalists themselves and their accumulation. But as things actually are, the replacement of the capitals invested in production depends to a large extent on the consumption capacity of the non-productive classes; while the consumption capacity of the workers is restricted partly by the laws governing wages and partly by the fact that they are employed only as long as they can be employed at a profit for the capitalist class. The ultimate reason for all real crises always remains the poverty and restricted consumption of the masses, in the face of the drive of capitalist production to develop the productive forces as if only the absolute consumption capacity of society set a limit to them.[20]

To say that 'the ultimate reason for all real crises' is found in the "restricted consumption of the masses" is not, of course, to understand the outbreak of crisis as having resulted from lowered wages, and not simply from the fact that wages only represent a restricted part of the value products. This is caused by the fact that the consuming power of employed workers are restricted by the economic laws of wages, and by the fact that they are "used only as long as they can be profitably employed by the capitalist class", but even if this is so, if "credit" – by which "general interrelations of the entire reproductive process" are developed – is excluded, does this not overlook the cause itself of

reasons that animate my 1937 article on 'Money Capital and Real Capital', in which I introduce Marx's many statements in that chapter (see my *Studies in Capital* as well as *UKC*, Vol. 3).

20 *Capital*, Vol. 3, pp. 614–15.

a sudden outbreak of crisis? Of course, when we theorise crisis generally, we must not theorise it simply as a commercial crisis or financial crisis. However, in theorising crisis generally, there is not the slightest reason why we should theoretically exclude how the expansion of the reproduction process proceeds by passing through credit.

Now, it goes without saying that the disproportions and imbalances between different productive sectors may have to be adjusted no matter what, even by crisis. However, this imbalance is something that is constantly passing through and adjusted by the movement of prices, and so we cannot say that this imbalance can be resolved by crisis necessarily. By contrast, the consuming power restricted by class relationships is nothing less than the ground of crisis, as something that indicates capital's inability to organise productive power through its own form. This is demonstrated in the aforementioned Chapter 15 of Volume 3. However, for a crisis to actually burst forth from this ground, it must come up upon apparatuses, which disclose to individual capitals how accumulation, as the total capital, turns into something meaningless. And is not the credit system precisely that which animates these apparatuses?

In very blunt terms, in *Capital* – in which profits of commercial capital are explained in opposition to industrial capital, and in which the concept of interest-bearing capital unfolds on the basis of commercial capital – there is an unavoidable sense that, for interest-bearing capital, and of course for commercial capital, rather than being developed from within industrial capital, they have been somehow externally added from the outside. As I have described earlier, while commercial credit is considered in a pure form as, "the credit that the capitalists involved in reproduction give one another",[21] this point does not unfold throughout the exposition in a consistent manner. We could thus say that the way Marx examines industrial capital followed by commercial capital hinders this exposition.

In demonstrating crisis within the framework of the fundamental principles, when we say that foreign trade must be abstracted, this is natural for the theory of fundamental principles. The same can be said for commerce, which, as something operated independently by commercial capital, only complicates the phenomena, causing us to lose sight of the problematic points. Thus, commerce must also be abstracted, which is not to say that it is the same thing as foreign trade, a point I will consider later. Therefore, while foreign trade will naturally be examined later, it must be abstracted within the fundamental principles. For, we must never be distracted by all the phenomena of the cir-

21 *Capital*, Vol. 3, p. 610.

culation process that are separate from the production process. However, this should not lead us to treat, in a same fashion, "the credit which the capitalists engaged in reproduction give to one another". On the contrary, this point has to be examined in relation to how, for individual industrial capitals, the fundamental determination that, "the true limit to capitalist production is capital itself," cannot be clarified by way of these apparatuses alone. As long as credit can appear as a pure form like this, it will not complicate problems needlessly like foreign trade or commercial capital.

3

Crisis must not be theorised simply as a monetary crisis or as a credit crisis because monetary crisis and credit crisis can appear even when they are separated or isolated from the reproduction process. The reason, for example, that the crises of the seventeenth and eighteenth centuries cannot illustrate the fundamental determinations for a theory of crisis is that these crises cannot be said to have appeared apart from the capitalist reproduction process itself. But when industrial capital enlarges the social reproduction process by mutually and elastically accommodating idle funds to each other, these credit relations of industrial capital are now already tied to the reproduction process, and are thus never separated from it. Quite the opposite takes place; they carry out the fundamental development of the capitalist reproduction process. As I pointed out earlier, credit relations are capitalist apparatuses which develop regulations of individual capitals by *social* capital, while the former enlarges the reproduction process until it cannot be expanded any further on the same scale, and does so in a capitalistic, social way.

In actuality, and similar to merchant capital or commercial capital, the banks, as an institution that mediates these credit relations, do not simply make the idle funds of industrial capital available. Funds which cannot be said to have arisen directly from the capitalist reproduction process itself are also made available to industrial capital. While it does not go so far as to consider these credit relations in themselves in terms of the theory of the fundamental principles, "the credit which the capitalists engaged in reproduction give to one another" is, theoretically speaking, a fundamental capital relation that goes one step further than the independently shared capital relation, which allows commercial capital to independently carry out the commercial activities of industrial capital. That relation is one between industrial capitalists, and even when these develop, they should not be located on the so-called outside of industrial capital as independent capitals like commercial capital. Of course, various lending and borrowing relations develop new determinations as loanable capital. In these relations, interest comes to be paid in a way that is similar to how rent is paid on the leasing of land. Here, industrial capitalists, as such, become loan capitalists to each other, but even when banking capital becomes independent as a mediating institution of credit, this basic point is not altered. The fundamental ground of banking capital in fact becomes clarified for the first time. More so than commercial capital, banking capital, which serves as the simple, mediating institution between industrial capitals, is a much simpler thing, and appears merely as a capital that possesses the form of so-called merchant capital.

Due to the fact that commercial capital is explained, in *Capital*, as if commercial capital were in opposition to industrial capital at the same time that it is often explained like merchant capital – that is to say, as something on the outside of industrial capital, as I have already discussed previously – it seems to me that this makes it difficult to explain loanable capital in such a pure form. At the same time, the capital as an automatically interest-bearing force is immediately viewed as the same thing as loanable capital, which is then explained as capital that is already commodified (see *Capital*, Volume 3, Ch. 21). Here, however, capital is not commodified. For loan capital, the value of capital is always passed onto the borrower. Capital is not sold as a commodity; rather, money – as funds – is commodified, and therefore sold for definite periods of time. Capital becomes commodified and sold as so-called fictitious capital on the basis of interest formed by loanable capital, and only when it becomes independent as something that automatically bears interest through the mediation of commercial capital.

My opinion on this point is that, in the same way that Marx treated commercial capital as if it were like merchant capital, and as a natural result of it, Marx must have explained loanable capital as something akin to money-lending capital, existing on the so-called exterior of the capitalist reproduction process. This misconception severely hinders the explanation of how the collision – between falling rates of profit of industrial capital and the sudden rise in interest rates – creates the momentum for the outbreak of crisis. As I have described earlier, if loan capital can be said to emerge from between industrial capitals themselves, then the explanation of this collision, as an explanation of crisis, decidedly cannot be reduced to a mere theory of credit crisis. Even if we were to suppose, like Marx, that, "the whole of society is composed only of industrial capitalists and wage workers", these relations still are able to be developed, and capital must also be naturally seen to develop these credit relations. It cannot be said, therefore, that, "a crisis would be explicable only in terms of a disproportion in production between different branches and a disproportion between the consumption of the capitalists themselves and their accumulation." Thus, while it is not mistaken for Marx to write that, "The ultimate reason for all real crises always remains the poverty and restricted consumption of the masses, in the face of the drive of capitalist production to develop the productive forces as if only the absolute consumption capacity of society set a limit to them", the essential meaning of this determination will not be truly grasped unless it is understood from within the relationships in which industrial capital brings out all of its abilities by mutually extending credit. As Marx says elsewhere, the limit of surplus production that constitutes the basis of capital's accumulation is, "*capital* itself, the existing level of the conditions of production and the unlimited desire of the capitalist to enrich themselves and to enlarge their capital, but by no means [is it] *consumption*, which from the outset is inhibited, since the majority of the population, the working people, can only expand their consumption within very narrow limits, whereas the demand for labour, although it grows *absolutely*, decreases *relatively*."[22] In fact, "crises are always prepared by a period in which wages generally rise, and the working class actually does receive a greater share in the part of the annual product destined for consumption."[23] To say that "the ultimate reason for all real crises always remains the poverty and restricted consumption of the masses" does not mean that crises could be averted if, "the working class receives too small a portion of its own product, and that the evil would be remedied if it received a bigger share, i.e., if its wages rose", or that crises could be averted by doing so.[24] In fact, the opposite is true.

Concluding Remarks

Even if we cannot confirm whether or not Marx himself believed, as Professor Kuruma did, that a theory of crisis necessarily remained incomplete within the categories of *Capital*, so long as we recognise that *Capital* addresses capitalism's general and fundamental determinations, it is impossible to claim that it must not develop a 'proper theory of crisis'. Of course, the actual analysis of crises, in connection to the world market, is found outside of the categories of *Capital*. By this we can infer that it is 'proper' to 'crisis' in Marx's systematic plan in *The Critique of Political Economy*. Yet, it is likely that a clarification of the determinations set by world-historical stages of capitalism would have to precede such

22 Marx, *Theories of Surplus Value*, Part II (1951), p. 492.
23 *Capital*, Vol. 2, pp. 486–87.
24 Ibid.

an analysis of the processes of concrete crises. While it is certain that a theory of crisis encompasses the formal determinations of world-historical development, or the concrete analysis of particular crises, these things must be given the name of special research on crisis. There is no reason why, in contrast to the general determinations set out by a text such as *Capital*, these concrete analyses should especially be given the name of a 'proper theory of crisis'. To say that a theory of crisis was never fully developed in *Capital*, and that it is therefore impossible to demonstrate the inevitability of crisis with the fundamental principles of political economy, would simply seem to suggest that *Capital*, as a scholarly legacy, has not been fully utilised.

Of course, the foregoing theorisation merely represents my own speculative attempts based on logic that I learned for myself from *Capital*. It represents neither my research into the history of crises, nor my individual research based on the examination of various scholarly discourses related to crisis. One may find points in my argument that do not understand the true intentions of *Capital* or that even violate historical facts. In speaking of a theory of crisis, however, I do not believe that proper respect is paid to *Capital* when the "various statements regarding crisis, which are scattered throughout *Capital*"[25] are merely gathered and strung together.

25 Kuruma 1936, p. 95.

APPENDIX 2

Capital and the Demonstration of the Inevitable Ground of Crisis

In my essay, 'Problematic Points in the Theory of Crisis in *Das Kapital*',[1] I argued that a theory of crisis in *Capital*, which introjects historico-concrete factors such as merchant capital into its theory, and which does not develop loanable capital in a pure form on the level of a theory of fundamental principles, is hindered by following a logical development and contains points that are extremely difficult to understand.[2] Here, however, I would especially like to pursue and clarify another difficult point, namely that of searching for the ground of the inevitability of crisis in a capitalist society, and in the development of the internal contradictions of the law of the tendency of the general profit rate to fall.

1

Volume 3, Part 3 of *Capital* theorises 'The Law of the Tendential Fall in the rate of Profit'. Chapter 15, 'The Development of the Law's Internal Contradictions', clarifies the process by which the tendency of the profit rate to fall, which accompanies an advance in the productive forces, appears in a specific form; it also clarifies the ground of the inevitability of crisis that cannot but accompany the phenomenon of crisis peculiar to capitalist society. It thus clarifies the development of the contradiction of the process, by which the productive forces advance by a method in which the endless increase of value, which represents the fundamental drive of the development of capitalist society, is restricted capitalistically. The point that requires careful consideration here, however, is that the increase of value, as the immediate purpose of capitalist production and as its fundamental drive, is not something that is exclusively dependent on the advance of productive forces, itself based on the improvements of methods of production. "Assuming the necessary means of production, i.e., a sufficient accumulation of capital, the creation of surplus-value

1 [See Appendix 1.]
2 [Originally published in *Keizai Kenkyū*, 3, no. 4 (October 1952).]

faces no other barrier than the working population, if the rate of surplus-value, i.e., the level of exploitation of labour, is given; and no other barrier than this level of exploitation, if the working population is given."[3] As clarified in *Capital*, Volume 1, Chapter 23, accumulation stemming from the transformation of surplus value into capital takes place in two ways, accumulation occurring with "the composition of capital remaining the same", and with "the changing composition of capital." The "law of the tendency of the profit rate to fall" thus appears as something in which falling rates of profit, on the one hand, are compensated by a rise in the mass of profit, on the other, so that accumulation always includes both of these aspects.

Of course, even in Volume 3 of *Capital*, Marx did not ignore these two aspects. This is true especially in the third section of Chapter 15 of Volume 3, "Surplus Capital alongside Surplus Population", but here these two aspects are theorised, by and large, as occurring simultaneously, which makes the logical development of this chapter extremely difficult, it seems to me. Once the advance of the productive forces takes place as something "accompanying the change in the composition of capital", so long as this is the case, a surplus population of workers – one that is relative to capital – will be created, and now it can be said that the products of capital, i.e., the means of production as well as the means of subsistence, will form, all on their own, the fundamental conditions for the transformation into capital. Therefore, if accumulation "accompanying the change in the composition of capital" also includes that aspect of accumulation which takes place "without a change in the composition of capital" and as the simple expansion of the scale of production, then the fundamental contradiction of capitalism will constantly be resolved while the accumulation of capital will advance infinitely. The problem is: To what extent will the relative surplus population, formed by the rising composition of capital, be able to transform the means of production and the means of subsistence, as capital's products, into capital? Of course, even in this scenario, capitalism, as that which proceeds through blind and anarchical commodity production, by no means displays a constant, even relation between the two. On the contrary, an excess or deficiency of the means of production and means of subsistence, as capital, constantly arises, and because of this there are times when the falling rate of profit cannot even be compensated for by an increase in the magnitude of profit. However, this kind of unevenness does not necessarily appear in a definite period of time. It rather appears as something that is unceasing, and unceasingly corrected by passing through the movement of prices.

3 *Capital*, Vol. 3, p. 351.

Capitalist production develops according to the so-called business cycle in which, after a more or less definite period of prosperity, it passes through crisis and falls into depression, and after a definite period turns back into prosperity once again. This distinctive process, viewed broadly – that is, as that which contains within it various cyclical processes, and as a total process of capitalist development – is one in which the expansion of the scale of production is steadily realised, on the one hand, with the advance of the productive forces based on the rising organic composition of capital, and, on the other, with the addition of the formation of a relative surplus population that accompanies these developments with the natural multiplication of the population. In this sense, it can be said that the advance of capital's accumulation is something that includes these two aspects, which can be said to have a mutually supplementary relationship to each other. However, this does not clarify why capitalist development proceeds cyclically through prosperity, crisis, and depression, or at least why prosperity and depression continue for a definite period and are both connected by crisis. It never clarifies the periodicity of crisis. We could even say that the actuality of crisis will never be grasped unless the inevitability of crisis is clarified in terms of its periodicity. Even if crisis phenomena can be said to present themselves in in the cessation of production resulting from price fluctuations and the disturbance of the reproduction process, this still does not address the inevitability of crisis in capitalist society. The inevitability of crisis is found where the cessation of production and the disturbance of reproduction break out periodically. What has to be clarified is how crisis necessarily appears with a periodicity and as a definite economic law of motion of the capitalist economy. It is regarding this point that I also have doubts as to whether the ground of crisis can be provided by Marx's famous prescription that, "the conditions for immediate exploitation and for the realisation of that exploitation are not identical".[4]

2

Following Marx's discussion of the above-mentioned restrictions placed upon the production of surplus value, his next point is that the production of surplus value does not necessarily guarantee its realisation. This is summarised in 'The Exposition of the Internal Contradictions of the Law', in *Capital*, Volume 3, Chapter 15. His argument, however, is not as simple as it may seem at first blush.

4 [Transl. note: *Capital*, Vol. 3, p. 352.]

Let us, therefore, delineate the problem more closely, allowing us to quote at length the pertinent passage:

> As soon as the amount of surplus labour it has proved possible to extort has been objectified in commodities, the surplus-value has been produced. But this production of surplus-value is only the first act in the capitalist production process, and its completion only brings to an end the immediate production process itself. Capital has absorbed a given amount of unpaid labour. With the development of this process as expressed in the fall in the profit rate, the mass of surplus-value thus produced swells to monstrous proportions. Now comes the second act in the process. The total mass of commodities, the total product, must be sold, both that portion which replaces constant and variable capital and that which represents surplus-value. If this does not happen, or happens only partly, or only at prices that are less than the price of production, then although the worker is certainly exploited, his exploitation is not realized as such for the capitalist and may even not involve any realization of the surplus-value extracted, or only a partial realization; indeed, it may even mean a partial or complete loss of his capital.[5]

Marx continues by pointing out that, "the conditions for immediate exploitation and for the realization of that exploitation are not identical", and that, "the former is restricted only limited by the society's productive power, the latter by the proportionality between the various branches of production and by the society's power of consumption". Regarding the 'society's power of consumption', Marx writes that it is, "neither by the absolute power of production nor by the absolute power of consumption but rather by the power of consumption within a given framework of antagonistic conditions of distribution, which reduce the consumption of the vast majority of society to a minimum level, only capable of varying within more or less narrow limits."[6]

The "exposition of contradiction", discussed in this section, is thus related to the impossibility of the realisation of the produced surplus value, precisely because it develops out of the opposition between the production and realisation of surplus value. Marx explains that the "total mass of commodities ... must be sold" and whether "this does not happen," is "restricted ... by the proportionality between the various branches of production and by society's power of

5 *Capital*, Vol. 3, p. 352.

6 *Capital*, Vol. 3, ibid.

consumption," and therefore realises that crisis is caused by this fact. However, when Marx says, almost verbatim, that, "a crisis could only be explained as the result of a disproportion of production in different branches of the economy, and as a result of a disproportion between the consumption of the capitalists and their accumulation", he says that we must, "leave aside those changes in price which prevent large portions of the total capital from being replaced in their average proportions."[7] Moreover, when Marx writes that, "the consumption capacity of the workers is restricted partly by the laws of wages and partly by the fact that they are employed only as long as they can be employed at a profit for the capitalist class", this point is not reducible to how commodities cannot be sold at a definite price, or to, "the power of consumption within a given framework of antagonistic conditions of distribution, which reduce the consumption of the vast majority of society to a minimum level, only capable of varying within more or less narrow limits", or else to the consumption power of the capitalist that is, "restricted by the tendency to accumulate." Especially when we consider, "the antagonistic conditions of distribution", this does not merely signify the economic "laws of wages". Rather, the explanation may have to include the fact that, "they are employed only as long as they can be employed at a profit for the capitalist class."[8] Had this explanation been included, then we could perhaps justify "leav[ing] aside" whether commodities "are not sold or '[sold] only in part'" in terms of prices. Or, here, too, are "price fluctuations, to the extent that they 'prevent large portions of the total capital from replacing themselves in their average proportions', to be 'disregarded'"?

The problem is that, if it includes how the consumption power of workers is "restricted ... by the fact that they are employed only as long as they can be employed at a profit for the capitalist class", we cannot say that this is simply a matter of, "the conditions for immediate exploitation", for there is already a problem implied in, "the conditions for immediate exploitation." The production of surplus value, as mentioned above, is determined by the rate of surplus value and the population of workers based on the assumption of sufficient accumulation. Similarly, "the conditions of immediate exploitation", which "are only limited by the productive power of society", are not only determined by the rate of surplus value. If "necessary means of production" and means of subsistence are produced, even if they are invested as capital, it will be impossible to realise productivity, which appears as a definite rate of surplus value, unless a labouring population is not adequately given. From this point of view, we

7 *Capital*, Vol. 3, p. 614.
8 *Capital*, Vol. 3, p. 615.

cannot say that commodities become an excess simply because of the conditions in which commodities "are not [sold] or [sold] only in part, or only at prices below the prices of production". The problem is not simply that excess appears as commodities. Rather, excess comes into being because it exists as capital, and for this reason, excess also exists as commodities. It means that both means of production and subsistence have been produced too much as capital for workers to be "profitably employed by the capitalist class." Already in "the first act of the capitalist process of production", capital is not able to "absorb unpaid labour" enough. In this way, the means of production and subsistence cannot avoid becoming excessive, even as commodities.

Generally speaking, crisis is explained as something resulting from the impossibility of selling commodities, or from selling them "only at prices below their production prices." This is true, but this is not simply because there is not a buyer. In a capitalist society, whether the "proportional relation of the different branches of production" or the "consumer power of society" forms a buyer of commodities, it is found within capital's reproduction process. It thus becomes impossible for the "proportional relation of the different branches of production" or the "consumer power of society" to form the buyer, if workers cannot be "profitably employed by the capitalist class". Most importantly, as we have already pointed out in the above-mentioned essay, whether or not workers can be "profitably employed" does not directly become a behavioural standard for individual industrial capitals. We think that this point reveals the special significance of loanable capital that accompanies the inevitability of crisis, but practically speaking, the essential problem does not appear with any real clarity, for excess capital is concealed by its inventory and stock which result from interventions by commercial capital, and especially by the speculations of merchant capital, which raise prices suddenly and speculatively. Moreover, credit relations themselves are enlarged in a speculative manner. All of these secondary factors are actually implied within the argument that crisis appears as the impossibility of selling commodities.

The above-stated points, which Marx described in Section 1, 'General', together with the relationship between the magnitude of advanced capital and the mass of profit, which he continues on to discuss, and the problem of the concentration of capital that accompanies the rising of the composition of capital, may all be interpreted as an endeavour to elucidate the fundamental cause of crisis through the various phenomena accompanying the increase in capital's composition. However, Marx writes that:

> the more productivity develops, the more it comes into conflict with the narrow basis on which the relations of consumption rest. It is in no way

> a contradiction, on this contradictory basis, that excess capital coexists with a growing surplus population; for although the mass of surplus-value produced would rise if these were brought together, yet this would equally heighten the contradiction between the conditions in which this surplus-value was produced and the conditions in which it was realized.[9]

Here, Marx risks resolving the relationship between excess capital and surplus populations in the period of crisis into the contradiction between the conditions of the production of surplus value and the conditions of its realisation. This then opens the way to explanations of crisis in terms of underconsumption or overproduction.

3

However, even in Section 2, "The Conflict Between the Extension of Production and Valorization", the advance of productivity that accompanies capital's accumulation is only developed in terms of the rising composition of capital, as "the development of the social productivity of labour".[10] The increased mass of employed capital is considered to be something that always takes place at the same time that an increase in the composition of capital accompanies a fall in the general profit rate. Marx writes that, "Once the rate is given, the absolute amount by which capital grows depends on its existing magnitude. But if this magnitude is given, the proportion in which it grows, i.e. its rate of growth, depends on the profit rate."[11] What this leaves out of consideration are the limits stemming from the labouring population. Instead, quite the opposite comes into view: "Insofar … as the higher rate of profit gives rise to an increased demand for labour, it leads to an increase in the working population and hence in the exploitable material which is precisely what makes capital capital."[12] This, however, merely supplements the formation of a relative surplus population that accompanies a rising composition of capital. Even from the perspective of an advance in accumulation, in which the development of the productive power of labour increases, "the mass and diversity of use values … which form the material substratum, the objective elements of capital," Marx only states that, "Since the mass of labour applied thus grows, and the mass of

9 *Capital*, Vol. 3, p. 353.
10 *Capital*, Vol. 3, p. 355.
11 *Capital*, Vol. 3, p. 356.
12 *Capital*, Vol. 3, p. 356.

surplus labour with it, the value of the capital reproduced and the surplus-value newly added to it grow as well."[13]

Thus:

> Simultaneously with impulses towards a genuine increase in the working population, which stem from the increase in the portion of the total social product that functions as capital, we have those agencies that create a relative surplus population.
>
> Simultaneously with the fall in the profit rate, the mass of capital grows, and this is associated with a devaluation of the existing capital, which puts a stop to this fall and gives an accelerating impulse to the accumulation of capital value.
>
> Simultaneously with the development of productivity, the composition of capital becomes higher, there is a relative decline in the variable portion as against the constant.
>
> These various influences sometimes tend to exhibit themselves side by side, spatially; at other times one after the other, temporally; and at certain points the conflict of contending agencies breaks through in crises.[14]

Thus, concludes Marx. The problem here, however, is that we cannot grasp why crises necessarily appear with a periodicity.

Here, what becomes visible is how the general tendencies of the development of the capitalist method of production, which are accompanied by the cyclical process of prosperity, crisis, and depression, are defined as a whole. But it must also be said that what remains unclear is why this cycle must pass through these distinct phases. When Marx says, "Capitalist production seeks continually to overcome these immanent barriers, but overcomes them only by means which again place these barriers in its way and on a more formidable scale", he defines the development of capitalist production methods based on a comparison between one cycle and the next, but he does not clarify how these contradictions and their solutions take place within a single cycle in which prosperity develops into crisis, and depression develops into prosperity. This is how I understand the problem at hand, which also stems from the fact that this chapter (i.e., Chapter 15), is titled 'Development of the Law's Internal Contradictions'. Rather than explaining the internal contradictions of capitalist methods of production itself, Marx only explains the internal contradictions

---

13 *Capital*, Vol. 3, pp. 356–57.

14 *Capital*, Vol. 3, p. 357.

and the exposition of the law of the tendency of the profit to fall, which can be said to be just one phenomenal appearance of the former contradictions.

Now, it goes without saying that the exposition of law of the tendency of the general rate of profit to fall can only be developed on the basis of the givenness of the labouring population. Put differently, Marx's observations go no further than showing how a rise in capital's composition, which brings about a fall in the profit rate, forms by itself a relative surplus population, which can be used in accumulation. If, in Marx's observations of the law of the tendency of the profit to fall, he considered the limits stemming from the labouring population, his observations would contain unnecessary complications. Ultimately, the development of capitalist methods of production itself points to the 'tendency of the general rate of profit to fall'. This, in itself, is not a problem to say. It is a problem, however, to say that the actuality of the development of capitalist methods of production is determined solely by the dimension of accumulation in which a constant fall in the general profit rate is said to present itself. What begs emphasis is less the 'Exposition of the Internal Contradictions of the Law', and more an "exposition of the internal contradictions of capitalist methods of production". Marx's definition that, "the *real barrier* of capitalist production is *capital* itself", as well as the above-mentioned definition that, "Capitalist production seeks continually to overcome these immanent barriers" surely comes to life when we consider these points. This is also further elaborated upon by Marx in Section 3 of the same chapter, titled 'Surplus of capital alongside surplus populations'.

4

In Section 3, however, we see the unavoidable influence of the exposition of Sections 1 and 2, described above. When Marx explains that the, "Overproduction of capital and not of individual commodities – though overproduction of capital always involves overproduction of commodities – is nothing more than over-accumulation of capital," he says that with the overaccumulation of capital, "we have only to take it as an absolute," and then assumes that, "no further additional capital could be employed for the purpose of capitalist production."[15] In other words, with the advance of capital's accumulation, Marx writes that:

15 *Capital*, Vol. 3, p. 360.

> [A]s soon as capital has grown in such proportion to the working population that neither the absolute labour-time that this working population supplies nor its relative surplus labour-time can be extended (the latter would not be possible in any case in a situation where the demand for labour was so strong, and there was thus a tendency for wages to rise); where, therefore, the expanded capital produces only the same mass of surplus-value as before or even less, there will be an absolute overproduction of capital.[16]

Additional capitals, therefore, become meaningless when, due to sudden rises in wages, relatively larger capitals are unable to produce more profits compared to the originally smaller capitals. In this way, Marx clarifies how, unlike the general case of a fall in the general profit rate, "a change in the composition of capital", as the cause of this special case, "would not be due to a development in productivity, but rather to a rise in the money value of the variable capital on account of higher wages and to a corresponding decline in the proportion of surplus labour to necessary labour."[17] For Marx, however, these points fall under what he calls, "the most extreme assumption".[18] However, the manner by which he defines this case as an "extreme," is based, on the one hand (and as I have previously described), on the assumption that the advance in capital's accumulation is accompanied by the rise in the composition of capital, and, on the other hand, on a definition of a method of "settlement" or "resolution" of the excess of capital.[19]

Thus, the first point is that this kind of fall in the profit rate cannot avoid being seen under "extreme" assumptions and conditions, arguably because it overlooks the point that capital's accumulation, which depends on a given composition of capital, advances quantitatively. Simultaneously, therefore, Marx is not able to explain why the "extreme" conditions necessarily appear with a definite periodicity. The problematic point is that the restrictions on the labouring population, by which capital accumulation is made meaningless for capital, are said to appear under "the most extreme assumption", and

16 *Capital*, Vol. 3, ibid.

17 *Capital*, Vol. 3, ibid.

18 *Capital*, Vol. 3, p. 364. [Transl. note. Marx writes, "Even under the most extreme assumption that might be made, absolute overproduction of capital is not absolute overproduction in general, not absolute overproduction of the means of production. It is an overproduction of means of production only insofar as *these function as capital*, and hence have to produce an additional value in proportion to their value that has expanded together with their mass, i.e., to have to valorize their value."]

19 *Capital*, Vol. 3, p. 362.

as long as the accumulation of capital is assumed to advance *constantly*, forming a relative surplus population that attends a constant rise in the composition of capital.

The second point pertains to the idea that this kind of fall in the profit rate immediately sets off a process of making capital idle. '[The] portion of ΔC that was already in their hands lie more or less idle, so as not to devalue their own original capital themselves and not constrict its place in the field of production, or else they would apply it so as to shift the idleness of the additional capital onto the more recent interlopers and onto their competitors in general, even at a temporary loss.'[20] By contrast, 'the part of ΔC that was in new hands would attempt to find a place for itself at the cost of the old capital, and would partly succeed in this, forcing a portion of the old capital to lie idle. It would compel this to evacuate its former place and would itself take the place of the additional capital that was employed only partially or not at all.'[21] However – and I am not sure if we can really say this based on the above-mentioned quotation alone, but – the competition between capitals here is one that occurs after investments in a given industry have already been made, and not for investments yet to come. If that were the case, then, overall, even if the profit rate were to fall, and even if only a smaller quantity of profit were to be gained by capitals that are relatively larger than before, we wonder whether this would necessarily cause individual capitals to lie idle. In fact, when Marx writes that, "The part of ΔC in the hands of old functioning capitalists would be allowed to remain more or less idle to prevent a depreciation of their own original capital", he should have perhaps explained how it is also withheld for future investments. Regardless of cases in which these capitalists seize a monopolistic position, in cases when they are not in this position, is it correct to therefore assume that ΔC is not invested and becomes idle, on its own, for individual capitals? What can be said minimally is that this additional capital of ΔC in this case will naturally be invested directly in industry, be used by commercial credit or loan capital, or in any case be used in some social form for the expansion of industry. In such a case, it seems to me that the profit rate would have to fall. Put differently, we cannot say that, for individual capitals, excess capital can be transformed directly – at least as a way of avoiding the fall in profit rates – into idle funds.

In fact, it is not necessarily true that, for individual capitals, if only a smaller profit is earned from the use of progressively larger capitals than before,

20 *Capital*, Vol. 3, p. 361.

21 Ibid.

this would directly lead to a "sharing [of] losses", in which "each seeks as far as he can to restrict his own share of this loss and pass it on to someone else."[22] What we can at least dismiss is the assumption that a fall in profit rates, due to sudden rises in wages, would allow "ΔC in the hands of old functioning capitalists ... to remain more or less idle". Rather, it "would [be] employ[ed], even at a temporary loss", or else it would be used by commercial credit or loanable capital, as we have already mentioned. Moreover, we think, "[t]hat portion of ΔC which is in new hands" would be invested "at the expense of the old capital", thus obtaining progressively smaller profits by the use of larger capitals.

I have written about this relation in a separate essay (Appendix 1), where I explained how the situation of "accumulation, as the total capital [that has become] something that is meaningless, is clarified for the individual capitalists" through the mediation of interest rates. Therefore, the "method of settlement" that transforms excess capital into idle funds does not take place immediately in the hands of individual capitals. Rather, in my understanding, it is settled and resolved by passing through the credit system, and thus social regulations that cannot be actualised individually are actualised with the transformation of the said idle funds into loanable capital. It is here, it seems to me, that we can clarify why crisis breaks out in a certain period on the basis of enlarged production, which socially uses the idle funds of individual capitals.

In *Capital*, Marx writes that, "The same causes that have raised the productivity of labour, increased the mass of commodity products, extended markets, accelerated the accumulation of capital, in terms of both mass and value, and lowered the rate of profit, these same causes have produced, and continue constantly to produce, a relative surplus population".[23] As an overall tendency, this description is fine, but nonetheless it also cannot clarify why crisis breaks out at a certain period, or why crisis is periodically and necessarily repeated.

5

Marx writes that, "Periodically, however, too much is produced in the way of means of labour and means of subsistence, too much to function as means for exploiting the workers at a given rate of profit."[24] However, so long as the profit rate is conceived as an incessant tendency to fall, which includes the rise in

22 Ibid.

23 *Capital*, Vol. 3, p. 364.

24 *Capital*, Vol. 3., p. 367.

the rate of surplus value and the formation of a relative surplus population, the periodic overaccumulation of capital that causes crisis has to be treated as that which happens under an "extreme" assumptions or conditions (as already described above), or else as that which develops out of, "a disproportion of production in different branches of the economy, and as a result of a disproportion between the consumption of the capitalists and their accumulation." This, however, is never explained as something that appears inevitably, with its own, determinate periodicity; it is only explained as something that appears occasionally. Moreover, while capitalist production, which has the principle of pursuing extra-profits by *constantly* seeking to introduce new methods of production, it is impossible to change the already invested capital – the fixed capital, in the form of means of labour in particular – so incessantly. Additional capitals are not always invested separately from old capitals. When a certain method of production prevails, old capitals are intermittently transformed into the latest means of labour – for example, during the time to replace the fixed capital that has been invested for the former period, and especially when there is an urgency to make replacements. The introduction of new methods by additional capitals have different meanings depending on whether or not they are introduced as a means of extrication from the awkward situations of the phase of depression after crisis. As Marx stated, if, especially after crisis, "The fall in prices and the competitive struggle ... impel each capitalist to reduce the individual value of his total product below its general value by employing new machinery, new and improved methods of labour and new forms of combination,"[25] this is when what Marx calls an "artificial surplus population" is added to a labouring population that has already become a surplus population through the suspension of production, providing the standard of the replacement and new implementation of means of labour, as fixed capital, for the next phase of prosperity. Thus, until the expansion of production is accompanied by an absorption of workers which reduces the surplus population, raises wages, and thus brings about a fall in profit rates, we should rather say that, based on these standards, capital's accumulation is found in its tendency towards quantitative advances. Moreover, in actuality, the profit rate that is said to fall due to a rise in wages is concealed by the interventions of speculation, which we have already described.

In phases of prosperity, an expansion of production is based on an already given composition of capital, one that, of course, is much higher compared to the level of composition in the previous period of prosperity, and that has

25 *Capital*, Vol. 3, p. 363.

already formed a relative surplus population through the simple renewal of means of production. This given composition of capital absorbs progressively more and more of the labouring population, along with the new construction and expansion of means of production, by realizing the phase of prosperity to extend production. This process of expanded reproduction with a given composition of capital is then turned into the phase of depression, where an excess of means of production and means of subsistence appears, which cannot be employed as capital with the given, existing composition of capital, and which forces individual capitalists to adopt new production methods to gain extra profits, resulting in the creation of an "artificial surplus population" in addition to the surplus population already brought into existence by the reduction and stagnation of production. The theoretical ground of crisis is to be clarified as the phase in the business cycles which necessarily, and periodically, unites these two phases. Simultaneously, what is clarified is how crisis, which manifests the contradictions between the forces and relations of production in capitalist society, is a process which is developed around the axis of the commodification of labour power, which is both the fundamental presupposition of capitalist society and the fundamental difficulty of capitalist society. While this does not directly signify the collapse of capitalist society, it is a manifestation that includes or connotes the possibility of this collapse. Explaining crisis in this way must be a task of the theory of the fundamental principles of political economy.

Guiding Comments

Makoto Itoh

1 A Basic Frame of Reference for the Subprime Crisis

In the blink of an eye, the American financial crisis that erupted in 2007 became a global economic crisis that threatened people's livelihoods. This global crisis was originally called the subprime crisis. After decades of negligence, economic crisis and all of its calamities had suddenly become an important concern in the mass media, as well as in everyday conversations around the world.

The subprime crisis had its direct origins in the collapse of the American housing market and in the speculative financial expansion surrounding the housing mortgage loan market until the autumn of 2006. That expansion lasted for nearly ten years and widely supported the US economic recovery, especially after 2002. By the end of 2006, the balance of US housing loans had reached 13 trillion dollars in total, roughly comparable to the amount of the American GDP. If the average housing loan can be assumed to have been about 300,000 dollars, then about 43,300,000 households (or about 43.3 percent of American households) were given the ability to purchase new houses. If one includes furniture and electrical appliances that accompany new home purchases, one can catch a glimpse of just how large the world-leading American consumption boom, and the consumer finance that fuelled it, were. Within that figure, the so-called subprime loans – that is, the housing loans to people without sufficient creditworthiness to be considered for prime loans – are estimated to have been about 13 percent of the total. Considering that the standard subprime loan was, on average, 200,000 dollars, these loans allowed roughly 8.5 million households to purchase new houses. As the housing market reversed and fell, the numbers of sluggish or failed repayments and resultant foreclosures increased sharply after 2007, leading to the large social problem of more than two million households being thrown out of their homes. (Michael Moore's *Capitalism* vividly captures this scenery on film.) In essence, in our age of capitalism, the financialisation of labour power can now be apparently added to the principle of the commodification of labour power, which, as Uno emphasised in this volume, is the basic source of contradiction of the capitalist economy. As a consequence, so many working-class households became expropriated through plundering and predatory housing loans.

On the other hand, the expansion of US housing loans in this period was characterized by a system of 'shadow banking', which mobilized global idle money funds. This was carried out by means of composing multiple and complex layers of securities based upon bundles of home mortgage loans, as well as upon derivatives to sell on the world market. When the US housing market began to fall and failures in repayment of housing loans increased, those layers of securities had to decrease their prices and ratings, and in the end created a huge amount of bad debt. As a result, the collapse of hedge funds affiliated with large European and American banks, as well as increased bank losses, which led to managerial crises, became increasingly frequent after the summer of 2007. All of this led to the historically largest-ever bankruptcy, when the American investment bank and securities firm Lehman Brothers collapsed in September 2008.

The impact and losses from the so-called Lehman Shock spread globally through the linkages that mediated financial institutions, the stock market and other financial markets.

Thus, the subprime economic crisis developed into a capitalist worldwide crisis, as Uno had pointed out on page 18 of this volume: "Originally, crisis always appeared phenomenally as a financial crisis, emerging, to a considerable extent, when payments on loans could not be met, and when loan funds were simultaneously uncollected to a considerable extent." Beginning in America, and then even in the European countries, public funds were injected into all financial markets, one after another, in emergency rescue operations, and central bank relief financing was mobilised. The shock spread to the real economy, and employment continued to worsen. (For more details, see M. Itoh [2009] [*From the Subprime to the World Crisis*], Seido-sha).

The former Federal Reserve Chair, Alan Greenspan, called this financial crisis a 'once in a century tsunami'. Greenspan's description captures the large and destructive scale of this calamity, but its essence was not really a natural disaster. The global crisis was rather essentially the contemporary expression of the fundamental contradictions and unstable self-destructiveness inherent in the capitalist economic system, brought about by the wide acceptance of capitalism's immanent tendency to pursue efficiency and rationality just for moneymaking, and through free and competitive markets, unleashed from the yoke of social regulation and control by neoliberalism after the 1980s.

The essential characteristic of the subprime crisis was thus very different from the Japanese economic crisis caused by the earthquake and giant tsunami in Japan in March 2011 (called "the Great East Japan Earthquake"), or the more recent world crisis caused by the pandemic of the new corona virus in 2020, both of which can be said to have been caused by actual, natural disasters such as terrible earthquakes, tsunamis, or serious plagues that destroy supply chains, transportation, and consumer demand in the real economy, and which were accompanied also by financial distress. Unlike these crises, the subprime crisis was entirely caused internally by the autonomous expansion of the capitalist market economy under neoliberalism, and especially originated from the US economy as its global center.

However, neoclassical micro-economics, which constitutes the theoretical foundation of neoliberalism, cannot advance an inquiry in such a direction. This is because micro-economics entrusts economic activity to competitive and free markets and believes that the price mechanism will realise a rational distribution and use of capital, resources and labour. From the perspective of this dogma, it is impossible to analyse, let alone to predict, a calamity like the subprime crisis, which has resulted in social costs and economic losses requiring enormous injections of public funds in relief. From the orthodox economic perspective, it may indeed be so that the only way to describe this crisis is as if it was something like a tsunami, which suddenly attacks the market from outside.

It is thus not strange that in opposition to neo-classical micro-economics, Keynesianism and the post-Keynesianism of Hyman Minsky [1982] *Can "It" Happen Again?* among others – which turns Keynes's financial instability hypothesis into a theory of financial crises – are being re-evaluated around the world. However, Minsky's theory has a strong tendency to emphasise a hypothetical model of alteration in psychological preferences within the financial system, which proceeds from a boom in favourable economic times to an increase in speculative investment and finance, which induces a crisis by the collapse of a bubble-like boom. However, it does not sufficiently explain why and how the development of the fundamental contradictions within the objective dynamics of capitalist accumulation must cause, by logical necessity, an increase in speculative financial and investment instability in a certain phase of industrial accumulation. It also does not explain systematically the development of the capitalist economy as a historically unique economic system that includes such internal contradictions. This is related to a basic flaw in Minsky's neo-Keynesianism: it is difficult to raise issues of the historical characteristics of the subprime crisis, or why and how such bubble crises have become frequently repetitive in the global economy since the 1980s, when neoliberal globalisation developed under the system of floating exchange rates.

The basic frame of reference for the analysis of the subprime crisis is thus largely difficult to find, not just in so-called neoliberal micro-economic theory, but also in macro-economics. Does this not remind us of the general absence of a proper theory of economic crisis in non-Marxist economics? This is a reason why even daily newspapers in Europe and America, like the *Guardian*, have run editorials acclaiming Marx's prescience. In 31 German universities, *Cap-*

ital reading circles are expanding. *Capital* actually offers rich observations and investigations about the fundamental inevitability of crises within capitalist economies, something that is very much desired as a basis of inquiry into the current world crisis. It is thus only natural to see a renewed interest in the theoretical potential of Marx's original political economy in his lifework, *Capital.*

Marx made deep and important theoretical contributions to the basic theories of crisis, but these contributions were relatively incomplete compared to his theories of value and money. This incompleteness, however, was in part a result of Marx's own scientific thoroughness; before the first edition of Volume I of *Capital* (1867), Marx drafted an enormous manuscript of it almost three times. Because of these weighty attempts, he was unable to complete Volumes II and III during his lifetime and entrusted the editing of these manuscript volumes to Engels. Thus, even if Marx's works show a breadth and depth of the author's theoretical insights, it is often difficult to read their internal consistency, especially in the field of theories of credit and crisis. As a result, they have given rise to competing views among Marxian theorists concerning the most fundamental source of contradictions of capitalism, and concerning the basic cause of crises and how to understand the fundamental connections between the functions of the credit system and the industrial cycles, including the phase of crisis. Marx's original plans for his lifework, articulated around the time he wrote the *Grundrisse* (1857–58) (his first draft of *Capital*), was also interpreted that *Capital's* theoretical system did not intend to include a proper theory of economic crisis.

Even if we limit the discussion to *Capital,* crisis theory has been generally regarded as a difficult problem among difficult problems. In response to this difficult problem, Kozo Uno (1897–1977) – a uniquely creative, systematic and original theorist, the pride of Japanese social science – challenged this difficulty in this volume *Theory of Crisis,* producing an influential classic of condensed and penetrating theoretical exposition.

It is said that our time is exactly like that of *Capital.* Our current socioeconomic problems force us to reconsider again the fundamental principles of the capitalist economy. In what sense is the calamity of economic crisis, which is so hard to understand with common sense, an inevitable result of the working of the principles of the capitalist economy? In this regard it is high time to read Uno's *Theory of Crisis,* among other texts, as a guiding frame of reference for re-examining the historical significance of the subprime crisis in our age.

2 Characteristic Contents of *The Theory of Crisis*

The first edition of *The Theory of Crisis* was published in 1953. This was one year after the publication of Uno's [*Principles of Political Economy*] (vol. I, 1950, vol. II, 1952), which restructured the total volumes of *Capital* into a theoretical system of basic principles for the total field of research in Marxian political economy. However, its main contents had already been made public in 1951, in an occasional lecture course at the Department of Economics of the University of Tokyo, entitled 'Theory of Crisis'. A revised version of this lecture was published as a textbook of an occasional lecture course at Hosei University in November 1952, called 'Principles of Political Economy'. The contents of these lectures were developed along the lines of Uno's pre-war research on crisis theory, which can be seen in essays such as ['The Inevitability of Crisis in Capitalist Society'] (*Kaizo*, February 1935) or ['Money Capital and Real Capital'] (*Keizaigaku*, February 1937), both of which are included in Uno Kozo [*Collected Works*], vol. 3 (Iwanami Shoten, 1973). However, according to Uno's own recollections, only when he lectured on 'Theory of Crisis' at the University of Tokyo was he able to go beyond just commenting on the related chapters in *Capital* and to clarify his own theoretical understanding to himself.

In other words, the content of what would become *Theory of Crisis* became clear to Uno as he was writing the second volume of his *Principles of Political Economy*. As he pushed forward with his rebuilding of the system of the principles of political economy in *Capital*, Uno grew confident in the possibility of completing Marx's theories of crisis as an indispensable part of the basic theory of typical industrial cycles. Moreover, the elucidation of the theory of crisis in this volume was also necessary for completing Uno's original system of principles of political economy.

This volume actually presents a more synthetic and thorough theory of crisis based upon Uno's original reinterpretation of Marx's theories of accumulation, profit and the credit system in his *Principles of Political Economy*. Moreover, it pursues methodological and logical problems in demonstrating, more thoroughly, the inevitability of crisis, specifically through an Introduction, five chapters, and two appendix essays, which are also included in this volume. Uno's original intention – to situate and complete Marx's *Capital* as basic principles of political economy – is substantially shown more clearly in *Theory of Crisis*. Simultaneously, by presenting *Theory of Crisis* as an important aspect of the fundamental principles of political economy, Uno's three-step methodology, which calls for more concrete research at the levels of both stages theory of capitalist development and the concrete analysis of the contemporary world economy and individual capitalist economies, is demonstrated more powerfully.

In this regard, the "Introduction" in particular, which Uno himself confessed to be 'disproportionately long' (p. 11), shows the book's special attractiveness and profundity, as it does not merely lead us into the main theoretical essence of the basic theory of crisis. Instead, Uno meticulously argues and raises several interesting problems that extend to the total methodology concerning his three-step approach based on the principles of political economy.

To wit, and in accord with his systematic divisions among the three dimensions of research in political economy, Uno stipulates that investigations of the phenomenon of crisis should be distinguished among three levels: first, its basic theory in principle; second, the theory of the stages of the historical metamorphoses of capitalist development; and third, the analysis of its individual, concrete and contemporary instances. Then, in order to examine which stage in capitalist development can properly serve as the historical basis of abstraction for the basic theory of typical cyclical crises in principle, Uno reviews the historical metamorphoses in crises through the birth, growth and maturity stages of capitalist development. Here Uno summarises his research on the history of crises with great concision, and in doing so supplements his theory of capitalist development in [*The Types of Economic Policies under Capitalism*], (1971). Through these investigations Uno concludes that one cannot establish the theoretical inevitability of crisis within capitalist economies by drawing from the common facets of crises in early and late capitalism, due to their connections to factors that were external to the capitalist economy, such as pre-capitalist agricultural social strata or wars. Uno stipulates that the demonstration of the inevitability of capitalist crisis, in terms of the principles of political economy, must rest on an abstraction from the cyclical crises repeated between the 1820s and the 1860s in England. He insists that the theory of crisis, as a composite that abstracts from the commonalities of historically different forms of crisis, throughout all stages of capitalism, remains insufficient as a basic theory of crisis, which should instead establish the theoretical inevitability of regular cyclical crises. According to Uno, the basic theory of cyclical crisis can be clearly abstracted from the liberal-stage of capitalist development, where accumulation of capital on the ground of commodified labour power was established and proceeded through the most typical industrial trade cycles as an essential part of principles of law of the autonomous motion of capitalist economy.

However, in contrast to the theoretical image of a purely capitalist and closed society that automatically reproduces its order in accordance with the principles of political economy that Marx identified in *Capital*, the actual development of capitalism in England, with its repetition of cyclical crises, depended heavily on foreign trade. Therefore, there is a methodological question of why it is possible to abstract away foreign trade within the principles of political economy, as *Capital* does. In his Introduction, Uno stresses this problem and offers the following solution. As Marx himself points out, the commodity economy developed out of trading relations between communal societies, forming a different economic order than the internal socio-economic communal orders. For the first time in human history, capitalism turned the commodity economy into a society's fundamental internal economic order, which was completely different from other social formations. As a consequence, commodity trading with other, exterior societies, as well as with non-capitalist various producers, became an order of economic relations that was homogeneous with society's internal economic forms of organisation under capitalism. This means that, for example, agricultural goods imported in exchange for English industrial goods could be interpreted essentially as substitutes for the use values produced by English capital through commodity relations. Qualitatively, this is not different than if one sector of English capital takes up agricultural production to trade with other industrial sectors. Quantitatively, it is much like the result of an expansion in productive power, which enables more use-values to be produced by the same social labour time. Thus, from the standpoint of a basic theoretical investigation of the self-reliant laws of motion of the capitalist economy, the world market can be understood as if it were a national market for a society, and in which all industrial sectors are organized and managed capitalistically. Uno's logic, which abstracts foreign trade from the basic principles, and which took its cue from Marx's *Capital* itself, serves as an important supplement to his methodology, which assumes a purely capitalist economy made up of only capitalists, wage workers and landlords, and which follows the historical and actual tendencies of English society up to the mid-nineteenth-century.

Continuing in this vein, Uno's Introduction additionally points out that while the speculative trade of commercial capital plays an important role in the actual outbreak of cyclical crises, this aspect is also abstracted from the basic theory of crisis. The reason is that the role of commercial capital is basically just to expand and accelerate the reproductive motion of industrial capital by undertaking a portion of its circulation process. This insight corresponds to the theoretical order of exposition of Uno's *Principles of Political Economy*, in which the theory of the "inevitability of crisis" is posited prior to the determination of commercial capital, and also disclosed and demonstrated within the exposition of the theory of credit.

The main text of this volume, *Theory of Crisis*, is made up of five chapters following the Introduction. The first three chapters are 'Prosperity', 'Crisis' and 'Depression', which constitute three main phases in the typical industrial trade cycle. Crises are always prepared by the accumulation of capital in the phase of prosperity and cause depression. The severe competition in the phase of depression then enforces reorganisation and innovation among capitals, so as to induce, in turn, the next phase of prosperity.

In the phase of prosperity, a positive and quantitative expansion of accumulation among capitals generally proceeds without difficulty and on the basis of existing fixed capital, and therefore the incentive for innovation to seek extra (or "super") profits by improving the methods of production tends to be weak. The replacement and renewal of equipment in fixed capital tends to be avoided in this phase, and the accumulation of capital generally forms a quantitative widening and expansion of production by maintaining, more or less, the same organic composition of capital (i.e. the value composition that reflects technological conditions in production between variable capital (v), invested in labour power, and constant capital (c), invested in means of production). In this regard, the phase of prosperity is characterized by a so-called 'quantitative boom' and a proportional expansion of employment, along with progressive accumulation.

The expansion of commercial credit and bank credit also promotes the process of capital accumulation in the phase of prosperity, and forms capitalist social mechanisms that mutually utilize idle money-capital and commodity-capital for the expansion of production. So long as commercial credit is easy to expand, the increase in demand for loanable money capital in bank credit remains slower than the supply from expanded circuits of industrial capitals, and interest rates remain lower compared to profit rates. This eventually works as a factor in facilitating speculative trading toward the end of prosperity. Especially when accelerated accumulation brings about an increased demand for the means of production and labour power, prices of raw materials and wages tend to rise at the end of prosperity, and speculative trading of raw materials becomes activated by utilizing more and more bank credit. The rise in prices of raw materials and wages also spreads to the means of consumption. Thus, generalized price increases tend to obscure, to some extent, the decline in profit rates resulting from a rise in wages at the end of prosperity.

However, the fundamental contradiction of capitalist production lies in the commodification of labour power, which capitalism cannot itself produce, or supply, as a commodity, and which cannot be avoided or concealed by relationships such as this. The increase in wages, which is a final result of the prosperous and quantitative expansion of capital accumulation, reveals an inevitable appearance of the intrinsic contradiction of capitalist production in the unavoidable form of excess-demand beyond the social capacity to supply commodified labour power. The quantity of profit inevitably decreases in spite of the increased quantity of capital, making the accumulation of capital excessive. Individual capitalists cannot stop accumulation as they are competitively forced to attempt to maintain the quantity of profit with greater amounts of capital.

As a result, industrial capital's demand for bank credit continues to increase, while, conversely, the supply of loanable money capital in bank credit decreases due to both a fall in profit and to delays in the return payment for loans. Now, a sharp rise in the interest rates of bank credit is inevitable. The fall in the rate of profit collides with the rise in interest rate. The excessive accumulation of industrial capital in relation to the laboring population is now forced to stop, mediated by the inverted appearance of a shortage of loanable money capital. The sacrificed sales, especially of speculatively stockpiled commodities, are then hurriedly carried out in order to escape the increasing burden of repayment with higher rates of interest, and usually signals the beginning of cyclical crises. As prices that had been held up by speculative stockpiling fall, a vicious circle spreads between the inability to repay for matured bills of exchange and the difficulty in selling commodities, thereby making the destruction of capital's value and cutbacks to production unavoidable, and forming a typical phase of crisis.

When the storm of crisis of inter-related insolvencies within the credit system settles, the phase of depression follows. In this phase, employment is reduced, creating a relative surplus population (expressing difficulty in commodified labour power to adjust supply in accord with demand in an opposite form compared to the case at the end of prosperity), and loanable money capital also becomes excessive as a sort of unemployed idle capital. As a result, both wages and interest rates fall to relatively low levels. Nevertheless, industrial capitals cannot thereby recover its profitability immediately because they are saddled with unused and idle equipment and must endure severe competition for survival, which is characteristic of the phase of depression. Individual industrial capitals are thus forced to stake their survival on finding extra profits through rationalisation and innovations in the methods of production. Towards the end of the recession, when the amortisation of fixed capital in the main industries generally progresses, thereby making the replacement of fixed capital easier, capitals begin to improve the general methods of production, thus cutting down the value of labour power by increasing the portion of surplus labour time relative to the necessary labour time required for the maintenance and reproduction of labour power. The production of relative surplus value thus progresses, restoring the rate of profit, and at the same time raising the organic composition of capital, creating additional relative surplus population. Thus, with renewed value relations, the basic conditions for the next phase of prosperity are prepared.

Chapter 4 argues that 'The Turnover Period of the Business Cycle', which forms the phases of prosperity, crisis and depression, is determined chiefly by the period of the renewal of fixed capital used in large-scale mechanised industry since the Industrial Revolution; the longer the prosperity, the shorter the depression and vice versa. This is demonstrated by the roughly ten-year period of the typical business cycles in the mid-nineteenth century.

The fifth final chapter, 'The Inevitability of Crisis in Capitalist Society', makes clear that the inevitability of crisis is not a mere mechanical necessity, but a historical phenomenon, which affects the various economic agents as something akin to a law of nature, but which is actually characteristic of the capitalist economy and repeated in typical form at a certain stage of capitalist development. At the same time, it is noted that although crisis and the inevitable collapse of capitalism share the same root in the commodification of labour power, crisis resolves that fundamental contradiction repeatedly within the actual dynamism to form business cycles in capitalist economic development. In this respect, the demonstration of the inevitability of crisis in the principles of political economy does not intend to prove the inevitability of capitalism's final collapse. Methodologically, Uno also cautions that the investigation of crisis, as a part of the principles of political economy, must also be performed in distinction from investigations of crises within the stages theory, as well as in more concrete levels of empirical analysis. Otherwise, it will not be able to serve effectively as a clear frame of reference for analyses of contemporary capitalism.

As a whole, the theory of crisis in this volume can be read as a positive theoretical result that evolved out of Uno's original and decades-long study of Marx's *Capital*. The significance of this evolution is exemplified, among others, in two essays in the Appendix, both included this volume. In referring to these two essays, let me summarize in what senses this volume intends to purify and complete crisis theories in *Capital*. There are three main points.

First, Uno methodologically differentiates the basic theory of cyclical crises from more concrete research into the metamorphoses of crises in both the stages theory of capitalist development and in the actual analyses of contemporary capitalist economies. Uno thus clarifies how research into Marx's theories of crises (in texts such as *Capital*) should be completed as a part of the fundamental principles of political economy. In preparatory manuscripts for *Capital*, such as the introduction to the *Grundrisse*, Marx outlines his plans for his lifework by listing the topics to be investigated: capital, wage labour, land ownership, the state, foreign trade, and lastly, 'the world market and crisis'. Also, in *Capital*, while giving various and important considerations to crises, Marx still states that 'the actual movement of competition lies outside of our plan, and we are only out to present the internal organization of the capitalist mode of production, its ideal average, as it were.'[1] As discussed in the first essay of the appendix, Samezō Kuruma interpreted such passages from Marx and concluded that one could not find a 'proper theory of crisis' in *Capital*. Against this, Uno pointed out that the basic theories of wage labour and land ownership, which were originally planned outside the scope of 'Capital in General', nonetheless came to be included in *Capital* as parts of the principles of political economy, and thus there was no reason why the basic theory of crisis should not also be incorporated there. For Uno, the problem was rather why a theory of crisis was not clearly developed and completed in *Capital*.

When the whole manuscript of the *Grundrisse* became available, it became apparent that the theoretical structure, as 'Capital in General', was indeed restricted to the general total social relation between capital and wage labour. Compared to the contents in the *Grundrisse*, the theoretical contents in *Capital* were clearly and greatly expanded to include competition between capitals, theories of crises based on the dynamics of the process of accumulation, as well as the principles of credit. Although *Capital* occasionally preserves the initial plan to provide only an 'an ideal average' of the capitalist mode of production's internal organisation within the framework of 'Capital in General', it has been ascertained further, in subsequent manuscripts, that Marx was gradually inserting theories of capital accumulation, competition and credit among capitals, as well as cyclical crises. (cf. M.Itoh [1973] [*Credit and Crisis*], The University of Tokyo Press). In particular, so long as we can separate the principles of political economy, as Uno argues, from more concrete levels of studies, either in the stages theory of capitalist development, or else in empirical analyses of contemporary economies concerning 'The World Market and Crisis', it is indeed important that we complete the proper and basic theory of cyclical crisis in *Capital* as one of our tasks for research – a task we've inherited from Marx.

Secondly, and related to the first point above, in this book Uno criticizes *Capital* for its dual and parallel explications of the fundamental cause of the inevitability of cyclical crisis and attempts to put them in order. As discussed in the second essay in the appendix, there are indeed two different types of basic theory to explicate the logical inevitability of cyclical crisis in *Capital*. For example, in Volume III, Chapter 15, Section 1, it is stressed that 'the conditions of direct exploitation, and those of realizing it, are not identical', especially because the latter condition to realize (or sell in a market) exploited surplus value is due to the anarchic imbalances between sectors of production and the restricted purchasing power (effective demand) of the working classes. On

1 *Capital*, Vol. 3, p. 970.

the other hand, in Section 3 of the same chapter, the limitations on the production of surplus value that accompanies excessive accumulation relative to the limit of working population, and the resulting fall in the rate of profit, is clearly presented as the fundamental cause of crisis. A majority of Marxist economists, including Soviet orthodox scholars, have relied on the former type of crisis theory in *Capital*, particularly of the underconsumption variant, and have ignored the latter type of over-accumulation theory of crisis in Marx. However, without referring to the process whereby the accumulation of capital runs into difficulties, the realization problem caused by a shortage of effective demand still always leaves open the possibility that it can be resolved by the progress of the accumulation of capital. Thus, this type of crisis theory – either the underconsumption or disproportionality variant – cannot theoretically establish the cyclical inevitability of crises, though it may suggest its possibility.

Therefore, this volume, unlike previously dominant such type of Marxian crisis theories, intends to purify Marx's over-accumulation theory of crisis in *Capital* in order to clarify consistently, in principle, why general overproduction and overall difficulties in realising commodity values occurs periodically and inevitably. At the same time, this volume demonstrates that the fundamental contradictions of capitalist production, exposed in periodic crisis, originates from the historical preconditions of capitalism based on the commodification of labour power, the axis around which Uno's entire theoretical view of the whole system of Marxian political economy revolves. This may be the most distinctive characteristic of Uno's theory of crisis.

As this book points out, there are two main reasons why Marx did not manage to complete and demonstrate his over-accumulation theory of crisis in *Capital*. On the one hand, since the restrictions to technological changes on existing fixed capital in the phase of prosperity tends to be neglected in the theory of accumulation of capital (especially in the first volume of *Capital*, and preceding the definition of fixed capital in the second volume), what has been left unclarified is the character of the quantitative expansion accompanied by a relatively constant composition of capital in the process of accumulation in prosperity. As a result, there is a tendency to assume that the process of capital accumulation always forms a ceaseless increase in the organic composition of capital accompanied by the formation of a relative surplus population. Thus, the theoretical inevitability of the over-accumulation of capital in relation to the limited labouring population, as a result of the quantitative expansion of production, is not presented clearly. On the other hand, in *Capital*, the theoretical mechanism of the credit system, through which the competitive accumulation of industrial capitals is mediated and regulated along with the movement of loanable money capital, was only investigated but not yet completed by Marx. It remains for us to theoretically study and examine further the difficulties of the overaccumulation of industrial capital, and how it turns into destructive crisis mechanically, through contrasting shortages of loanable money capital.

Thirdly, therefore, and unlike most preceding Marxian theories of crisis, Uno's theory of crisis in this volume stresses the importance of Marx's theory of credit in Volume III, Part V in *Capital*. It intends to demonstrate the inevitability of cyclical crisis in the principles of political economy through an intricate investigation of the mechanisms and dynamics of the opposing movements between interest rates and profit rates, which are observed especially in chapters on 'Money Capital and Real Capital' in that Part of *Capital*.

According to Uno, in order to clarify the law of motion of interest rates suitably for this task, it is necessary to revise Marx's theory of the credit system into a theoretical mechanism, one that is essentially internal to the mutual utilization of idle capital among industrial capitalists themselves, and not as a mechanism that mediates transactions between the external origins of loanable capital by 'money capitalists', on the one hand, and industrial capitalists, on the other. In this sense, Uno's theoretical reworking of the theory of interest and the credit system in his *Principles of Political Economy*, together with his preparatory work on theories of accumulation and profit, clearly serve as theoretical premises for the arguments presented in this volume. Marx's unfinished efforts in *Capital* to develop a theory of interest, including the credit mechanism as an essential part of the logical explication of business cycles and crises, were fully utilized for the first time by Uno's reworking. In this volume, Uno thus systematically demonstrated the principles of how business cycles repeatedly form phases of prosperity and depression through crisis, and as manifestations of capitalist production's intrinsic contradiction based on the commodification of labour power, a contradiction which also never fails to appear as a crisis of financial credit.

In these ways, Uno's *Theory of Crisis* realised an unprecedented breakthrough, surpassing earlier Marxian theories of crisis.

In the midst of the repeated and disastrous series of cyclical and speculative bubbles and collapses, including the subprime crisis – all of which are deeply rooted in monetary and financial instability in capitalist economies in our age – Uno's characteristic theoretical contributions in reworking the crisis theory of *Capital* are all the more worthy of broader attention.

3 The Flavour of a Classic

There are two types of classics in political economy. One is a voluminous work that is full of historical illustrations and examples, and that offers multifaceted and rich theoretical explorations. The other is a condensed work that leaves its mark through a purified and high level of theoretical consistency. To take an example from Iwanami's paperback series of classics, Adam Smith's *Wealth of Nations* (1776) is a good example of the first type and Ricardo's *Principles of Political Economy and Taxation* (1817), which purifies and consistently completes Smith's labour theory of value, is a distinguished example of the second type. Marx's *Capital* offers another well-known example of the first type. It takes over Smith and Ricardo's labour theory of value and critically overcomes their theoretical weaknesses and limitations scientifically, while building up a vast and rich theoretical structure to elucidate the historical specificity of capitalism's laws of movement, together with a vast array of historical facts, which serve as examples and illustrations. Uno's *Principles of Political Economy* intends to purify and re-condense the very essence of Marx's rich and complex theories in *Capital* through original and creative theoretical insights and attempts. Uno clearly worked with the aim of performing an operation on Marx that resembled what Ricardo had done with Smith.

Theory of Crisis in this volume was also a part of this project of reworking Marx. As touched on above, *Capital* offers deep and multifaceted inquiries into crisis, but mostly as incomplete and complex theories. Uno contributed towards a creative re-systematisation of Marx's theories of crisis, weaving them into a classically complete and concise theoretical work. At times, Uno's works are said to be hard to understand. However, if readers accustom themselves a little to Uno's unique style, in which positive definitions are drawn out of layers of so-called dialectic negations, many will no doubt be deeply impressed by the brevity and clarity of his theoretical framework. As the contents of this volume were originally prepared for undergraduate lecture courses, they were no doubt intended to be clear enough to be understood even by beginner students not yet majoring in economics. Both professional economists and general readers alike have broadly appreciated the many publications of *Theory of Crisis* in Japan as a rare classic, as it clears up mysteries of economic crises that are so hard to understand with common sense. This appreciation doubtless derives from the clarity at the book's core.

That said, the attraction of this book is also found in the flavour of Uno's creative intellectual vitality, his scientific speculation, and the challenging thrill of research that one does not obtain from typical, introductory textbooks. Supporting this attractiveness, there is, on the one hand, Uno's deep and wide scholarship, which he learned from studies on the history of business cycles and crises, as well as from other theories of crisis, not only those of Marxists like E. Varga and M.I. Tugan-Baranowski but also those of outstanding non-Marxist scholars in this field like A. Spiethoff and M. Bouniatian, as well as from the analysis by the League of Nations, *The Course and Phases of World Economic Depression* (1931). On the other hand, there are probably few readers unimpressed by Uno's challenging attempts – carried out through his reading and re-reading *Capital* – to reach certain satisfying solutions for difficult or inconsistent theoretical points left-over in *Capital* in order to complete its essence as principles of political economy. Thanks to these attempts, *Theory of Crisis* also serves as a useful and indispensable reference guide to understand what *Capital* is, and how to read its rich and heartfelt theories. What attracts us to this volume substantially originates from the attraction of *Capital* itself.

Clearly, this volume is a work which earns high marks for its completeness compared to theories of crisis in *Capital*. Nevertheless, it cannot be said that it left nothing left over for further investigation. For instance, are the roles of speculative trading promoted by elastic credit mechanisms, as well as the function of commercial capital toward the end of prosperity, not essential in causing destructive and acute cyclical crisis, even though Uno's *Theory of Crisis* omits them in the basic principles? Is it not also desirable theoretically to investigate more clearly the logic of these dynamics of general price levels in relation to variations in the relative value of money through business cycles?

In addition, there are certainly important research tasks which have been explicitly left outside the scope of this volume, such as the study of the metamorphoses of crisis in the stages theory of capitalist development, and the further concrete analyses of crisis in the contemporary capitalist world economy after the first World War. Regarding these tasks, and as not a few works by Uno's successors have shown, the attractiveness of Uno's classic masterpiece is found in its power to stimulate, induce and encourage research to follow it.

And that is not all. This slender volume presents us with a broad and deep theoretical perspective that recognizes how the nature of commodity exchange, originating from inter-social exchange and connecting to pre-capitalist communities, also underlies the autonomous nature of the motion of the capitalist economy as something that is relatively independent from political and other social superstructures, and thus creates a special society for which foreign trade is no longer something alien to its intra-social economic order. As Uno suggests (p. 27–32 in this volume), this special character of the capitalist commodity economy must have served as the material foundation for Marx's formulation of the historical materialist synthesis of human history, and for his connections and distinctions between the economic base and the political superstructure.

At the same time, this small book also has broad and important significance in terms of its reinterpretation and clarification of the core of all three volumes of *Capital* to form the contradictory source of cyclical crises, which originates from the commodification of labour power as a sort of Achilles' heel for capital, and as the fundamental premise of the capitalist economy. Such theoretical insights of Uno's in this volume have provided not a few vantage points from which to analyse and reconsider multiple crises in both contemporary socialism and capitalism, and it will no doubt continue to do so in the future.

For example, Soviet-style socialism understood the crisis-generating contradiction of the capitalist economy as originating from the anarchical imbalances among the various sectors of production and the limited shortage of mass consumption, which leads to overproduction. Soviet-style socialism thus sought to overcome these contradictions with centralised state planning of the economy. Against this, Uno's crisis theory takes the position that the basis of capitalist contradiction lies in the commodification of labour power. This implies that socialism should strive among all to tackle the task of socially recovering and liberating the human subjectivity of labourers alienated under capitalism. Although Uno did not express an open criticism against Soviet socialism, already in 1953, in his famous article, "Economic Laws and Socialism" – a full three years before de-Stalinization in the Soviet Union took place in 1956 – Uno criticized Stalin's view of utilizing the law of value in political economy for the construction of socialism just like laws in the natural sciences. There is no doubt that Uno's theoretical contributions to Marxian political economy, such as those found in this volume, together with his sharp criticism against Stalin's view, impressed many readers who felt discomfort with, or antipathy towards, Soviet orthodox Marxism, as well as to the Soviet-style of social system. *Theory of Crisis* in this volume harbours an appeal, an appeal for a turn in the basic task of socialism beyond capitalism, a turn, so to speak, from "things" to "human beings."

Uno believed that the development of capitalism after the late nineteenth century had slowed or even reversed the historical tendency to realize a more and more purified capitalist society in England and had become greatly affected by agricultural peasant problems and world wars. The elucidation of the phenomenon of crisis, such as the great world crisis in the inter-war period, or the explanation for the absence of crisis in the long boom period from World War II to the 1960s, had to take into sufficient consideration factors that were exterior to the capitalist economy (for example, as stressed on p. 25.). For this reason, among others, Uno maintained that, in investigations of crises as concrete historical phenomena, the direct application of the basic theory of crisis, like the one in this volume, must deliberately be avoided. Thus, as for the investigation of economic crises under contemporary capitalism, Uno stressed the influence of factors exterior to the capitalist market economy, such as wars and economic policies that were against socialism, and he was thus rather cautious against the direct application of the principles of crisis theory in relation to his three-step methodology, a point that is reiterated in Uno's Introduction to this volume.

The Introduction can also be read to suggest that, for historical studies in economic crises, either as parts of the stages theory of capitalist development or of more concrete analyses of contemporary capitalist economies, there is room for a consideration of the significance of theoretical possibilities pertaining to causes of crises that accord with the overproduction of commodities due to underconsumption or disequilibrium, or further with speculative instabilities of money and the credit system, in addition to a more complete basic theory of cyclical crisis in this volume as frames of reference based on *Capital*.

Nevertheless, Uno's successor, Tsutomu Ouchi, attempted to use – rather straightforwardly – Uno's basic theory of crisis, while also recognising the effectiveness of Keynesian policies in his [*State Monopoly Capitalism*] (1970). Ouchi argued that the Keynesian policy of a mild inflation successfully keeps real wages in check and thus extends the prosperity phase of capital accumulation in the post-War world.

However, when a serious economic crisis occurred in the advanced economies in 1973–75, Keynesian policies were of little use, and rather worsened the situation by promoting vicious inflation. In its background, accumulation of real capital in advanced economies through the post-War long boom became excessive by that time in relation to easily mobilizable labouring populations within each economy and primary products in the world market. The resultant rise in wages and prices of primary products caused difficulties of capital accumulation and a fall in the rates of profit. Thus, the basic theoretical logic that causes crises due to excessive capital accumulation, specifically in connection with the commodification of labour power – which is demonstrated in this volume – has powerfully resurfaced from the depths of history into the contemporary world.

At that time, difficulties arising from the excessive accumulation of real capital, which caused rises in wages and prices of primary products, coincided with the collapse of the Bretton Woods international currency system, and tended to induce an enormous expansion of the supply of currencies and credit, so as to promote a vicious inflation or inflationary crisis. This contrasts with the classic and typically deflationary cyclical crises shown in this volume. Although the features of the inflationary crisis in 1973–75 were shown in excessive currency and credit – which promoted a destructive and general shortage in commodities necessary for the production of oil and other raw materials and semi-products, forming quite the opposite of features manifested in classical crisis (such as those presented in this volume) – they were nonetheless concrete phenomena suitably analyzed by utilizing Uno's crisis theory as a powerful frame of reference.

As the basic tone of economic policies in the advanced countries changed from Keynesianism towards neoliberal globalisation, the introduction of new information technology to the workplace, the pressures of privatisation of public corporations, and the loosening of labour protection regulations accompanied by an increase in the number of irregular workers, the weakening of labour unions, and the recreation of a relative surplus population as a result of 'rationalisation', all worked together against working conditions among the mass of labouring populations, as if there had been a prolonged and large-scale phase of depression, such as it is described in the chapter on Depression in this volume. Industrial firms became multi-nationalized thanks to a neoliberal relaxation of restrictions on the movement of capitals across borders, then moved factories to China and other developing countries. The accompanying negative influence on employment through industrial hollowing-out was further added to the stagnation of consumer demand in the advanced economies. As a result, the surplus of idle money capital could not be easily absorbed by industrial capitals for the real expansion of production, including investments in equipment and machineries. Thus, the co-existence of idle loanable money capital, idle capacity of production in industrial capitals, alongside a relative surplus labouring population, continued to characterize the prolonged stagnation in advanced economies. This explains why global relays of speculative bubbles and collapses are so easily repeated in the age of neoliberalism since the 1980s.

The subprime crisis discussed at the outset of this essay is to be analyzed as a further development of contemporary crisis based upon such an unstable and financialized world economic order, revealing the deepening contradiction intrinsic to capitalism rooted in the financialisation of labour power, a further evolved contradiction of the commodification of labour power in our age. From this point of view, conventional interpretations of the contemporary capitalist crisis – as it is said, for example, to arise from either mere errors in fiscal and financial policies, or from the sins of excessively greedy speculative capitalists who did not behave within rules or moderation, or the views of the crisis as a consequence of the speculative instability inherent in capitalist money and finance in general – are all clearly inadequate. This is also true even when these interpretations are seen against the background of a stagnation in the rate of profit due to the intensification of international competition among industrial firms. The current crisis has an aspect which must be understood by following the dynamic of contemporary capitalist accumulation, which has its origins in the contradictory and basic difficulties in treating human labour power as a commodity. Despite Uno's somewhat reserved tone at the time of its writing, the significance of this book, as a basic frame of reference to be applied for investigations into contemporary capitalism, seems to be increasing.

The substantial contents and theoretical implications of Uno's *Theory of Crisis* are thus no doubt rich and attractive, tempting us to broad and relaxing applications for the most urgent issues of our own age. This surely captures the flavour which this volume shares with the great classics in the field of the social sciences.

December 2009, revised March 2020.
(Translated by Guy Yasko and edited by Makoto Itoh and Ken Kawashima.)

SUPPLEMENTARY ESSAY

Uno Kōzō's *Theory of Crisis* Today

Ken Kawashima and Gavin Walker

> ... surplus capital *alongside* surplus population [... *überflüssiges Kapital neben überflüssiger Bevölkerung*].*[1]
>
> KARL MARX

•••

> When faced with the disclosure of the intrinsic interconnection [of the capitalist system], the vulgar economist ... prides himself in his clinging to appearances and believing them to be eternal. Why then have science at all? But there is also something else behind it. Once the interconnection has been revealed, all theoretical belief in the perpetual necessity of the existing conditions collapses, even before the collapse takes place in practice.[2]
>
> KARL MARX

•••

> It is possible to say metaphorically that crisis manifests the circle in which the whole mode of production moves with an immobile movement.[3]
>
> ÉTIENNE BALIBAR

∴

---

* All translations are ours unless otherwise indicated. An earlier version of this piece appeared in *Viewpoint* magazine, Issue 6: Imperialism (2018), https://www.viewpointmag.com/2018/02/01/surplus-alongside-excess-uno-kozo-imperialism-theory-crisis/.

1 Marx, *Capital*, Vol. 3, in Marx and Engels 1975–2004 [hereafter *MECW*], Vol. 37, p. 240; Marx, *Das Kapital*, Bd. 3, in Marx and Engels 1956–90 [hereafter *MEW*], Bd. 25, p. 252.

2 Marx, 'Letter to Kugelmann of 11 July 1868', in *MECW*, Vol. 43, p. 69.

3 Balibar 1970, p. 291.

The Specificity of Crisis Theory

Uno Kōzō's *Theory of Crisis* was first published in 1953, a complex moment not only in Japan, just a year after the end of the US Occupation, but also in the communist world with the death of Stalin, an event that ushered in a new era to the Soviet Union, and which inaugurated a period of crises and upheavals in the world socialist movement, soon to experience not only the revelations of the Twentieth Congress of the CPSU, but also the events of Hungary in 1956, the Sino-Soviet split, the 'Bandung era', the movements of decolonisation and national liberation. This period, therefore, would equally mark a turning point in the global history of Marxist theory, previously fixed to the long aftermath of 1917, the experience of World War II, and the initial organisational and political culture of the socialist movement. The pivotal moment of the 1950s, therefore, saw extensive new developments in Marxist thought that paralleled and reinvestigated the problems of the capitalist economy in the postwar period within this intense cauldron of politics internal to the world socialist movement itself: the problem of monopoly and the concentration of capital, the questions of world capitalism, imperialism, and uneven development, the problem of crisis and the particular relation of *politics* to the *logic* of crisis within Marx's critique of political economy.

In the midst of this complex moment emerged Uno's *Theory of Crisis*. From the outset, this text was situated not only in the midst of the aforementioned global situation, but also at an important moment in the development of Uno's work itself. *Theory of Crisis* was also released almost exactly one year after he had completed his most influential and major theoretical work, his two-volume theory of the fundamental principles of political economy, *Principles of Political Economy*, the first volume of which was published in 1950, and the second in 1952.[4] But two moments intervene in this periodisation. First of all, already in the pre-war period, in 1935, Uno had undertaken an extensive analysis of the Marxian theory of crisis, resulting in his essay, "The Inevitability of Crisis

4 This crucial text has not yet been translated into other languages. See *Principles of Political Economy* in Uno Kōzō, *Collected Works of Uno Kōzō*, hereafter *UKC*, Vol. 1. The second, abridged version of *Principles of Political Economy* (in *UKC*, Vol. 2) has been translated by Thomas Sekine (see Uno 1980). Although this second version contains important independent insights, its compact nature eliminates numerous crucial theoretical formulations present in the original two-volume edition. These editions should not be seen as 'versions' of the same text, but as independent theoretical works. In this sense, we can only hope that the original two-volume *Principles of Political Economy* will be translated into many languages in the future.

in Capitalist Society",[5] published in *Kaizō* [*Reconstruction*], one of the major journals of Marxist theoretical inquiry of the time. Over the nearly twenty years since the publication of this early essay, Uno's work had taken up all the major thematics of Marxist theory and political economy: the methodological discussions of the 'order of exposition', economic policy and the development of world capitalism, the analysis of the agrarian question and the problem of the transition, the concept of the value-form and the accompanying analyses specific to value theory, not to mention numerous topics in the analysis and exegesis of Marx's work as a whole.

But between the publication of the first volume of *Principles of Political Economy* in 1950, and the second volume in 1952, Uno began to revisit the theory of crisis and its centrality for Marxist theory and political economy. Beginning with an occasional course of lectures to the Tokyo University economics department in 1951,[6] Uno began to undertake something quite different from his early work on crisis theory – which, while important, remains to a large extent a preparatory exegetical reading of the place of crisis theory in Marx – beginning to develop and formalise his original contribution to the Marxian analysis of the phenomenon of crisis around a series of points that he continued to expand on in a number of writings that followed the appearance of *Theory of Crisis* in 1953. It is necessary here to point out, therefore, two specific points on which Uno's analysis came to be located.

First, Uno's work on crisis expresses a general problem in Marxist theory: how to explain crisis both as a *necessity* (or inevitability), in other words, as something *cyclical*, and also as a *contingency*, something that joins the question of crisis to political arrangements, ideological factors, and other seemingly 'irrational' elements that appear on the level of *historical* crises?[7]

Secondly, Uno attempts to formalise and concretise the Marxian theory of crisis, which, since its inception, has been divided largely between two separate explanations of the formation of crises: an excess commodity theory of crisis (so-called 'overproduction' due to 'underconsumption' or 'disproportion') and an excess capital theory of crisis.[8] The former, taken in its broadest sense,

5 Uno's, 'The Inevitability of Crisis in Capitalist Society' was originally published in the October 1935 issue of *Kaizō* (republished in UKC, Vol. 3, pp. 128–46).

6 On this moment, see Uno's reflections in *Shihonron gojūnen* (Uno 1981, Vol. 2, pp. 964–5). Itoh Makoto points out this moment also in his afterword to UKC, Vol. 5, p. 450.

7 On this point, see Takumi 2000, pp. 104–7; see also Nakamura 2007.

8 For a general presentation of the main variants of crisis theory and a defence of Uno's mature theory of crisis, see Itoh 1980, esp. pp. 119–49. For reasons of space and topicality, we cannot address the relation of Uno's theory to the many existing Marxian theories of crisis, but for a general overview of the diversity of crisis theory, see Howard and King 1992, Clarke 1994, and

emphasises that crises stem from the disproportion of production in various branches of the economy and the accompanying restricted consumption of the masses. The latter, on the other hand, emphasises that crisis erupts through the 'absolute overproduction of capital in a ratio to the labouring population', and that this leads to regular periodic and cyclical crises. As Makoto Itoh, among others, has pointed out, the essence of the difference between these two broad positions, which are both represented in Marx's work, particularly in Volume 3 of *Capital*, concerns their *order of priority*, or logical position within the structure of *Capital* as a text. Essentially, the excess capital theory of crisis asserts that 'excess commodities in the market and difficulties of the realisation of surplus value' are not the *cause* of crisis, but the *result* of cyclical crises caused by the excess accumulation of capital. In the excess commodity theory, this positioning of cause and effect is reversed, an argument that sees excess capital and a falling profit rate as *effects* of the deeper crisis of the overproduction of commodities beyond the demand for their consumption.[9]

With the background of Marx's incomplete and partial crisis theory as his guide, Uno attempted to complete the systematisation of a version of the excess capital theory of crisis, focusing particularly on the position of the labour power commodity. The excess commodity theory of crisis, which emphasizes the cause of crisis in the sphere of circulation and in the failure to realize surplus value in the exchange process, cannot explain why crisis should be *repeated*, periodically and inevitably. In contrast to such an explanation, Uno specifically attempted to develop the unfinished connections in Marx's theory of crisis between the excess capital theory and the inability of capital itself to produce labour power *as a commodity by means of capital*. By attempting to formalise this linkage, Uno theoretically emphasises the cause and foundation of crisis as *internal to the capital-relation itself*, a point that we should understand not only theoretically but also *politically*.[10]

Shaikh 1978. In the *Theory of Crisis*, Uno specifically responds to other Marxist studies of crisis, especially in the stage of imperialism, by Tugan-Baranowsky, Eugen Varga, Henryk Grossman, and others in Japan (for example, Suzuki Kōichirō, Kuruma Samezō, and prewar economic historians such as Yamada Moritarō). Uno was also aware of Paul Sweezy's *The Theory of Capitalist Development* (1942) and Maurice Dobb's *Political Economy and Capitalism* (1937), and in fact wrote short reviews of both works during the time he himself was writing the *Theory of Crisis*. On this latter point, see *UKC*, Vol. 11, pp. 181–2, 184–5.

9 Itoh 1980, pp. 94–5, 119–30.

10 Our thinking on this question is part of a broader project especially influenced by Nagahara Yutaka's re-reading, re-writing, and re-coding of Marx and Uno. See in particular his essays collected in Nagahara 2008 and 2016.

The Actuality of Uno's Crisis Theory

After the outbreak of the 2008 financial crisis, and its ongoing reverberations, we believe that Uno's *Theory of Crisis* offers a powerful and important critique of existing interpretations of the cause of crisis, pointing us toward possible political responses to the immediate conjuncture. For example, one of the most common and prevailing ideological formulas behind the typical understanding of the 2008 crisis is that the world of finance is completely autonomous from the 'real economy' of manufacturing and industry, that Wall Street and its 1% has become completely severed from 'Main Street' and its 99% of working-class and middle-class populations.

This way of thinking has led to a general conception of capitalist crisis, widely shared in a variety of political spaces, in which Main Street is believed to function in a healthy state so long as irrational financial speculation is curbed on Wall Street. This manner of understanding the phenomenon of crisis thus ineluctably banishes from thought the notion that Main Street can actually only thrive precisely through exuberant financial speculation on Wall Street, and that it is the *fusion* and not the separation of finance and the so-called 'real economy' that contains the hidden cause of capitalist crisis. As Slavoj Žižek points out, it is around this banishment from thought, this conceptual foreclosure, that the populist factions on both the right and left converge in shared criticisms of state bail outs; the populist left says that bail-outs merely protect the banks while sacrificing the masses, while the populist right sees the banking bail-out as an unforgivable form of state intervention and 'socialism' that goes against the logic of free competition, preventing 'the market' from returning to its supposedly 'natural' stability.[11]

In contrast to these superficial conceptions of crisis that have attained a certain status as 'common-sense' in recent years, Uno's *Theory of Crisis* provides a systematic and trenchant critique of the current ideology of the separation of finance from production. This ideology, in fact, has epistemic roots that extend back to the very origins of modern political economy itself. It was the classical political economists such as Smith and Ricardo who standardised the theorisation of the phenomena of crisis merely as a phenomenon of commodity circulation, where defaults on payments on commodities based on unrealisable prices stemming from speculation broke up the reproductive process of capital, sending everyone into a mad dash for liquidity. The cause of crisis was thus explained away as a problem of commodities not being sold even though

11 Žižek 2009.

they were produced, which led the classical political economists to assert that the cause of crisis was ultimately found in the separation of buying and selling. In this way they unwittingly reproduced a way of thinking of crisis that was closer to the reality of an earlier historical era of mercantilism.

What they failed to explain theoretically was how the very possibility of grasping, in thought, the existence of commodities as products of labour was itself based on an incessant overcoming of a specific social and historical restriction placed upon capitalist production methods, namely that for capitalist production to exist at all, capitalist production must consume as a commodity something that capital cannot produce as a commodity directly: the peculiar commodity of labour power.

The ideological ruse of the classical political economists was that, while this social restriction on capitalist production was especially clear, for example, during phases of economic prosperity, when industry widened its scale of production and thus needed to absorb more and more workers, it was equally clear that industry could not assume that workers would necessarily 'be there' for capital in the right numbers, since workers are not moveable in the same way that, say, machinery as commodities are, they nonetheless disavowed this fundamental vulnerability of capitalist production by theoretically treating labour power merely as a commodity as a product of labour.

This was not simply a diabolical plan on their part; rather, it was a theoretical blindness, because all they could see were the immediate phenomenal forms of the commodity and money. Because labour power could be bought and sold just like any other commodity, with a use value and an exchange value, they theoretically understood labour power in precisely the same manner, as a commodity that was a product of labour. What the hitherto existing political economy failed to take into account was the specifically *capitalist* nature of labour. Unlike a slave economy, in which the worker's body itself is sold as a commodity, the formation of the 'doubly-free wage labour' – free to sell its work to the highest bidder, and simultaneously free or *available* for exploitation – at the advent of the capitalist era connotes a situation in which what is sold as a commodity is the *capacity, potential*, or *force* to work within definite limits and for a definite period.[12] And unlike various pre-capitalist forms of labour, in which the compulsion to work is generated by means of certain forms of 'extra-economic coercion' (directly feudal landed property relations, seigneurial systems of ground rent in kind, direct relations of force and violence to compel serf labour), the formation of labour power is only possible

12 See on this point Walker 2016, Chapter 4.

when what is commodified – that is, circulated as a commodity – is not labour *in general* but the specific capacity to work 'piecemeal' or 'for a determinate period'.[13] This difference furnishes us with the essential problem of the labour power commodity, a commodity that is bought and sold in the labour market, but that can never be located in a stable presence. It is on this point that Uno's intervention into the excess capital theory of crisis finds its basis, a point closely linked to what Marx called 'the deepest and most hidden cause of crisis', that is, the cause of its *inevitability or necessity*.[14]

'The Deepest and Most Hidden Cause of Crises'

For Marx, this oversight of the bourgeois economists was not something neutral, something simply to do with divergent modes of theoretical inquiry. Rather, this oversight concerns something directly political: in order to avoid the problems posed for the theory of crisis by the form of the labour power commodity, bourgeois political economy also had to disavow the reality of class struggle endemic to capitalist production, concentrated in the commodification of labour power. Althusser once pointed out that the identification of this lack of 'vision' or 'sight' is the key to the 'reading protocols' Marx utilises to explode the presumptions of bourgeois political economy. As Althusser argued, however, the problem is not that bourgeois political economy contained an

13 See here the important remarks in Marx, *Capital*, Vol. 1, in *MECW*, Vol. 35, p. 178; Marx, *Das Kapital*, Bd. 1, in *MEW*, Bd. 23, p. 182.

14 With regard to the present crisis, while various new phenomena of crisis can be identified and contexualised in the present (e.g., 'financialisation', 'debt economy', 'gig economy', etc.), the point that Uno's theory of crisis emphasises is how capitalist crisis formally or structurally repeats the origins of the capitalist mode of production in the present, but in an inverted and perverted form. While historically 'contexualising' the present crisis – 'historicism' – serves many purposes, it does not necessarily serve a crucial, political purpose *of and for Marxist theory*, of grasping the historical and materialist 'replay' of the origins of the capitalist mode of production in the present repetition of crisis – its historicity – *which throws the state, as well as its representations of the present, into a crisis of its own.* Once crisis can show, logically, how capitalism's interconnections necessarily lead to the repetition of crisis in – and of – the present, the historicity of capitalism is revealed in its transitory finitude. As a result, 'All theoretical belief in the perpetual necessity of the existing conditions of capitalism collapses, even before the collapse in practice'. The collapse of belief in capitalism marks the possibility and necessity of revolution. Uno's text, written in immediate post-Occupation Japan, continues to give us a precise and prescient guide to understanding the present repetition of crisis, in much the same way that Marx's analysis of crisis in *Capital* was relevant and meaningful for Lenin's enduringly prescient analysis of imperialism.

'oversight' whereas Marx emphasised a 'sight', a 'presence' of a certain problem in contrast to its 'absence'. Rather, the point is that bourgeois political economy's *sight itself*, its entire mode of vision, was predicated on a set of formulations that prevent or restrain the figure of labour power from coming to the surface: bourgeois political economy is structured through a 'vision' that is itself already identical with a certain 'non-vision', a constitutive inability to recognise the problem *as a problem*.[15]

What this means, essentially, is that because the labour power commodity must be *assumed to be given and present*, but cannot be produced *directly by capital*, the entirety of the history of struggles over land enclosures, the factory system, the life-and-death struggles of the workers 'thrown onto the market' by the decomposition of the previous social relations, and so forth is involved in this process of transforming into a commodity that which capital must consume absolutely in order for capital to be 'itself' despite capital's fundamental inability to produce labour power as a commodity directly.

It is significant that Uno often insisted on speaking of the *commodification* (*shōhinka*) of labour power, rather than simply treating it as an already presupposed commodity – this active sense, or sense of *process*, is important, precisely because what the bourgeois economists ignored at the outset of the capitalist era was the *ongoing process* of violence, capture, and discipline covered over or hidden by the product of labour. Marx in fact *tore open* this concealed relation precisely by emphasising that the labour power commodity remains always in a state of flux and precariousness that symptomatically reveals the necessarily contingent process of becoming or not becoming a commodity, a process, moreover, that can only be managed by ideological state apparatuses and social institutions of the sort Foucault discussed in his lectures on biopolitics.[16]

More broadly, however, Marx argued that this historical and social restriction endemic to capitalist production – that capital must consume labour power as a commodity but cannot produce labour power as a commodity directly – represents nothing short of what he called the 'deepest and most hidden cause of crisis'. Marx writes:

---

15 Althusser 1970, pp. 20–1.

16 On the deep connections between the contingencies endemic to the commodification of labour power, on the one hand, and the myriad ways in which biopolitical organisations attempt to tame those contingencies through power and knowledge production of populations, on the other, see Kawashima (2019), "The Hidden Area of Marx and Foucault", in *positions: asia critique*, vol. 27, no. 1, February 2019, pp. 115–44.

> The fact that bourgeois production is compelled by its own immanent laws, on the one hand, to develop the productive forces as if production did not take place on a narrow restricted social foundation (*auf einer bornirten gesellschaftlichen Grundlage*), while, on the other hand, it can develop these forces only within these narrow boundaries (*den Schranken dieser Bornirtheit*), is the deepest and most hidden cause of crises (*der innerste und geheimste Grund der Crisen*), of the crying contradictions within which bourgeois production is carried on and which, even at a cursory glance, reveal it as only a transitional, historical form (*historische Uebergangsform*).[17]

Here we should note something crucial: the homology between the narrow social 'foundation' [*Grundlage*] on which production rests and the 'secret' or 'hidden' 'cause' or 'ground' [*Grund*] of crisis. The basic restriction that production faces is contained in the fact that labour power must be *indirectly* produced in order to overcome its inherently limited nature, and this indirect production must be effected through all sorts of 'narrow' social bases: the nation, race, gender, physical attributes of bodies, language, ideology, the historical restrictions of consumption for subsistence, and so forth. This *Grundlage*, on which labour power must be dealt with (because it is restricted to the physical corporeality and finitude of the worker), exists in a constant interchange with the cause or *Grund* of crisis, the spasms and seizures that capital must endure when it becomes a barrier to itself.

The major contribution of Uno's theory of crisis, it seems to us, is how he focuses our thinking of this 'deepest and most hidden' cause or ground of crisis identified by Marx in the process of the commodification of labour power, while elaborating upon the way this deep cause becomes concealed by economic phenomena produced from within the unfolding of the accumulation process. Uno therefore identified precisely how the 'narrowness' (*Bornirtheit*) of capital's own 'boundaries' or 'barriers' (*Schranken*) stem from 'limits' (*Grenzen*) thrown up by capital itself, a reflexive relation back upon its own foundations that always returns to the 'ontological defect' of the labour power commodity.[18]

---

17 Marx, *Economic Manuscript 1861–1863* (*Theories of Surplus Value*), in MECW, Vol. 32, p. 274 [translation modified]; Marx, *Zur Kritik der Politischen Ökonomie* (*Manuskript 1861–1863*), in *Marx-Engels Gesamtausgabe* [hereafter MEGA], Bd. 3.4, p. 1276.

18 For an extensive theoretical development of this 'ontological defect' (*sonzaironteki kashi*), see Nagahara 2008.

In a theoretical tour de force, Uno demonstrates this concealment in his analysis of the accumulation process, and what he calls 'the direct cause of crisis' found therein. The direct cause of crisis is specifically identified in the accumulation phase of economic prosperity, when production processes 'widen' based on generous extensions of credit and the establishment of low interest rates, which allow capitalists to keep production going without fear of selling their products of labour to final consumers. With widened production, prices of raw materials become inflated while larger and larger numbers of workers are absorbed in production, the latter of which raises wage levels and consequently pulls down profit rates.

The tendency of profit rates to fall as a result of rising wages, however, is itself concealed by exuberant speculations by commercial creditors on the prices of increasingly overstocked commodities that continue to be produced without concern for final sales, itself made possible due to the availability of credit to manufacturing. With credit mediating finance and industry, the conditions for the *possibility* of crisis in the separation of buying and selling now appear across industries, precisely at the moment when the forecasted and speculated upon prices of these commodities become impossible to realise, leading to the phenomenon of excess capital in the form of unsold commodities, which in turn leads to defaults on payments and panic among banks and creditors, who scramble for hard cash and cut back on lines of credit while increasing interest rates as a last ditch attempt to compensate for rampant defaulting of payments. Rising interest rates then collide with falling profit rates, resulting in the inability of capitalists to reinvest in production and maintain production on the same scale. The social reproduction process is interrupted and production grinds to a halt. The resulting phenomenon of excess capital in the form of excess means of production and means of consumption now exists alongside a growing mass of unemployed workers, a point that connects us to the crucial question of *population.*

The separation between excess capital and a growing surplus population thus becomes the volatile ground upon which the historical origins of capitalist production are repeated in a new phase of prosperity with the commodification of labour power. The possibility for the commodification of labour power is secured, however, only on the basis of the formation of a relative surplus population *during the phase of depression*. The significance of the formation of a relative surplus population is that while capitalist production must circulate and consume labour power as a commodity despite being unable to produce it directly, its own methods of production lead to the emergence of an available mass of workers who have nothing except their labour power to sell as a commodity. This is precisely where capital attempts to *indirectly* 'produce' labour power, through the formation and maintenance of this 'available mass'. The cycle of accumulation can only be shown to be logically sutured as a circuit-process, therefore, by *presupposing* theoretically the commodification of labour power. Nonetheless, as Uno argues, the suturing of this cycle in theory remains *stained* or *scarred* by capitalist production's fundamental Achilles' heel, the ontologically scarred labour power that becomes 'incarnated' in capital's body.[19]

To repeat the basic point of Uno's theory of crisis, however: this cycle operates *through*, and not in spite of, the existence of this Achilles' heel. At the same time, the Achilles' heel is occluded in thought by the phenomenon of unsold commodities whose prices are exuberantly speculated upon at the zenith of prosperity, itself the result of credit and industrial financing. One of Uno's major contributions to a theory of crisis is thus found in his analysis of credit in the accumulation process, and the role of credit in bringing about what contemporary economic discourse calls exuberant speculation. It is this wild speculation that artificially raises prices and makes the realisation of surplus value difficult or impossible.

The very conditions of possibility that lead to this difficulty in realising surplus value, however, are themselves formed by capital's social and historical restrictions in attempting to bypass or overcome – without resolving – the problem of the commodification of labour power. Yet, at the same time, it is precisely the existence of excess capital in the form of unsold commodities – which Marx extensively analyses in Volume 3 – that stands rusting before our eyes in the most phenomenal form. This *hides* or *conceals* the deep cause of crisis. As Uno writes,

> [T]he true cause of crisis phenomena is concealed within accumulated, overstocked commodities accumulated in the expectation of a rise in price through the speculations of merchant and commercial capital. The direct cause of crisis is the fact that the forecasted price is not realised and defaults on payments arise. Phenomenally speaking, it thus looks like the

19 'The worker receives the equivalent of the labour time objectified in him, and gives his value-creating, value-increasing living labour time. He sells himself as an effect. He is absorbed and incarnated into the body of capital [*wird er absorbiert vom und inkarniert in das Kapital*] as a cause [*Ursache*], as activity [*Tätigkeit*]. Thus the exchange turns into its opposite, and the laws of private property – liberty, equality, property – property in one's own labour, and free disposition over it – turn into the worker's propertylessness and the dispossession of his labour [*Eigentumslosigkeit des Arbeiters und Entäußerung seiner Arbeit*]'. See Marx, *Grundrisse der Kritik der politischen Ökonomie*, in MEW, Bd. 42, p. 575; Marx, *Economic Manuscripts of 1857–1858* [*Grundrisse*], in MECW, Vol. 29, p. 64.

> root of crisis is found in the fact that, while commodities have been produced, they cannot be sold. (*Theory of Crisis*, p. 44)

What is at stake in Uno's *Theory of Crisis*, therefore, is a thinking of how the deep cause of crisis in capitalism is necessarily tied to the original, yet compulsively repeated, historical restriction of capitalist production in having to consume labour power as a commodity despite the inability of capitalist production to produce labour power as a commodity directly. This historical restriction on capitalist production signifies nothing less than the very origins of the capitalist commodity economy, and is deeply linked to the original and irrational emergence of capital as a social relation, in the form of the 'so-called primitive accumulation'.[20]

At the same time, however – and it is on this point that Uno shows us what is truly at stake for *theory itself* – this deep cause of crisis becomes occluded in thought by the very methods of capitalist production, once labour power is (and theoretically can be assumed to be) consumed as a commodity, a conceptual physics of concealment central to capital, in which, in Marx's terms, 'the process vanishes in the result'.[21] On the basis of the commodification of labour power, capitalist accumulation cannot help but conceal the deep cause of crisis with a more phenomenally immediate 'direct cause', namely in the production of excess capital. The task of historical analysis according to Uno, therefore, is to shed light on how this occlusion takes place practically and not just logically in order to demonstrate, theoretically, that capitalist production cannot take place except through class struggle.

Crisis and the Theory of Populations Peculiar to Capitalist Society

At this point we must take up Marx's theory of 'the law of population peculiar to the capitalist mode of production' (*der kapitalistischen Produktionsweise eigentümliches Populationsgesetz*),[22] because it is precisely through this mechanism that Marx demonstrates how the motion of capitalist accumulation also produces the social conditions of capitalist reproduction. But how and in what ways does Marx demonstrate this? In Volumes I and III of *Capital* especially,

20 For an analysis of the significance of the 'so-called primitive accumulation', linked to this theoretical reading, see Walker 2011a, pp. 384–404.

21 Marx, *Capital*, Vol. 1, in MECW, Vol. 35, p. 190; Marx, *Das Kapital*, Bd. 1, in MEW, Bd. 23, p. 195.

22 Marx, *Capital*, Vol. 1, in MECW, Vol. 35, p. 626; Marx, *Das Kapital*, Bd. 1, in MEW, Bd. 23, p. 660.

Marx shows how, on the basis of the transformation of labour power into a commodity, capitalist production unavoidably leads to the overproduction of capital itself and crisis. Uno has especially clarified how this can *only* occur at the zenith of the accumulation phase of prosperity. What is the resulting phase of accumulation? It is a phase of depression, during which time two things generally take place on the road to the renewal of capitalist production. First, the technical composition of capital is reorganised with better and more efficient machinery. This process, however, is restricted by time, and cannot simply take place automatically; in this regard, the time it takes to replace old machinery with new machinery determines the temporal length of the phase of depression. Partly because of the difficulty in selling off old fixed capital, workers are laid off during phases of depression, forming what Marx called a relative surplus population. It is called this because this population now stands in a relationship of relative excess to the level of demand for a regular labouring population and thus is located in a general separation or at a distance from capitalist production. This population is not an absolute social surplus, but a surplus that can only be grasped in its *relationality* to capitalist production, from which it has been cast out as the most easily disposable commodity: capital can always dispose of the worker's physical body during the phase of depression, in which capital attempts to shed as much labour power as it can. And this relationality is in essence contained within capital itself, a circular or cyclical relation that stems from the fact that 'labour power is the form under which variable capital exists during the process of production' (*Arbeitskraft ist die Form, worin das variable Kapital innerhalb des Produktionsprozesses existiert*).[23]

In its relative separation from production, however, this relative surplus population now forms a social mass of workers who, theoretically, once again have nothing but their labour power to sell as a commodity, establishing and setting in motion a cyclical process of disposal and re-capture of labour power. In this way, Marx theorises the law of populations peculiar to capitalist production, namely that while capitalist production cannot produce labour power as a commodity directly, it can produce a relative surplus population, which functions as a *mechanism* for capital to bridge this gap *indirectly*.[24] This mass of bodies must then sell their potential to labour – their labour power – in order to consume their daily necessities, in other words, a certain quantum of the means of subsistence that capitalist production can produce directly. Thus capital, through the form of population, turns a direct barrier to itself into

23 Marx, *Capital*, Vol. 1, in MECW, Vol. 35, p. 585; Marx, *Das Kapital*, Bd. 1, in MEW, Bd. 23, p. 616.

24 We have theorised this elsewhere as a 'mechanism' for the *axiomatic traversal* of capital's limits to itself. See Walker 2012, pp. 15–37, and Walker 2016, Chs. 5 and 6.

a new *threshold* of accumulation, transforming this Achilles' heel into a new beginning or commencement. In doing so, the 'narrow limits' or the social and historical restrictions of capitalist production are again overcome *without being resolved*, thereby establishing the conditions for another phase of prosperity.

Let us now summarise several key points in the above discussion. First, for Uno, the concept of crisis must be differentiated between a *fundamental* cause in the commodification of labour power, and a '*direct* cause' in the collision between falling rates of profit and rising interest rates, and in the phenomenon of speculation on excess capital in the form of overstocked commodities, which conceals from thought or covers over the tendency of the rate of profit to fall. What is most visible and taken as the cause of crisis are high prices on overproduced commodities; when these cannot sell, the immediate result is a chain reaction of defaults on payments, and thus further investments in production cannot take place. Another way to put this is that the direct cause of crisis is about the *phenomenal form of crisis*. This phenomenal form of crisis, however, conceals the *ontological form of crisis* of capitalist production itself in the commodification of labour power. Crisis for Uno, therefore, has to be understood on at least two levels: the phenomenal level and the 'ontological' level.[25]

Second, however, in Uno's theoretical elaboration of the inevitability of crisis, crisis as a phase of capitalist accumulation does not mark the end of the capitalist system; rather, it is merely a passing phase that mediates the phases of prosperity and depression. It is during the phase of depression (in addition to the phase of crisis) that a relative surplus population is formed, which allows Marx to theoretically show how capitalist production can, as it were, compensate for its original and fundamental inability to produce labour power as a commodity by producing a relative surplus population, which creates the general social milieu, the 'narrowly restricted social foundation' for the commodification of labour power.

Yet even so – and here is where Uno's analysis of the relationship between excess capital and surplus populations becomes crucial – the commodification of labour power cannot be assumed to take place automatically on the road to renewal and prosperity *simply* because a surplus population has been produced as compensation for capital's inherent historical restriction. The reason is that,

25 It is precisely on this point that Nagahara develops the aforementioned formulation of the 'ontological defects' of capital centred around the questions of labour power and land. Needless to say, land is equally a decisive problem here, and we should simply state that for reasons of length and topicality, we cannot extensively enter into how the phenomenon of crisis intersects with the agrarian question, except to point out the importance of this connection. See here in particular Ōuchi 1954.

precisely because capitalist production has ground to a halt during the phase of depression, it is as if a 'dead zone' or void appears or intervenes between excess capital and surplus populations. There is no money to be exchanged for labour power at this moment in the cycle. There is only decaying and dying – the 'moral degradation' and the devaluation of capital.

Thus, Uno's reading of Marx shows another way to think this conceptual sequence of 'the first time as tragedy, the second time as farce',[26] for the tragedy of capital's inability to directly produce labour power as a commodity now becomes transmuted – in the theory of crisis – into farce, where capital still cannot presuppose its own ability to capture labour power as a commodity *even through* capital's enormous power to produce a relative surplus population as compensation for capital's fundamental historical restriction (the originary and primal 'tragedy'). The difference between tragedy and farce here is found precisely in the ambiguous phrase, regularly repeated in Chapter 15 of Volume 3 of *Capital*: *an excess of capital exists alongside* (*neben*) *a surplus population.*[27] Alongside, but it is a relation of a non-relation, for here there is no exchange. Alongside (*neben*) draws a relation, but also a suspension; it implies that something is 'corollary', an 'accessory', tangential, auxiliary, and so forth. Two things *accompany* each other, but cause and effect are held in stasis – 'alongside' reminds us of Balibar's point, placed at the outset of this chapter: crisis furnishes the entire mode of production with a specific form of movement, but this movement is also linked to a particularly perverse form of immobility, a tension, an inertia; nothing happens, which is precisely the void in which to think the renewal of the political from within Marx's logic. Not even the production of a relative surplus population can guarantee capitalist reproduction once, that is, we grasp the principles of the inevitability of crisis. At this point, not even a god can save capitalism.

In this way, the historical origins of capitalist production are concentrated inwards towards its own pure drive, compulsively repeated at the level of the logic inherent in capital itself, in which the historicity of capital's contingent formation is constantly and desperately repressed, covered over by the *phenomenal* necessity of its logic. The 'ontological' crisis of capitalist production is more accurately its *hauntological* crisis.[28] On the theoretical level, Uno cla-

26 Marx, *The Eighteenth Brumaire of Louis Bonaparte*, in *MECW*, Vol. 11, p. 103.

27 See Marx, *Capital*, Vol. 3, in *MECW*, Vol. 37, pp. 239–65; Marx, *Das Kapital*, Bd. 3, in *MEW*, Bd. 25, pp. 251–77.

28 On the hauntology of capital, see in particular Derrida 1994, but also Nagahara 2008, in which this 'conjuring trick' (*escamotage*) of capital is theoretically developed at length and related to the form of crisis.

rifies how this takes place in the phase of prosperity, which is itself based on the phase of recession. Crisis is thus itself a period, phase, or *plane*, we could say, that expresses the difference and inserts itself in the interval between the phases of prosperity and recession. To speak of the hauntological crisis, however, is to return once again to the more fundamental or ontological form of crisis, located in the labour power commodity, a hauntology that is a central question of the nature and concept of necessity or inevitability itself – here Uno reminds us that the cycle of capitalist reproduction is never simply a mechanical cycle, but a profoundly *historical* one.

Labour Power as the 'Indispensably Disposable' Commodity

One of the most important problems that characterises and distinguishes Uno's theory of crisis from the broad field of texts in the history of Marxist theory devoted to the issue of crisis is his insistence on the meaning and complexity behind the phrase 'the commodification of labour power'. For Uno, this phrase is the key to the entirety of Marx's work, but also the pivotal element in a capitalist commodity economy itself. Around this phrase an entire series of problems and relations are concentrated: the logic of capital and history of capitalist development, the origin of capital and its repetition, the inside and outside of capital as a social relation, and the peculiar dynamics by which these instances are inverted into each other. But Uno also adds to this phrase a singularly complex concept, one that is deceptive in its *apparent* simplicity. This is what Uno referred to as the *muri*: the (im)possibility, the impasse, the contradiction, ir/rationality, nihil of reason, and the forced nature of the commodification of labour power.

In this peculiar turn of phrase, Uno specifies that capitalist production, which attempts to form a pure circle of inputs and outputs, always contains this contradictory *muri* in the commodification of labour power, which is something that is 'passing through' the entire circuit. But this *muri* is also an exceptionally polyvalent term: the commodification of labour power is also treated by Uno as itself the particularly (im)possible phenomenon of capitalism, because as Nagahara Yutaka and others have suggested, capital requires certain degrees of *force* or *forcing* in order to undertake the 'indirect' production of this thing that marks capital's fundamental Achilles' heel and allows it to compensate for it. Therefore, we should immediately note something important – this *muri* identified by Uno in no way suggests that somehow capitalism is grounded in something 'truly impossible' or that it secretly 'does not work'. It means, in fact, the exact opposite. Capital *works* because of the dynamism and tension that exists in this peculiar space, wherein labour power cannot be directly produced (a barrier that *should be* absolute) and yet this Achilles' heel *tends to be overcome* by means of the form of the capitalist law of populations.

We have attempted on a number of other occasions to develop this concept of *muri*, a term that indicates a deep and complex field of problems.[29] For the time being we will simply note that this term points toward crucial linkages between the theory of crisis and the general broad concerns of Marxist theory. It indicates, for instance, the (im)possible closure of Marx's theoretical exposition of the logic of capitalist accumulation, signifying the possibility and impossibility to assume the closure of the logical circle that capitalist reproduction represents; it reveals the necessary historical contamination of the logic, a structure in which capital must foreclose itself as a sphere of rationality, only paradoxically, on the basis of a '*nihil* of reason' on – and through – which the fundamental principles of capitalist commodity economy rest and cannot but dwell.

Further, when we think of labour power as a commodity in relation to the cyclical nature of capitalist crisis, we are presented with its *double and contradictory nature*. In the phase of prosperity, labour power is the most *indispensable* commodity, for no other commodity can produce new values within capitalist production. Yet, once this indispensable commodity is consumed in the course of capital's circuit-process, capitalist production is already on the way towards an outbreak of crisis at the zenith of prosperity, which is also to say that once labour power is consumed in production as the most *indispensable* commodity, capitalist prosperity is already moving in the direction of capitalist crisis and depression, when labour power now transforms into the opposite phenomenon, namely into the most *disposable* commodity. This is why labour power appears as the contradictory embodiment of being *indispensably disposable*. What Uno calls the *muri* is a formulation that expresses the conceptual dynamics of how labour power could exist as both indispensable and disposable in the same space and time.[30]

---

29 We have dealt elsewhere with the extensive development of this term, but it remains an irresolvable and endless theoretical problem. See in particular Walker 2016, Kawashima 2005, and Walker 2010.

30 For a concrete and historical analysis of how the contradictory embodiment of labour power as indispensably disposable can, and has, become mapped onto the 'axiomatics' of ethnicity and race, as well as onto diverse forms of colonial exploitation and domination, see Kawashima 2009.

Imperialism and Crisis

Uno's *Theory of Crisis* concerns not only the *logical* position of crisis within the analysis of capital. It also provides us with extremely important analytical tools for historical research. These tools, however, are not always explicitly articulated. Rather, we ourselves must derive them from the systematic intervention Uno is making, precisely because these concepts often appear or are developed in the interstices of his argument and imply a careful understanding of the politicality that lurks beneath the surface of this seemingly formalist inquiry. First, Uno clearly emphasises over and over again that the *principles* of political economy, or the (relatively) pure logic of capital taken in isolation, must never be mistaken for a direct reflection of actual history or the historical process taken as the history of capitalist development, with all its inherent contingencies and singularities. In the way theory functions in the natural sciences, so here the pure principles represent a theoretical artifice that can help us navigate the Heraclitean flux of actually existing historical phenomena – in this sense, Uno takes over and develops the implications of Marx's well-known formulation: 'in the analysis of economic forms, neither microscopes nor chemical reagents are of use. The force of abstraction must replace both (*Die Abstraktionskraft muß beide ersetzen*)'.[31] Uno's *Theory of Crisis*, therefore, is not simply about how the phenomena of crisis, its inevitability, must be understood, in the final instance, merely on the level of principle or in the logical system of *Capital*. Uno goes to great lengths to emphasise that in our actual world, these principles cannot be *directly* applied to understand our present. The minimal reason is that capitalism historically developed into the stage of imperialism after 1870s, and with this shift, the *form of crisis* changed in a way that, in Uno's words, 'distorts' (*waikyoku sareru*) the demonstration of the inevitability of crisis on the level of pure theory. The key change in the form of crisis in the stage of imperialism is that while crises still break out periodically (thereby revealing their inevitability), they do not break out with the regularity that they did in the era of laissez-faire capitalism, when crises broke out, between the 1820s and 1860s, every ten years (thereby revealing a periodicity and repetition that could be formulated into an object of knowledge).

In the stage of imperialism, however, the phenomena of *chronic recession* and *chronic unemployment* become the historical norm. There are many reasons for this, but we can mention the key ones briefly. Here, Uno argues for the analytical need to produce a theoretical articulation between Marx's *Capital*

31 Marx, *Capital*, Vol. 1, in MECW, Vol. 35, p. 8; Marx, *Das Kapital*, Bd. 1, in MEW, Bd. 23, p. 12.

and Lenin's *Imperialism: The Highest Stage of Capitalism.* With the rise of finance capital, the export of capital to colonies and foreign markets can take place easily, bringing back huge profits to the financial centres to the point where it becomes unnecessary for capital to transform the entirety of society under the axiomatics of a specifically *capitalist* commodity economy. Large agricultural swaths of the world still locked in relatively backward forms of social organisation and general commodity economic activity no longer pose an *obstacle* to capitalist development, but instead can be shaped and coded to accelerate capitalist development by virtue of becoming part of an expanding relative surplus population, thereby, for example, contributing to an overall depression of wages. Both national and the colonial agricultural populations now constitute strata of an expanding formation of *an international relative surplus population.*

How can this be explained? We know that the relative surplus population theoretically must be formed during phases of depression. As we pointed out earlier, moreover, the temporal length of the phase of recession is greatly influenced by the time it takes to sell off old machinery (fixed capital), and to replace old technologies with newer, more productive and efficient ones. It is precisely on this point that the development of capitalism into a specific stage of imperialism becomes significant. For, with the rise of finance capital, monopolistic investments in increasingly larger and larger forms of fixed capital raise the organic composition of capital exponentially, primarily because the dominant industries during this era are steel production and other extractive and chemical industries (e.g., coal and oil). The significance this holds for a theory of crisis is that phases of depression thus become dragged out or elongated over extended periods of time because of the huge difficulties in selling off and replacing such large forms of fixed capital. Today, to take one example, we might think of this phenomenon precisely in the new 'ruins' of the United States, the vast and abandoned rust belt of Pittsburgh's steel mills, the empty plants of Detroit, the deserted factories of upstate New York and elsewhere. This is one of the key reasons why recession in imperialism cannot help becoming chronic in nature, why the relative surplus population expands to include national and foreign agricultural populations, and why unemployment generally becomes chronic.

Third, as Lenin is quick to remind us, the export of capital to colonies leads to world war over regional supremacy in international markets. This is an important point for an understanding of capitalist crisis, because war increasingly also becomes a means to extricate national economies out of chronic depression. As Uno pointed out, it is on this point that the nature and function of the armaments and munitions industry is extremely important (here we might think about why Korean colonial populations were considered an 'indispensably disposable' workforce in the Japanese military-industrial complex after 1937 and during World War II).[32] At the same time, it also shows how the analysis of the phenomenon of crisis cannot simply be undertaken with the pure theory or internal logic of the fundamental principles of a capitalist commodity economy alone. In other words, we cannot simply rely on Marx's analysis in *Capital* to grasp the *historical* nature of capitalist crisis, but must also and equally grasp Lenin's analysis of imperialism and place it into relation with the pure theory of crisis and its 'fundamental causes'.

Finally, in speaking of war as a means to extricate an economy from chronic depression, we must therefore speak of how the work of the state and para-state institutions come to work for the reproduction of capitalist production, and to work in the service of trying to realise in 'actual' history what Uno has demonstrated to be impossible to realise even on the level of capital's logic, namely the ideal or perfected expression of the business cycle and a logically pure circle of capitalist accumulation. (Here is where Uno departs radically – to the left – of the likes of Schumpeter and his metaphysical ideals of 'creative destruction', for example.) The state and para-state institutions produce precisely this fantasy of being able to actualise in history that which is demonstrably impossible on the theoretical level. How they produce this fantasy demands a thinking of the state's relation to the economy, which is emphatically not simply as a superstructural result of the economic base. Rather, it shows us a way to think the state's *subservience* to the economy; the state and para-state institutions working as agents *for* the economy (we might think here of the old Althusserian formulation of 'determination in the final instance', but an instance 'that never arrives'). This is to say that the state demotes itself from an autonomous political power over the economy, but only to *promote* the economy through a vast production of *signs of the economy*.[33] Here, we develop this point by means of a decisive formulation in *Anti-Oedipus*, wherein Deleuze and Guattari write of the imperial state: 'Never before has a state lost so much power only in order to enter with so much force into the service of the signs of economic power'.[34] From what standpoint does the state enter with so much force into 'the service of the signs of economic power'? They mention: 'From the standpoint of the flow of "free" workers: the control of manual labour and of wages; from the standpoint of the flow of industrial and commercial production; the granting of

32 On the pre-history of this question, see Kawashima 2009.

33 This point ought to lead also to another reading of Nicos Poulantzas's final work, *State, Power, Socialism*, particularly his important reflections on the dual character of the state and economy (1978, pp. 163–99), but we will leave this cross-reading for another instance.

34 Deleuze and Guattari 1983, p. 252; Deleuze and Guattari 1972, p. 300.

monopolies, favourable conditions for accumulation, and the struggle against overproduction'.[35] All of these moments alert us to the bizarre role of the state, which must always appear to function – institutionally, in its relation to the law, in its apparently autonomous internal organisation, in its independent political relations – at a distance from the social relation of capital, while nevertheless serving as the guarantor or formative force for the 'narrow social basis' upon which the capital's dreadful *commencement* is constantly repeated in the commodification of labour power. What the state does is effectively recode the *economic* content of capital's own dynamics and redeploy this content in another social vector, in essence operating as a force to conceal or *overcode* capital's austere logical violence, appearing phenomenally to overwrite this logical violence so that it should appear as a reflection of *the natural state* of social relations.

Keeping Deleuze and Guattari's earlier analysis of the form of the state in mind in relation to the phenomenon of crisis requires us to think through the problem of how labour power as a commodity is *represented* or *included* on the level of the signs of the economy, and *as a method* by which capitalist crisis can be managed but never eliminated. In other words, how might the contradictory character of labour power as the indispensably disposable commodity be coded as a sign of the economy? For instance, elsewhere we have analysed how designations such as 'manual labour' versus 'skilled labour', 'factory worker' versus 'day worker', 'modern' and 'feudal', 'developed' and 'backward', 'particularity' and 'universality', 'national' and 'foreign', all historically produced categories of knowledge, become mapped onto the production of national and ethnic signs of economy such as 'Korean' and 'Japanese'.[36] The production of knowledge and the microphysics of power that accompanies it thus need to be taken into account as a critical way to understand how capitalist crises are managed *through the form of the nation state*, and represented ultimately as something that is accidental and contingent. This is where Uno's basic theoretical question, 'How to demonstrate the inevitability of crisis?', has political meaning for us today.

We have seen the wide variety of problems in Marxist theoretical work addressed by Uno's *Theory of Crisis*. All of these problems concern not only theoretical questions but also political problems and political projects. Here, we have to point out that Uno's work, which often appears highly abstract, functioning at a level that might seem to exclude the concrete demands and tactical

35 Deleuze and Guattari 1983, pp. 252–3; Deleuze and Guattari 1972, p. 300.
36 See Kawashima 2009 and Walker 2011b.

complexities of politics, may appear formalistic but this is only an *apparent* formalism. In fact, Uno's crisis theory is consciously positioned *against* the excessive formalism of much Marxist theoretical work. Uno's formalism is produced to combat tiresome historicism and to open up more deeply onto the question of the *historicity* of capital in the commodification of labour power.

In order to return with this point to the beginning, and think about where this analysis of crisis can lead us, let us quote from Uno at some length, in a later reflection on the nature of crisis theory and its position within his own overall theoretical system:

> In recent years, I have attempted to theoretically purify the economic theories of *Capital* on the level of principle – on the one hand, my intention has been to break through to new paths of cooperation and interchange between the field of the economic and the other forms of social scientific research, but on the other hand, related in another sense to this same problem, I have also tried to escape from the formalism that often constrains or holds back the extension of possibilities for research in political economy. I am of course fully aware that I alone would be incapable of such a massive task, but nevertheless, even within the narrow confines of my own research, I feel that I must consider my theoretical project always in relation to this larger problem of social scientific research in general. For the majority of Marxists who believe that every single word and phrase proposed in *Capital* is unchangeable and sacrosanct, my attempt to theoretically purify it has been considered something shocking or outrageous, and for a large portion of this group, my work has been turned into something that absolutely must be denounced for political reasons.
>
> Of course, I do not imagine that I have a perfect understanding of all aspects of the theorisations present in *Capital*, nor do I think at all that *Capital* is a mistaken work – every single thing that I have attempted to do stems solely from my personal understanding of *Capital*. This is precisely because I think that unless we ourselves purify the theory of principle latent in *Capital* to the extent that it can be effectively utilised in the analysis of imperialism, and in relation to questions such as the concrete analysis of Japanese capitalism, it will be impossible to avoid lapsing into formalism, and a realisation of effective cooperation between political economy and research in other areas of social scientific critique and cultural knowledge will be impossible. It is this theoretical process that will open new modalities for the settling of the theory of the principles of political economy, the logic of capital itself. We cannot blame Marx for errors that result from the fact that he could not possibly have known of the stage

> of imperialism, but it is nevertheless a fact that capitalism possesses this imperialist stage, and it is necessary that political economy, as a historical science, is able to clarify its nature.
>
> When we speak of the inevitability of crisis, the inevitability of war, the inevitability of revolution, and so on, we utilise this same identical word 'inevitability' or 'necessity' (*hitsuzensei*), but these three formulations cannot be proven or legitimated through identical, or even similar, methods, because the *content* of this word 'necessity' differs in each case. Although Marx's own considerations on this point remain unclear and undeveloped, we can at least say that, since he had no knowledge of imperialist war, he confronted a different set of facts than we do with respect to the problem of the inevitability of warfare. Thus, we must also say that he obviously had a different understanding than our own regarding the relation or split between the inevitability of crisis and the necessity of revolution. In the case of the inevitability of crisis, I believe that it can be proven, indeed that it *must* be proven, on the level of the theory of principles of political economy, at the level of the logical structure of capital, but if it is so, *how* should this inevitability be proven? It is precisely this question that has an intimate and inseparable relation to the purification of the principles of political economy, and it is the theory of crisis that provides the touchstone of these principles themselves.[37]

Uno's *Theory of Crisis* provides for us a way to think not only about Marx's *Capital* as a theoretical structure – it also provides us with the conditions of possibility for a renewal of politics in the face of our current situation. While theory therefore appears timeless and eternal, it emphatically does not mean that the interconnected totality of the laws and norms constituting capitalist society is itself timeless and eternal. Paradoxically, the theoretical eternality of the laws is precisely what allows us to grasp the historicity and finitude of the capitalist mode of production itself, as it is compulsively repeated in the present in the specifically capitalist mechanism of the commodification of labour power.

For Uno, the commodification of labour power *is* the ultimate or root cause of capitalism's inevitable crisis; it is capitalism's *original crisis*, if you will. This means that the violence of the phenomenon of capitalist society's economic crises is itself a derivative expression of the more basic, violent crisis that surrounds the political, social and even cultural question of labour power as a

37 Uno, 'Kyōkō no hitsuzensei wa ika ni shite ronshō sareru beki ka' ['How Should the Necessity of Crisis be Proven?'], originally published in the January 1959 issue of *Shisō*, reprinted in *UKC*, Vol. 4, here pp. 143–4.

commodity. Put differently, fundamentally economic expressions of the phenomena of crisis (e.g., falling profit rates colliding with rising interest rates, defaults on payments, over-production and under-consumption, phases of depression, mass unemployment, etc.) do not lead to the inevitable collapse of the system. It does mean, however, that to actualize a true collapse of the capitalist system, the root cause of capitalist crisis itself must be overcome (*aufheben*). To overcome capitalist crisis is to overcome the inter-connected totality of capitalism's basic economic laws of motion, which fundamentally pivot around the commodification of labour power. This fact, that capitalist crisis is inevitable and a part of capital's fundamental composition, transforms for us into a vector of politicization once we locate its 'deepest' cause in the 'impossibility' of the commodification of labour power. Insofar as this commodification is always volatile and necessarily unstable, Uno taught us that crisis might also serve to educate us politically towards another necessity: the necessity of revolution against the forces and forms of capitalist society.

Bibliography

Althusser, Louis 1970, 'From *Capital* to Marx's Philosophy', in *Reading Capital*, by Louis Althusser and Étienne Balibar, translated by Ben Brewster, London: Verso.

Bagehot, Walter 1910, *Lombard Street: A Description of the Money Market*, London: Smith, Elder & Company.

Balibar, Étienne 1970, 'Elements for a Theory of Transition', in *Reading Capital*, by Louis Althusser and Étienne Balibar, translated by Ben Brewster, London: Verso.

Clarke, Simon 1994, *Marx's Theory of Crisis*, London: Palgrave.

Deleuze, Gilles and Félix Guattari 1972, *L'Anti-Œdipe*, Paris: Minuit

Deleuze, Gilles and Félix Guattari 1983, *Anti-Oedipus*, translated by R. Hurley et al., Minnesota: University of Minnesota Press.

Derrida, Jacques 1994, 'Apparition of the Inapparent: The Phenomenological "Conjuring Trick"', in *Specters of Marx*, translated by Peggy Kamuf, Chicago: University of Chicago Press.

Dobb, Maurice 1937, *Political Economy and Capitalism*, London: Routledge.

Howard, Michael C. and John E. King, *A History of Marxian Economics, Vol. 2: 1929–1990*, Princeton: Princeton University Press.

Itoh, Makoto 1980, *Value and Crisis*, New York: Monthly Review Press.

Karatani, Kojin 1995, *Architecture as Metaphor: Language, Number, Money*, translated by Sabu Kohso, Cambridge, MA: MIT Press.

Karatani, Kojin 2020, *Marx: Towards the Centre of Possibility*, translated and edited by Gavin Walker, London: Verso.

Kawashima, Ken C. 2005, 'Capital's Dice-Box Shaking: The Contingent Commodifications of Labour Power', *Rethinking Marxism*, 17, no. 4: 609–26.

Kawashima, Ken C. 2009, *The Proletarian Gamble: Korean Workers in Interwar Japan*, Durham, NC: Duke University Press.

Kawashima, Ken C. 'The Hidden Area Between Marx and Foucault', *positions: asia critique*, "The End of Area: Biopolitics, Geopolitics, History," edited by Naoki Sakai and Gavin Walker (vol. 27, no. 1, february 2019)

League of Nations 1931, *The Course and Phases of World Economic Depression*, Geneva: Secretariat of the League of Nations.

Marx, Karl 1951, *Theories of Surplus Value*, edited by Karl Kautsky, translated by G.A. Bonner and Emile Burns, London: Lawrence & Wishart.

Marx, Karl 1990, *Capital*, Volume 1, translated by Ben Fowkes, New York: Penguin.

Marx, Karl 1991, *Capital*, Volume 3, translated by David Fernbach, London: Penguin.

Marx, Karl 1992, *Capital*, Volume 2, translated by David Fernbach, London: Penguin.

Marx, Karl and Friedrich Engels 1956–90, *Marx-Engels Werke* [*MEW*], 43 Bds., Berlin: Dietz Verlag.

Marx, Karl and Friedrich Engels 1975–, *Marx-Engels Gesamtausgabe* [*MEGA*], 65 Vols., Berlin: Dietz Verlag.

Marx, Karl and Frederick Engels 1975–2004, *Collected Works of Karl Marx and Frederick Engels* [*MECW*], 50 Vols., Moscow, London, New York: Progress Publishers, Lawrence & Wishart, and International Publishers.

Mitsuhiko, Takumi 2000, 'Kyōkōron no saikōchiku: Uno taikei no genkai o doko de koeru ka' ['The Reconstruction of Crisis Theory: From Where do we Overcome the Limits of Uno's System'], in *Marukusu riron no saikōchiku: Uno keizaigaku o dō ikasu ka* [*The Reconstruction of Marxian Theory: How to Revive Unoist Political Economy*], Tokyo: Shakai Hyōronsha.

Nagahara, Yutaka 2008, *Warera kashi aru mono tachi: Han-'shihon'ron no tame ni* [*We, the Defective Commodities: For an Analytics of Anti-'Capital'-ism*], Tokyo: Seidosha.

Nagahara, Yutaka 2016, *Yasagure tachi no gaitō: Kashi sonzai no seijikeizaigaku hihan josetsu* [*The Rabble on the Streets: An Introduction to the Political Economy of Damaged Life*], Tokyo: Koshisha.

Ōuchi, Tsutomu 1954, *Nōgyō kyōkō* [*Agrarian Crisis*], Tokyo: Yūhikaku.

Ōuchi, Tsutomu 1984, *Nihon Keizairon* (*jō*), Tokyo: Tokyo University Press.

Poulantzas, Nicos 1978, *State, Power, Socialism*, London: Verso.

Sekine, Thomas 1980, *Principles of Political Economy: Theory of a Purely Capitalist Society*, Sussex: Harvester Press.

Shaikh, Anwar 1978, 'An Introduction to the History of Crisis Theories', in *US Capitalism in Crisis*, New York: URPE.

Sweezy, Paul 1942, *The Theory of Capitalist Development*, New York: Monthly Review Press.

Tugan-Baranowski, M.I. 1931 [1894], *Promyshlennye krizisy v sovremennoi Anglii, ikh prichiny i blizhaishie vliyaniya na narodnuyu zhizn* [*Industrial Crises in Contemporary England, their Causes and Immediate Influence on National Life*], Japanese translation, City: Publisher.

Uno, Kōzō 1935, 'The Necessity of Crisis in Capitalistic Society', *Kaizō*, February.

Uno, Kōzō 1950–77, *Uno Kōzō chosakushū* [UKC], 11 Vols., Tokyo: Iwanami Shoten.

Uno, Kōzō 1980, *Principles of Political Economy*, translated by Thomas Sekine, Sussex: Harvester Press.

Uno, Kōzō 1981, *Shihonron gojūnen* [*Fifty Years with Capital*], Vol. 2, Tokyo: Hōsei Daigaku Shuppankyoku.

Uno, Kōzō 2016, *Types of Economic Policies Under Capitalism*, translated by Thomas T. Sekine, edited by John R. Bell, Chicago: Haymarket Books.

Walker, Gavin 2010, 'Muri to iu iki to "kyō" no seisan' ['The Threshold of the *muri* and the Production of the Commons'], *Jōkyō*, Part 1 (May) and Part 2 (October).

Walker, Gavin 2011a, 'Primitive Accumulation and the Formation of Difference: On Marx and Schmitt', *Rethinking Marxism*, 23, no. 3: 384–404.

Walker, Gavin 2011b, 'Postcoloniality and the National Question in Marxist Historiography: Elements of the Debate on Japanese Capitalism', *Interventions*, 13, no. 1: 120–37.

Walker, Gavin 2012, 'The World of Principle, or Pure Capitalism: Exteriority and Suspension in Uno Kôzô', *Journal of International Economic Studies*, 26: 15–37.

Walker, Gavin 2016, *The Sublime Perversion of Capital*, Durham, NC: Duke University Press.

Yasuharu, Nakamura 2007, 'Dai-kyōkō-gata kyōkō no riron' ['A Theory of "Great Crisis"-type Crises'], in *Marukusu riron kenkyū* [*Research in Marxian Theory*], edited by Obata Michiaki et al., Tokyo: Ochanomizu Shobō.

Žižek, Slavoj 2009, *First as Tragedy, Second as Farce*, New York: Verso.

Works Cited in *Theory of Crisis*

Compiled by the translator.

Arnold, Thurman Wesley et. al., *The Aspirin Age, 1919–1941*, Simon and Schuster, 1966.

Bouniatian, Mentor. *Geschichte Der Handelskrisen In England: Im Zusammenhang Mit Der Entwicklung Des Englischen Wirtschaftslebens, 1640–1840*, (1908).

Bagehot, Walter. *Lombard Street: a description of the money market*, London: Smith, Elder, 1910.

Ellison, Thomas, *The Cotton Trade of Great Britain*, 1886.

Kuruma, Samezō. 'On the Confirmation of Marx's Theory of Crisis', *Studies in Crisis Theory*, Okuryūkan (1949).

Marx. *Capital*, Vol. 1, Penguin Books, 1990.

Marx. *Capital*, Vol. 2, Penguin Books, 1992.

Marx. *Capital*, Vol. 3, Penguin Books, 1991.

Marx. *Grundrisse*, Penguin Books, 1973.

Marx. *Theories of Surplus Value*, Progress Publishers, Parts I, II, and III, 1968.

Marx. 'Preface to *A Contribution to the Critique of Political Economy*', International Publishers, 1989.

League of Nations. *The Course and Phases of the World Economic Depression*, 1931.

Lenin, V.I. *Characterisation of Economic Romanticism*, 1897, in *Collected Works of V.I. Lenin*, Verso Press, 2019.

Spiethoff, Arthur. 'Krisen', translated by Yoshiyuki Mochizuki, Tokyo: Sanseido, 1936.

Spiethoff, Arthur 'Typical Cycles and Alternating Cycles of Business Alternations'.

Suzuki, Kōichiro. 'On the Plan of *Capital*', in *Shisō*, 1948 (December).

Teramura, T. 'Preparations for the publication of a scientific edition of *Theories of Surplus Value* in the Soviet Union', in *Keizaigaku Zasshi* (Osaka University of Commerce), 25, no. 4.

Tugan-Baranowski, Mikhail Ivanovich. *Studien zur Theorie und Geschichte der Handelskrisen in England*, (1894/1901), Jena, G. Fischer Publishers.

Uno Kōzō. *Uno Kōzō Complete Works*, Volumes 1–11, Iwanami Shoten, 1973.

Uno Kōzō. *Principles of Political Economy: Theory of a Purely Capitalist Society*, translated by Thomas Sekine, Sussex: Harvester Press, 1980.

Uno Kōzō. *The Types of Economic Policies under Capitalism*, translated by Thomas Sekine, Haymarket Books, 2016.

Uno Kōzō. *Theory of Method* (*Hōrōron*), UCZ, vol. 9

Uno Kōzō. *'Capital' and Socialism* (1958), UCZ, vol. 10.

Uno Kōzō. 'On the Method of Political Economy', *Shakai Kagaku Kenkyū* (University of Tokyo), vol. 2, no. 1, included in my *Studies in the Theory of Value*, republished in UKC, Vol. 3

Uno Kōzō. 'Money Capital and Real Capital', *UKC*, Vol. 3

Varga, Eugen. *World Economic Crises, 1848–1935*, translated by Michio Nagasumi, Vol. 1, Part 2, Tokyo: Keiō Shobo, 1938.

Index

Accumulation of capital 49, 52–53, 61, 65–67, 70, 72–74, 76, 82–84, 97, 101, 110–113, 138, 142, 144, 150, 152, 155, 164–165, 168, 176, 185–186, 190
  and the commodification of labour power 187
  and falling rate of profit 71
    see also *Falling rate of profit*
  and finance capital 34, 115
  and *muri* 193
  excessive 81, 166, 169–170, 180
  in late-developing countries 25
  in seventeenth and eighteenth centuries 33
  in phase of prosperity 52–58
  in post-war long boom 174
  in relation to organic composition of capital 52, 145–146, 153–154
    see also *Organic Composition of Capital*
  new 99, 103, 105
  vis-à-vis stages of capitalist development 50
Althusser, Louis 183, 184n16, 196
Armaments 7, 25
Arnold, Thurman W. 4n3, 5n5

Bagehot, Walter 19n19
Balibar, Etienne 177, 191
Bank system 39, 61n4, 62, 80, 158
  Banking Act of 1844 79n3
  Bank of England 79n5, 80n3
Boutanian, Mentor 19n16, 21n20
Business cycle 18, 20, 21n20, 31, 51–52, 61n4, 63n5, 98n2, 99n2, 106, 111, 146, 157, 167, 170, 172, 196

Capital
  banking 141
  commercial XIX, 12, 36, 38–39, 41, 48, 70, 74, 86, 91, 98, 108, 137, 139–141, 149, 164, 172, 187
  destruction of 52–53, 91–94, 100–101, 111, 166
  excess of 72–74, 76–78, 80–82, 84–86, 88–91, 93, 95–96, 98, 137, 145, 149–150, 153–155, 157, 166, 174, 179–180, 183, 186–188, 190–191
  fictitious 141
  finance capital 9–10, 15, 25, 34, 56–58, 57n2, 88n9, 115, 122n2, 125–126, 128n6
  fixed 26, 53–58, 59n3, 60, 63, 67, 70, 71n1, 92, 100–102, 106, 110–113, 114n4, 115, 156, 165, 167, 189, 195
  idle 39n32, 59–62, 70, 74–76, 96, 110, 140, 154–155, 158, 165–166, 170, 175
  industrial 12–13, 33, 36n31, 37–41, 40n33, 45, 61–65, 70, 74–78, 81, 84, 88n9, 89, 91, 94, 98n2, 104, 107–108, 110, 122n2, 138–140, 142, 149, 165–166, 169–170, 175
  interest-bearing 61, 108, 137, 141
  loanable XIX, 12, 39–41, 61–62, 70, 74, 76, 78–79, 81, 84, 88n9, 89, 91, 95, 97–98, 104, 108, 110, 114n4, 137, 141, 144, 149, 154–155, 165–166, 169–170, 175
  merchant 11–13, 19, 33, 36–41, 40n33, 45, 48, 60–61, 61n4, 65, 70, 74, 77, 86, 91, 93, 98n2, 107–108, 140–141, 144, 187
  money-lending 13, 37–38, 39n32, 40n33, 108
  shortage of 77–81
Capital (Marx's)
  method of 13, 14
  on absolute overproduction 153
  on amoritization 53n1
  on commercial credit 137
  on competition 96
  on cycles 151
  on dialectical method 124
  on excess capital 87n8
  on exchange 8, 29n26
  on fixed capital 110
  on general law of accumulation 47n36
  on industrial cycles 113n4
  on joint-stock companies 122n2, 128
  on labour theory of value 117–118, 118n1
  on law of populations 84n6
  on manufacturing 107
  on narrow basis of consumption 147–148, 197
  on poverty 142
  on primitive accumulation 128n6

on rate and mass of profit 71n1
see also *Falling rate of profit*
on relative surplus population 99n2, 151
on reproduction schemes 48, 54
on reproduction process 138
on tendency of the rate of profit to fall 136–137, 146–147
on unpaid labour 83
plan of 131, 135n15, 136, 142, 161, 167
Capitalist commodity economy 7, 9–15, 17–18, 44, 79, 188, 192–193, 195–196
Chronic depression 26, 120, 126, 195–196
Class XV, XVI, 11, 49, 50n37, 83, 84n6, 96, 113n4, 127, 138–139, 142, 148–149, 158, 168, 181, 183, 188
Commercial credit 39, 40n33, 61n4, 97, 104, 139, 154–155, 164–165, 186
Commodity economy 7–13, 17–19, 27, 29–30, 34, 36–37, 42–46, 48, 50, 87–88, 117, 119, 122
Crisis
agricultural 3n2, 26
and collapse 123–128
and commercial capital 36–41
and credit 139
see also *Credit*
and foreign trade 27–36
see also *Foreign trade*
as phase of accumulation 70–94
capitalism's general 26n25
cause of in prosperity 52
financial 18, 158, 160
imperialism and 194–197
in stages of capitalist development 17
industrial 3n2
inevitability of XVIII, 18, 42–49, 116, 123–128, 144, 152, 167, 179, 180, 198
periodicity of 21, 23, 27, 30, 32, 48, 51, 112, 114n4, 119, 127, 146, 151, 153, 156, 194
Credit 23n22, 24–25, 48, 54, 57n2, 58–64, 65n6, 68, 70, 74–75, 91, 113, 114n4, 138–142, 149, 154–155, 158, 161–162, 164, 166, 168–170, 172, 174–175, 186–187

Deleuze, Gilles (and Felix Guattari) 196–197
Dobb, Maurice 180n8

Ellison, Thomas 101n3
Engels, Friedrich 79–80, 132, 135, 161
England 6, 9, 13–15, 18–20, 22–28, 30–35, 39n32, 40, 63n5, 64, 79–80, 99n2, 100n3, 102n4, 112, 120, 124, 127, 134–135, 163, 173

Falling rate of profit 71, 74–75, 77, 84, 141, 145, 180, 186, 190, 200
Foreign trade 21–22, 25, 27–35, 133, 139–140, 163–164, 167
Foucault, Michel 184
France 20n20
Fundamental Principles of Political Economy XIV, XIX, XX, 11–15, 16n14, 17–18, 21n20, 24, 27–30, 34–38, 39n32, 49, 51, 57n2, 61n4, 114n4, 123–125, 128–130, 136, 139, 143, 144, 157, 162, 167–168, 178
Funds 19–20, 38, 39n32, 40n33, 41n33, 53–56, 57n2, 58–65, 66n6, 68, 70–71, 74–79, 80n3, 97, 104, 108, 110, 140–141, 154–155, 159

Germany 6, 9, 14–15, 23–25, 34–35, 63n5, 64n5, 130
Greenspan, Alan 159
Grossman, Henryk 180n8

Historical crisis
after World War One 25
of 1793 21n20
of 1819 20
of 1929 3–7, 25, 26n25
of 1937 25
of 1973 174–175
of nineteenth century 22
South Sea bubble 19–20
Subprime mortgage crisis (2007–2008) XVI, 160
Tulip crisis 19–20
Historical materialism 28–29
Historical stages of capitalist development 3, 10–12, 14–15, 17–18, 46, 50, 57, 63, 86, 113–114, 121, 125, 128–130, 134, 142, 162–163, 167–168, 172, 174
imperialist stage XII, XVI, 57n2, 115, 126, 178, 180n8, 183n14, 194–196, 198–199
mercantilist stage 20, 113, 125, 182
liberal stage 27, 35, 113, 124–125

Holland 18, 20n20, 21n20
Hoover, Harry 3, 6

Industrial reserve army 47n., 55, 71, 83, 84n6, 99n., 112–113
Industrial revolution 9, 15, 20, 21n20, 27, 106, 108–109, 113, 167
Interest rate 61–64, 71, 74–77, 79–80, 84, 88–89, 97–98, 104, 109, 137, 141, 155, 165–166, 170, 186, 190, 200
Itoh, Makoto XIII, 57n2, 158–159, 168, 180

Japan VI, XII, XIII, 6, 25, 130, 159, 178, 180, 183, 196, 198
Joint stock company 25, 115, 122n2, 128n6
Juglar, Clement 21n20

Kawashima, Ken 184n16, 193n29, 196n32
Keynes, Maynard 160
Kuruma, Samezō XIX, 7n7, 132–134, 142, 167, 180n8

Labour Power XII, XX, 16, 26, 40, 42–51, 55, 57–59, 66–67, 71–73, 78–79, 81–93, 98–99, 101, 104, 106–110, 112, 118, 163, 165–167, 180, 182–193, 197–200
  and land 106
  and *muri* 72–73, 192–193
  and primitive accumulation 55
  and reproduction process 49
  and wages 67, 98n2
  as ground of crisis 49–51
  commodification of XII, XIV–XVI, 44–47, 88, 112, 118, 157–158, 165, 167, 169–170, 173–175, 184–188, 190, 192, 197–200
  financialization of 175
Lapavitsas, Costas XV, XVI, 57n2
Late-developing countries 9, 14–15, 25, 27–28, 130
League of Nations 7
Lenin, V.I. XII, 50n37, 129, 152

Malthus, Thomas 47n36
Military 26, 88n9, 196
Minsky, Hyman 160

Nagahara, Yutaka XIII, 180n10, 185n18, 190n25
Nagatani, Kiyoshi XIII
Natural Sciences 14, 16n14, 173
Neoliberalism XVI, 159–160, 175

Oki, Kōsuke XIII
Organic composition of capital 47, 50, 52, 55–56, 57n2, 66, 73, 101, 146, 165–166, 169, 195
Ouchi, Tsutomu XII, 174, 190n25

Poulantzas, Nicos 196n33
Primitive accumulation 55, 107, 113, 128n6, 188
Purely capitalist society XIX, 15, 24–25, 28, 36n31, 49, 61n4, 117, 118n1, 120–122, 122n2, 127, 128n6, 163–164

Ricardo, David 171, 181

Sekine, Thomas XIII, 178n4
Smith, Adam 171, 181
Spietoff, Arthur 19n15, 20n20, 21n20, 63n5, 95, 103n5, 103–104
Social reproduction process 20, 30, 43, 50, 64, 70, 75, 78–79, 93, 95–96, 140, 186
Stalin, Josef 173, 178
Suzuki, Kōichiro 131n2, 180n8
Sweezy, Paul 180n8

Relative surplus population 47, 49, 66–67, 73, 84n6, 99n2, 101, 109, 114n4, 145–146, 150–152, 154–157, 166, 175, 186, 189–191, 195
Revolution 16n14, 124, 127, 183n14, 199–200

Social sciences 10, 16n14, 17n14, 120–121, 176
Socialism XVI, 85n7, 86n7, 174, 181
  Soviet-styled 173, 196n33

Theory
  and praxis 16n14
  currency 80n3
  of business cycles XVII, 18
  of credit system 169–170
  of finance 61
  of fundamental principles of political

economy see *Fundamental Principles of Political Economy*
of landed property 135
of modern colonialism 128n6
of stages of development see *Historical stages of capitalist development*
of underconsumption or disproportion 169
Tugan-Baranowski, Mikhail 22n21, 23n22, 24, 31n28, 100n2, 180n8

United States of America 5–6, 9, 14–15, 21n20, 22, 24–25, 26n25, 102, 158–160

Varga, Eugen 5n6, 26n25, 180n8

Walker, Gavin 182n, 188n20, 189n24, 193n29
War 18–21, 27, 120, 163, 173–174, 195–196, 199
American civil 22, 103n4
Crimean war of 1853 22
world war one XII, 3, 24–26, 172, 174
world war two XII, 3, 7, 25, 173, 178, 196

Yamada, Moritaro 180n8

Žižek, Slavoj 181

www.ingramcontent.com/pod-product-compliance
Lightning Source LLC
LaVergne TN
LVHW022208200926
848481LV00006B/1892
* 9 7 8 1 6 4 2 5 9 7 9 0 5 *